THE WAR BEHIND ME

# THE WAR BEHIND ME

## VIETNAM VETERANS CONFRONT THE
## TRUTH ABOUT U.S. WAR CRIMES

### DEBORAH NELSON

BASIC
BOOKS

A MEMBER OF THE PERSEUS BOOKS GROUP
NEW YORK

Copyright © 2008 by Deborah Nelson
Published by Basic Books,
A Member of the Perseus Books Group

Books published by Basic Books are available at special discounts for
bulk purchases in the United States by corporations, institutions, and
other organizations. For more information, please contact the Special
Markets Department at the Perseus Books Group, 2300 Chestnut Street,
Suite 200, Philadelphia, PA 19103, or call (800) 810-4145, ext. 5000, or
e-mail special.markets@perseusbooks.com.

Designed by Timm Bryson

Library of Congress Cataloging-in-Publication Data
Nelson, Deborah
   The war behind me : Vietnam veterans confront the truth about U.S.
war crimes / Deborah Nelson.
      p. cm.
   Includes bibliographical references and index.
ISBN 978-0-465-00527-7
1. Vietnam War, 1961–1975—Atrocities. 2. Vietnam War, 1961–1975—
United States. 3. Vietnam War, 1961–1975—Veterans—United States. 4.
War crimes—Vietnam. I. Title.
DS559.2.N45 2008
959.704'3—dc22

                                                       2008015814

10 9 8 7 6 5 4 3 2 1

*To* MOLLY *and* ANNA,
*and for* THEIR GENERATION

# CONTENTS

# INTRODUCTION

On November 12, 1969, the Dispatch News Service carried investigative reporter Seymour M. Hersh's first article on the My Lai massacre.[1] In the weeks that followed, photographs appeared in print and on television. The army announced a full-scale inquiry that, four months later, confirmed the magnitude of the slaughter and the cover-up.[2] The tragedy and its fallout are in every credible history book on the Vietnam War.

The army launched a second important inquiry in the wake of Hersh's exposé. But this one would receive no public notice. The chief of staff quietly assembled a team of officers to collect information on other war-crime allegations that had been reported internally or elsewhere. The men culled investigation files, surveillance reports, press accounts, court-martial records, and congressional correspondence. Each month they summarized what they'd found and sent a memo up the chain of command.

They operated in secret for five years. During that time, they amassed nine thousand pages of evidence implicating U.S. troops in a wide range of atrocities.[3] In contrast to the My Lai investigation, their inquiry led to no major actions or public accounting. In fact, the Pentagon kept the entire collection under wraps, even after the war ended.

In 1990, Kali Tal, founder of *Viet Nam Generation*, a small journal of contemporary history and literature on the 1960s, was tipped to the papers' existence. She requested a declassification and Freedom of Information Act review. After a year had passed, the National Archives and Records Administration notified her that the documents were available for inspection.[4] She found the records deeply disturbing and posted a short notice in her journal to alert others. She did not pursue the matter further, and the boxes returned to the storeroom shelves.

A decade later, Cliff Snyder, a Vietnam specialist on the Archives staff, brought the cartons to the attention of Nicholas Turse, a visiting military historian.[5] While researching them for his dissertation, he came across a 1968 massacre and other cases he believed to be newsworthy. In 2005, he contacted the *Los Angeles Times* about them. I was the newspaper's Washington investigative editor at the time, so his e-mail was relayed to me. We joined forces soon afterward to investigate the long-buried reports.[6]

When I proposed the project to John Carroll, then the *Los Angeles Times'* top editor, his first question was whether a few rogue units committed most of the crimes. That had been his impression as a young Vietnam War correspondent, and a commonly held view. The most notorious was the Americal Division, responsible for My Lai and a lengthy list of less-known atrocities.

The Tiger Force, an elite army platoon, became a late addition to the club with the *Toledo Blade*'s Pulitzer Prize–winning series in 2003 that documented a seven-month killing spree in which scores perished.[7]

The archive collection contained hundreds of sworn statements from soldiers and veterans who committed or witnessed rapes, torture, murders, massacres, and other illegal acts. There were letters from soldiers, statistical reports, and case summaries.[8] When we hand-entered the data into a spreadsheet, it became clear the problem was much bigger than a few bad men: Every major division that served in Vietnam was represented. We counted more than 300 allegations in cases that were substantiated by the army's own investigations. Some had never been revealed; others had been publicly disputed while the army remained silent about its findings. Five hundred allegations couldn't be proven or weren't fully investigated.[9] According to officers who helped compile the records, those numbers represented only a small fraction of the war crimes committed in Vietnam.

Many veterans tried to alert the Pentagon and the public to the problem in the early 1970s at forums sponsored by such groups as Vietnam Veterans Against the War. Most famously, John Kerry, then a leader in the organization, testified on Capitol Hill on April 22, 1971, that U.S. forces had "raped, cut off ears, cut off heads, taped wires from portable telephones to human genitals and turned up the power, cut off limbs, blown up bodies, randomly shot at civilians, razed villages in fashion reminiscent of Genghis Khan, shot cattle and dogs for fun, poisoned food stocks, and generally ravaged the countryside of South Vietnam in addition to the normal ravage of war. . . ." [10]

Within days, the declassified records show, the White House quietly requested a list of war-crime investigations from the army.[11] The staff at the Pentagon was ready with a lengthy response that reported 213 suspects and included confirmed cases of acts from the litany cited in Kerry's testimony.[12] Yet the Nixon administration went ahead with an aggressive backroom campaign to discredit as fabricators and traitors Kerry and other veterans who spoke out about war crimes. The president and White House aides worked closely with a rival organization, Vietnam Veterans for a Just Peace, to publicly condemn the allegations.[13] "The big lie" became the group's familiar drumbeat. Years later, the founder of the group would boast, "Americans got the message that a motley crew of exaggerators and frauds didn't speak for Vietnam veterans."[14] The impression stuck. By the mid-1980s, the whistle-blowers largely had been silenced, and conventional wisdom held that atrocities in Vietnam were overblown.[15] The controversy resurfaced in 2004, when Kerry ran for president. His old detractors ran ads demanding that he disavow his 1971 testimony, confident they would play to a receptive audience; their efforts contributed to his defeat.[16] All the while, the army had evidence in its files that he had spoken the truth.

But this book isn't about Kerry. It's about setting the record straight for the many ordinary men who were ignored, threatened, or disbelieved. It's a place for them to tell their stories again, now with the full force of the army's own investigation findings behind them. Years ago, many of them hoped their accounts would pressure the Pentagon to stop "all the wrong killing," as a soldier wrote in a private letter to then army chief of staff Gen. William C. Westmoreland in 1970.[17] The war ended without an accounting or acknowledgment of the war crimes they witnessed. Their retelling comes at an equally important time when, having failed to address the past, we're destined to repeat it.

WITNESS STATEMENT
(AR 195-10 - TB PMG 3)

| PLACE | DATE | TIME | FILE NUMBER |
|---|---|---|---|
| Sherman Oaks, California | 28 Feb 70 | 1300 | 70-CID046-26104 |

| LAST NAME, FIRST NAME, MIDDLE NAME | SOCIAL SECURITY ACCOUNT NO. | GRADE |
|---|---|---|
| HENRY, James Daniel | | Civilian |

ORGANIZATION OR ADDRESS
3576 Sepulveda Boulevard, Sherman Oaks, California

SWORN STATEMENT

I, James D. HENRY, WANT TO MAKE THE FOLLOWING STATEMENT UNDER OATH:

First of all I would like to make it clear that the purpose of this interview and the purpose for devulging the names of the persons who were involved in the incidents which will be described in this tape is not to "get" any of the individuals who were involved in any of these incidents; that the purpose is not to embarrass any of the families or any of the persons who were involved in these incidents, but solely to make sure that these kinds of incidents do not occur again; second, that there is no defamatory intent on my part, nor is there any intent to injure any individual or their reputation or their standing in the community; third, that the conditions attached to this interview under which names will be given are as follows: First, that I understand that the individuals to whom I am speaking are licensed investigators of the Criminal Investigation Division of the US Army and that the information which will be given here is for official use only and will not be released except at a trial; that in fact permission is expressly denied to use this material in any other way except in a criminal investigation for the purpose of bringing other persons to trial or at a trial itself; and finally that all of the information that follows and all of the names which will be given of individuals who were involved in any particular acts are given on information and belief.

My name is James D. HENRY. I was inducted into the US Army on March 12, 1967. I went to Ft Polk for basic training, and I was later transferred to Ft Sam Houston, Texas, for the rest of basic training and AIT. From there I got 12 days leave and following that, I was sent to Vietnam. I arrived in Vietnam the last of September or August 1967. I was assigned to HHC, 1/35th Inf, 3d Bde. I spent a couple of weeks in base camp with Hq Co and then I was assigned to B Company, 1/35th Inf. This was in Duc Pho, Vietnam. From there we went up to Chu Lai. We operated west of Chu Lai, and on the 8th of October 1967, we got into a fire fight. It was my first fire fight and at that time I witnessed a 12 year old boy executed for no reason by a medic. I didn't actually see the boy executed. Somebody caught him up on a hill and they brought him down and the Lieutenant asked who wanted to kill him, who wanted to shoot him. Two guys, an RTO and a medic said that they did. The RTO kicked the boy in the stomach and the medic took him around behind a rock and I heard one magazine go off complete on automatic. This took place during a rainstorm. At that point the Captain called up and asked what happened. The shooting was reported as a KIA. The Captain asked where the body was and they said it was going down the river. Nobody told the Captain it was a 12 year old boy who was unarmed and didn't have anything on but shorts. After that we stayed in the field a couple weeks and we went into base camp on Hill 488 I think. I'm not sure about that hill number. 1st Platoon went out on a night ambush from there. I was told by men of the 1st Platoon that they raped and executed five women which they caught in their ambush. Men of the other platoons later went down and saw the bodies. From there we went to LZ Baldy which was made our base camp. Of course, the company spent almost all thi

| EXHIBIT | INITIALS OF PERSON MAKING STATEMENT | PAGE 1 OF 10 PAGES |
|---|---|---|
| Incl. 1 of 1 | | |

ADDITIONAL PAGES MUST CONTAIN THE HEADING "STATEMENT OF___ TAKEN AT___ DATED___ CONTINUED." THE BOTTOM OF EACH ADDITIONAL PAGE MUST BEAR THE INITIALS OF THE PERSON MAKING THE STATEMENT AND BE INITIALED AS "PAGE___ OF___ PAGES." WHEN ADDITIONAL PAGES ARE UTILIZED, THE BACK OF PAGE 1 WILL BE LINED OUT, AND THE STATEMENT WILL BE CONCLUDED ON THE REVERSE SIDE OF ANOTHER COPY OF THIS FORM.

DA FORM 2823
JAN 68

70-156

The sworn statement of former army medic James Henry
that launched a secret three-and-a-half-year investigation.

## CHAPTER ONE

# WHAT WAS RIGHT THEN

Jamie Henry swings open the door. He is a striking figure: tall, lean, and strong, with gray hair and a handsome face as craggy as the Sierra Nevada mountains that loom to the east. He leads his two visitors with their heavy bags to the dining room table in his small, comfortably worn house. Over a pot of coffee, he slowly pages through the records we have brought. His wife, Patty, who has been with him since he returned from Vietnam, hovers anxiously in the background.

Thirty-seven years earlier, Henry reported to military officials that members of his company executed nineteen unarmed children and adults in a tiny hamlet on the central coast of Vietnam.[1] The massacre occurred on February 8, 1968, a month before U.S. troops opened fire in My Lai to the south. The army accused him of lying and, as far as he knew, did nothing with the information. Now, decades later, he holds the declassified file of a three-and-a-half-year internal inquiry.

"I had no idea," he says.

Henry's case had been among the hundreds of declassified war-crime accounts collected by the Army Staff in the 1970s and kept secret for the better part of three decades. His own typed, ten-page sworn statement was tucked into one of several fat folders labeled "Henry Allegation." As far as he knew, the statement had been the beginning and end of the investigation. Yet the file reveals more than one hundred interviews, conducted by army investigators across the country with former members of his company, and a final report sent up the chain of command with signatures of top brass at the Pentagon.

As Nick Turse and I set out to investigate the contents of the long-hidden archive for the *Los Angeles Times,* Henry's case quickly rose to the top. It did not stand out in terms of lives lost or brutality—nearly every case in the collection contained its own horror. But for reasons not yet clear, it was one of the most aggressively pursued and mysteriously dropped.

We also were drawn to Henry himself. The records showed that he had earned a Bronze Star for valor while serving as a battlefield medic in Quang Nam province from 1967 to 1968.[2] Fellow members of B Company, 1st Battalion, 35th Infantry, 4th Infantry Division described him as honest and brave in their interviews:

"On numerous occasions, he would repeatedly disregard his own personal safety to administer aid to a wounded soldier. He knew military medicine. He was fast and sure of himself. I am certain that several men in B Company owe their lives to James Henry."

We found Henry largely through providence. Someone in the federal bureaucracy had neglected to take a black marker to the names and Social Security numbers in the investigative files before placing them on the public shelves at the National Archives in College Park, Maryland. Armed with that data and a people-finder database, *Times* researcher Janet Lundblad could find almost anyone. There would be some notable exceptions that would test the luck and limits of my own gumshoe skills. But Henry wasn't one of them. Janet easily traced him to a small town in the gold-rush foothills of the Sierras.

Nick called Henry in September 2005 to ask if he would be willing to meet with us. His wife took a message. He was a logger and out in the field, Patty explained. We waited a few days for a response. He had to ponder the request. With Patty's encouragement, he finally sent an e-mail agreeing to an interview.

"A long time ago I tried to put . . . the war behind me and move on with my life," he wrote in his e-mail. "To be honest, I don't relish going back there now, after all these years, but if you think talking to me will be useful in some way, then I am fine with that."

---

The table nearly fills the cozy dining room off the kitchen, and our documents cover its surface. But Henry, lost in his reading, has been transported to another place. He has returned to a part of his life that he had "put in a closet and locked the door."

He was nineteen in 1967, done with high school and trying to figure out what to do next. He lived at home with his mom, worked at a dismal state hospital, and moonlighted as a hippie at San Francisco's Haight-Ashbury district. It was more about pot than peace, he confesses. When the draft letter arrived, he initially refused induction and was arrested. After a six-month tangle with the Selective Service, he emerged with conscientious objector status.

"No religious designation," he says. "The first and only one I know of."

The army still sent him to Vietnam, but as a medic instead of a rifleman.

He arrived in the fall of that year, part of a 100,000-troop surge that brought U.S. forces close to the half-million mark.[3] The numbers on the other side of the ledger were rising at an even more precipitous rate: 9,378 Americans killed in combat, an 87 percent increase over the prior year.[4] Quang Nam province was an enemy stronghold. Snipers, land mines, and booby traps infested the bucolic landscape of farms and foliage. Military maps denoted the most treacherous zones with Wild West nomenclature, such as "Arizona Territory" and "Dodge City." By the end of the war, more American lives would be lost in Quang Nam province than any other.[5]

"The first day in B Company, the first patrol I went on, we walked across this rice paddy. These guys had all been there a long time and I was just green as could be, and coming down the other path on the berm are these two young girls. Young—eighteen, nineteen, twenty. The guy in the lead immediately stops her and puts his hand down her pants. This goes on for—they're making jokes, and we pretty much all stayed in line. I just thought, 'My God, what's going on?'

"She didn't move and the girl with her didn't move. They just put up with this. A couple of minutes later he has a good laugh and we go walking on down the berm. It was my first day in the field with an infantry company. I just knew I can't have a fit right here, because I don't know what's going on. But I was just really appalled. It went downhill from there on."

"Welcome to Vietnam," Patty Henry says from a corner of the room. She is a pretty woman with a soft spray of lines around her eyes. She is relieved that he's finally talking about Vietnam after years of silence.

When not in combat, the troops were on patrol. They combed the countryside for enemy enclaves and searched hamlets for hidden stockpiles of weapons and food. They'd rarely find a military-age man in the village, only women, children, and old people. The men disappeared, some to stay out of harm's way, others to avoid service in the Republic Army, many to join the elusive local resistance that picked off Americans from their invisible perches in the trees.

"Most of the time we were getting our butts kicked," Henry says. B Company suffered heavy casualties with few clear gains. The orders to search hamlets gave way to orders to burn them to the ground. "Search and destroy" became the mantra. The malevolence caught like their cigarette lighters to grass hooches. Several men stabbed a pig to death for sport. When Henry objected, they told him to shut his mouth if he wanted to live long. Another time, a soldier shot a water buffalo repeatedly with an M-16, until the young medic stopped him and used an M-14 to put the animal out of its misery.

By October, some of the men turned their sights on civilians: a shirtless young boy led behind a rock and executed on a lieutenant's orders; a prisoner beaten and tossed over a cliff; five defenseless women gunned down and reported as enemy killed in action.[6] Henry overheard a lieutenant ask permission to test-fire his weapon and went to investigate. The officer and other soldiers had discovered a Vietnamese man sleeping in a hut, shot him dead, and now were using the body for target practice. By some estimates, members of B Company killed as many as thirty unarmed Vietnamese in the five months leading up to the massacre. No one stopped them.

On February 7, 1968, the battalion commander, Lt. Col. William W. Taylor Jr.,[7] ordered B Company to fight what many of the men believed to be a senseless suicide mission. From his helicopter overhead, he ordered them to advance on snipers hiding in a line of trees. "Really good snipers," Henry recalls. Five men died, including a popular lieutenant.

The next morning, the troops were rousted from their uneasy sleep with another unwelcome directive: Conduct a sweep of nearby fields and hamlets for enemy forces. Kill anything that moves, they were told. A man hiding in a spider hole in a field became the first casualty. Henry was with a small group of soldiers that found him. Later, a couple soldiers "held him down while a willing APC [Armored Personnel Carrier] ran over him with the right track. It didn't kill him the first time, so they backed over him again."

They marched on toward a nondescript hamlet of grass hooches. They met no resistance and found only women, children, and old people in town. As others searched for hidden stashes of enemy supplies, Henry took a break. He stepped into a hut, dropped his heavy medical bag onto the floor, unbuckled his bandolier, and lit a cigarette.

Voices crackled on a company radio parked nearby. Henry heard Lt. Johnny Mack Carter, one of the platoon leaders, report that that his men had rounded up nineteen civilians. Carter asked their captain, Donald C. Reh, what to do with them.

Reh, a West Point graduate and career officer, had joined B Company in November, after the first spate of civilian killings. Henry liked him and considered him a decent person. But Reh had not intervened in the APC incident. And now he gave a response that took Henry's breath away: "He said that higher said to kill anything that moves."[8]

Did Reh really mean for Carter to kill the civilians? Henry spotted the captain and took a couple steps toward him, hoping to get him to take back his words.

"I don't know why I suspected that Carter could do it, but I suspected that he could."

As Henry moved, he thought Reh might be trying to get Carter back on the phone. Henry peered over a short hedge, where women and children huddled as Carter and others took aim. Soldiers dragged a naked teenager from a hooch. "She was brought out by two guys, and she was thrown into the pile. . . . There were babies in there too . . . She was just thrown on the pile and they started shooting."

Within minutes, the massacre was finished. Reh was back on the horn, ordering his men to move out, with no hint of what had just transpired. At camp that night, emotions ranged from disbelief to disgust.

"I think they kind of accepted the ones and the twos and this over there, but this is just going way too far, rounding people up—old men and little children and women and just—I think it was just a total shock to the company. I think they just went, 'We can't do this.'"

The next day, Lt. Col. Taylor dispatched B Company to help two other companies engaged in a fierce battle with Vietnamese troops from the north. The battalion reported three hundred enemy and nineteen Americans killed in action (KIA), including three from B Company. The massacre faded into the background after that. But Henry made a promise to himself.

"From the minute it happened I was determined to do something about it. The minute—thirty seconds after the shooting stopped, I knew that I was going to do something about it. And I knew I couldn't do anything about it there."

Henry returned from Vietnam in September 1968. Upon landing at Fort Hood, Texas, he quickly made an appointment with an army lawyer to report the massacre. To his dismay, the lawyer admonished him to keep his mouth shut until he got out of the service. The lawyer warned of "a million and one charges you can be brought up on for blinking your eye."

That day or the next, he was contacted by an agent from the office of the Criminal Investigation Division[9] at Fort Hood. More commonly known as CID, it is the army's detective bureau, the lead agency for investigating serious crimes, including war crimes committed by U.S. soldiers on foreign soil. Henry discovered that the agent had already been briefed by the lawyer. "He wanted to know what I was trying to pull, what I was trying to put over on people, and so I was just quiet. I told him I wouldn't tell him anything and I wouldn't say anything until I got out of the army, and I left."

As Henry reads the documents, the old feelings return. "I never wavered on it. The lawyer was wrong and this stuff was going on and we had to get it stopped, and I never once thought of not doing anything about it. . . . I wanted to make a big stink about it and the public to know what was going on."

Henry received an honorable discharge in early 1969, moved to Los Angeles, enrolled in a community college, and met Patty. He helped form a local chapter of Vietnam Veterans Against the War.

"I'm not antimilitary," he says.

Patty adds, "Jamie's goal was the atrocity thing. Not so much antiwar but to report the atrocities."

He stares at the opening pages of the army file on the Henry allegation. There is a flurry of memos on February 21, 1970—two years after the massacre and seventeen months after his meeting with the agent at Fort Hood. The memos originated not at CID but in the army's Office of the Chief of Information at the Pentagon. The press staff had received an inquiry from CBS News about an upcoming article in an obscure muckraking magazine on an "alleged atrocity/massacre."[10] They tracked down an advance copy, notified CID, and sent alerts up the chain of command.

"Not very good news!" read a handwritten note attached to a staff memo summarizing the article for Gen. Bruce Palmer Jr., then the vice chief of staff under Gen. William Westmoreland.

Henry's accusations surfaced at an inopportune time for the army. Reporter Seymour Hersh's explosive exposé on the My Lai massacre three months earlier had unleashed a flood of atrocity claims by returning soldiers and veterans. Worried about the impact on public support for the war, the Nixon administration had begun monitoring the reports closely while searching for an effective strategy to contain the damage.

Within hours of receiving notice, CID agents contacted Taylor and Reh. Taylor denied knowledge of any massacre by his troops and insisted he had never issued an order to kill civilians. Reh, through a lawyer, declined to discuss the matter with investigators.[11]

Patty Henry says men in sunglasses began stalking her and Jamie. The couple spotted two in a parked car down the street as they left another veteran's house. "Dark sunglasses," she recalls. "Total James Bond." Henry read a one-page statement at a Los Angeles news conference sponsored by Vietnam Veterans Against the War on February 27, 1970, and Patty is certain that she spotted two undercover army operatives in the audience. She gets her proof thirty-five years later. In the file, there's a memo dated

February 28, 1970, from a press officer in Washington, D.C., stating that an officer in Los Angeles reported "very little of interest transpired during Henry's meeting with the press."

Attached to the memo is a copy of Henry's statement: a one-paragraph summary of the massacre followed by a five-paragraph condemnation of military leaders for ignoring atrocities. "My motivation can be stated quite briefly: I want the murder of Vietnamese stopped and I want the military to stop putting Americans in the position of becoming murderers," the statement says.

A short story ran inside the *Washington Evening Star*[12] two days before the press conference, and it's included in the file. So is a letter demanding an investigation, sent by Sen. Ogden R. Reid, a Democrat from New York, to army Secretary Stanley R. Resor. A CID investigator contacted Henry the day of the press conference, and they met soon afterward. Henry provided a ten-page typewritten statement with names, dates, and details. The investigators questioned him a few more times. Then CID stopped calling, and the press and the politicians moved on.

"We tried to get as much publicity as we could, and it just never went anywhere. Nothing ever happened. We published that article, nothing happened. Went to CID, nothing happened," Henry says, gloom suddenly clouding his face. Maybe the same would come of this retelling.

In late January 1971, he traveled to Detroit in the bitter cold to repeat his account at the "Winter Soldier Investigation," a forum on atrocities sponsored by Vietnam Veterans Against the War. More than one hundred veterans participated.[13] The event received little coverage, but their stories became the basis for John Kerry's Senate testimony that atrocities were "day-to-day" occurrences in Vietnam.[14] That modest victory was soon overtaken by other events. The movement had been infiltrated by poseurs—undercover FBI agents looking for dirt and a handful of veterans who made up or embellished their combat experiences.[15] The Nixon administration capitalized on the discrepancies and worked closely with a charismatic veteran (a future Swift Boat leader) from a rival veterans group that challenged the atrocity allegations.[16] The public attacks, a whisper campaign, and the movement's own failings drove veterans like Henry into the closet and led to the popular perception, which persists today, that their ranks were "packed with pretenders and liars."[17]

Henry dropped out—tainted, disillusioned, and defeated.

Nick and I take Jamie and Patty to dinner and then call it a night. We return the next day so he can finish reading the file. He looks discomfited when we arrive.

"I was kind of in a turmoil this morning about it," he eventually discloses. "I guess it is, it's just I don't know if it's going to—people are going to go, 'God, it's coming back.'" He pauses. We wait. "That was all I wanted to say."

He is paging through the thick stack of sworn statements that CID collected from fellow members of B Company. Henry hasn't talked to most of them since Vietnam. He had no clue that investigators interviewed so many of them.

"He says it happened!" Henry exclaims as he reads one of the first statements in the CID file. Dozens more follow.[18] (The documentary excerpts here and throughout the book reflect word usage, spelling, and grammar as they appear in the records.)

Staff Sgt. Wilson "Punchy" Bullock:

> As we made the sweep, my platoon came upon about three or four houses. The houses were fired into and then entered.

This was when about 19 VC Suspects were captured. They consisted of women, children, babies and two or three very old men. All of these people were lined up and killed. That is, they were put in to a slight depression in a huddle and were shot. Before the shooting took place, I heard a woman screaming and the screams appeared to be coming from one of the houses. When the shooting started, I turned and walked away. When it, the shooting, stopped, I began to return to the site when I observed a naked Vietnamese female run from the house to the huddle of people, saw that her baby had been shot. She picked the baby up and was then shot and the baby sot again. The unit was then moved out and the people left there. I don't know if they were all dead or not. Just after the shooting, LT CARTER came walking by me and when he looked at me, he said, "I had to do it", or something like that.[19]

Robert D. Miller, the radiotelephone operator for Lt. Carter:

We went in shooting but we had no problem getting into the village, as the personnel that were in the village was women and children. The only male that was in the village was one old man with a white beard. Once we were in the village we rounded up all the vietnamese that were there into a group and I believe that they were nineteen (19) of them, all women and children except the one old man. . . . After we rounded up all the Vietnamese, my Platoon Leader LT CARTER called my Company Commander CPT REH on the radio and advised him that we had nineteen Vietnamese rounded up and ask CPT REH what he should do with them. CPT REH replied over the radio "I already gave

you the operation order this morning". LT CARTER ac-
knowleged the transmission by CPT REH, signed off the
radio. At this time LT CARTER ask for two volunteers. I believe that everyone knew what was going to happen so no
one volunteered except one guy known only to me as
"Crazy". A few minutes later, while the Vietnamese were
huddled around in a circle LT CARTER and "Crazy" started
shooting them with their M-16's on automatic. As the
shooting started a young girl who was naked came running
out of a nearby hooch to where the Vietnamese women
and children were being shot. When she got to where they
were she was also shot and she fell onto the rest of the bodies. When this occurred I couldn't take anymore so myself
and a . . . SSG [staff sergeant] that we called "Punchy" ran
from the area so that we could not see anymore what was
going on.[20]

Gregory Newman, a member of the mortar platoon, whose
statement was a Q and A with investigators:

"The order of the day was to search and destroy and kill
anything in the village that moved. . . ."

Where were you during the incident?

"I was in the area of the corrals with the 4th Platoon
killing livestock."

What did you see pertaining to the Vietnamese female?

"I saw her taken from a hootch nude by a couple of
GI's. . . . She was a young girl about 19 years . . . She was
placed with the other civilians and shot."

Concerning the rest of the civilians, did you see them
shot?

"No, I saw them begging before they were shot and later I saw them dead. . . . Most of them were old men and women. Some were two or three years old."

. . . Who issued the order to kill anything that moved in the village?

"CPT REH."[21]

Jose Victor Davila-Falu, a rifleman, whose interview was conducted in Spanish and then translated:

He noticed that upon entering the hootch he saw the woman and the young girl were naked. He also stated that he saw the woman performing oral sodomy on the Sgt from the APC unit. He further stated that just a few moments after rentering the hootch he heard what sounded like shots and the young girl screamed and started running out of the hootch. They tried to stop her but she ran out anyway. They went to the front entrance to the hootch and saw the young girl thrown herself in front of the guns that were being fired into the crwd of civilians and she herself was killed. DAVILA-FALUE stated that . . . looking out the front entrance of the hootch, it seemed to him as if he saw everyone firing into the group of civilians and further stated that he couldn't believe what he was seeing . . . DAVILA-FALU stated that prior to this particular operation beginning, they had received orders allegedly from "higher up" to kill everything that breathed.[22]

All over the hamlet and back at the command post outside town, members of B Company heard the exchange between

Carter and Reh on their radios, followed by the sound of weapons firing. Their recollection of the precise words varied somewhat—but their meaning and the outcome were the same.

One allegation surprises Henry: Two members of the company told investigators that the battalion commander issued the operation order that Reh passed on to Carter. However, they gave markedly different versions of the exchange.

Myran Ambeau, a rifleman, told investigators that he was positioned five feet away from the captain when the battalion commander radioed from a helicopter overhead:

> The battalion commander told the Captain, "If they move, shoot them". The Captain verified that he had heard the command, he then transmitted the instructions to LT CARTER. LT CARTER verified that he understood and told the Captain that he would tell them to DeeDee (go away). [Vietnamese detainees sometimes would be told to "DiDi" as a pretext for shooting them as "fleeing" suspects.] There was no further radio communication after the Captain verified his response. Approximately three minutes later, there was automatic weapons fire from the direction where the prisoners were being held.[23]

Gary A. Bennett, who served as Reh's radiotelephone operator, told investigators that Reh called Taylor for instructions, that Taylor replied that it was a "search and destroy mission," and that the message was relayed to Carter. Bennett insisted that Taylor's order didn't mean that civilians should be killed, and he denied knowing a massacre had occurred. Investigators wrote that

Bennett seemed "vague and evasive" and that he refused to sign a sworn statement.[24]

Henry cannot believe that CID conducted such an extensive investigation. He is astounded that top brass at the Pentagon were monitoring the case—and that they all knew he was telling the truth yet remained silent. The inquiry lasted three and a half years. The lead investigator sent his final report up the chain of command in 1974. He concluded that evidence supported charges against nine members of B Company in connection with twenty-eight Vietnamese deaths and a corpse mutilation. The confirmed allegations included the killings of the young boy shot behind a rock, five women in an ambush, an unarmed man in the "target practice" incident, two old men shot in the chest, a man tossed under an APC, and "eighteen" civilians in a hamlet. (For unknown reasons, the investigator counted the massacre as eighteen deaths, even though many statements indicated that nineteen or more perished.)

The list of suspects in "founded murder offenses" did not include Reh or Taylor.[25] In a separate memorandum, the lead investigator explained that he had consulted with the regional staff judge advocate—a military lawyer—about their cases.[26]

"Concerning COL TAYLOR . . . it was determined that there was not sufficient cause," the investigator wrote, adding that the two witness statements "tending to involve TAYLOR" were not strong enough evidence to support any criminal charge. "Further, the information obtained indicates that if TAYLOR did communicate with REH concerning the 18 prisoners, his instructions were not followed in that the alleged reply by TAYLOR was to shoot the prisoners if they moved. If this remark was made by TAYLOR, it does not constitute an order to kill the prisoners in the manner in which they were executed."

The report did not say how Carter's actions may have differed from those intended.

Regarding Reh, the memo said the evidence supported a charge of dereliction of duty for failing to investigate the shooting but not a murder charge for ordering it.

"The statements that implicate REH in a radio transmission concerning the disposition of the villagers do not reflect that he issued any direct order for their murder."

The file ended with the final report. Henry tells us that the army never summoned him to testify—a strong indication that no one was prosecuted, as he almost certainly would have been a witness for the prosecution. That doesn't seem to make sense: Why would the army invest years building a case—go to the effort to find and interview scores of ex-soldiers—only to lock the file away in a drawer and do nothing?

In Henry's view, little about the war makes sense.

"All we wanted to do is survive this and get out. Nobody wanted to quit. Everybody wanted to do their job. When we were told to attack, we did. It was a fight. But it was pretty obvious that we weren't going to accomplish what that government wanted us to accomplish, especially the way we were going about it. I mean, going around killing all the people that we're supposed to be saving isn't going to work. If they weren't enemies before we got there, they were enemies after we got there."

As we pack up to leave, we tell Henry that we plan to contact other members of his company. We'll let him know what we find out.

"I imagine that a lot of people had problems with this," he says. "They can't tell anybody. They can't say, 'Dear, that's what I did in the war.'"

We have one more stop before we head back to the East Coast. Janet Lundblad, the *Times* researcher, traces Capt. Reh to Auburn, an old Wild West town of twelve thousand that lies thirty miles northeast of Sacramento. We exit I-80 and drive unannounced to his house.

Reh's service record showed that he left the army in 1978. An Internet search turned up photographs of Reh in Vietnam posted on the official 35th Infantry Web site, apparently taken in the weeks and days leading up to the massacre.[27] In the first one, a young man in a foxhole poses with an inflatable Santa. The sand around them is so white it looks like snow. The caption says the picture was taken December 25, 1967. In another picture, he sits on a box holding a metal cup. His hair is longer and his smile faint. The caption: "Probably early Feb 1968, after a real tough night fighting Charlie trying to overrun our position."

Elsewhere on the 35th Infantry Web site, members posted their war stories. Both Reh and Taylor contributed to riveting reprises of the February 9, 1968, battle—and the days leading up to it.[28] Not surprisingly, neither of them mentioned the massacre. Taylor's name appeared on a narrative that summarized February 8 in just two sentences. There was no major contact, only occasional sniper attacks and "burning of deserted villages."

Reh wrote a separate account that devoted only half a sentence to February 8: "Bravo Company received its mission, the night before (days just blended together) to move out the next morning. . . ."

I drive to Reh's address in Auburn, but no one is home. We take a spin around the quiet neighborhood of single-family houses, but his driveway's still empty on our next pass. We dawdle over sandwiches at a diner packed with a hungry after-church crowd. Back in the car, I try him on my cell phone. A woman answers and, after several unsuccessful attempts to get me to state my business, hollers for Reh to pick up the phone.

When he answers, I explain that we're in town working on a story about declassified army investigation records from the Vietnam War. We found his name in one of the case files. We'd like to show it to him and talk about it.

Reh pauses for about three beats. "I have nothing to say." Click.

We stop in downtown Sacramento to pass time before checking into our hotel rooms at the airport. We wander through the park by the state capitol, past a rose garden and a wedding party. We emerge from conversation to find ourselves in the middle of a Vietnam memorial, staring into the probing face of a bronze soldier sitting on his helmet. Not quite knowing what to make of this coincidental encounter, we linger to read the plaques and then leave.

A week after our visit, Henry sends an e-mail:

> After you guys left, I was very distressed. I just sat in my chair physically shaking for about an hour. I was reliving all of that and the thought of bringing all of that up again and going through all of that, all over again, and my mind just raced in a million directions all at the same time. Fear was involved in a lot of it.
>
> When Patty got up, she could see that I was in trouble, and she never really said anything, just handed me a hand written note that said,
>
> "Our lives begin to end the day we become silent about things that matter."
>
> Martin Luther King, Jr.

I carried that in my pocket all week and read it often.
That helped. It didn't take me back to being 23 years old
and bullet proof, but it helped me get through my thick
head that what was right then, is right now.

———————

Johnny Mack Carter doesn't hesitate.

"I'm not interested," he says and slams down the phone before
I have a chance to give him more than my name and affiliation.

Lundblad had located Carter in Palmetto, Florida, the same
place that an army investigator had recorded his flat denials in a
sworn statement taken March 3, 1970.

"As best as I can recollect, the area appeared to be deserted and
I do not recall any civilians being picked up and categorically
stated that I did not order the killing of any civilians, nor do I
know of any being killed," Carter told them.[29]

The army stonewalled our request for records showing what
happened to the case after the lead investigator filed his final report. So Nick and I are moving down the list of nine suspects and
four dozen witnesses in search of answers. Carter was the lead suspect in the massacre, so his refusal to talk to us is a major setback.

The man nearest Carter in the moments leading up to the massacre would have been his radiotelephone operator. We know
from the records that Robert D. Miller gave investigators a highly
detailed account of Carter's role in the slaughter.[30] He now lives
in Pittsburgh. I dial his number and leave a message that only
hints at the subject. When he calls back, "at my wife's urging," he
knows Nick and I want to talk about the massacre.

"I remember distinctly what happened," Miller says. "It has
bothered me the rest of my life."

His recollection tracks his sworn statement, even in the finer details, though he hasn't read it since the day he signed it. There were nineteen Vietnamese: one white-haired old man and the rest children and women. Carter radioed Reh and then gave the signal to start shooting, Miller says. The rest of the scene has been playing in his mind on a continuous loop ever since.

"I see the babies, the little kids, the naked woman. I see their bodies twitching, and I have nightmares," he says. "I feel guilty. I didn't do anything. It was just horrendous. There was no one to report it to. They were your officers. That was as high as you could go."

Later, when Carter and another soldier involved in the massacre began harassing a young Vietnamese woman in his presence, Miller didn't hesitate.

"I pulled my rifle on them. They stopped. I told the woman to go. She smacked me across the face, because she didn't know what was happening. They were grabbing on her. I gave the radio up after that. My mind just started shutting off."

He had volunteered for radio duty, because he thought it would keep him out of combat. Until the massacre, he never imagined there could be something worse than dodging bullets or watching a buddy die.

"Combat was bad, and losing your friends was bad," he says. "But they was innocent people."

I ask about the investigation. We know from the date on his statement that CID waited until 1972 to contact him and that the agents who visited him were not the same ones who questioned Carter. CID generally dispatched investigators from the closest army base, a practice that gave the interviews a potluck quality.

Miller says he balked initially: "I told them I wouldn't want to go public, because it would hurt the country."

With their assurances, he eventually agreed to provide the sworn statement we found in the file. But that wasn't the end of the story, Miller says. Sometime later, a middle-aged white colonel in full dress uniform appeared at his door "out of the clear blue sky." He trudged up the steep staircase to Miller's apartment and sat down in the living room. Miller doesn't recall his name, only that he said he was from Washington, D.C., and claimed he knew Capt. Reh personally. He seemed eager to excuse the massacre. He pointed out that the Vietnamese had killed Americans. He asked about Miller's intentions.

"The colonel was there to find out if I was going to go public," Miller says. "He called me, 'You crazy Vietnam vets.' I got appalled. So I threw him out of my house."

If silencing Miller was his intention, the colonel got his wish. Soon after his visit, CID agents stopped by Miller's apartment to re-interview him, but he refused to say anything more.

"I'd had a few drinks and was keeping quiet. I said I'd be a hostile witness."

That was the last he heard from CID. Miller says he became an alcoholic in the ensuing years, his marriage fell apart, and he suffered a nervous breakdown. He sought counseling in the 1980s, gave up drinking, and remarried. Still the nightmares continued. He says he couldn't talk about the massacre until 2001 or 2002, when he finally told his psychiatrist.

"I remember when I told my shrink, he was speechless," Miller says. "I told my shrink, 'There's proof of this somewhere. Something like that could never get away without proof.'"

The final report concluded that an "indeterminate number" of soldiers participated in the massacre but named only two suspects. We'd already struck out with one of them. That left Pvt. Frank Bonilla, better known as "Crazy," a skinny nineteen-year-old from Hawaii, the youngest soldier in the company. Investigators wrote that they couldn't find him and closed the case without questioning him.[31]

Lundblad locates Bonilla on the island of Oahu. Nick and I call him. He's now fifty-eight and works at a hotel. Bonilla tells us he had no idea the army was looking for him. He returned to Oahu in 1969 after his tour of duty ended, he says. But he quickly relocated to the Big Island to get away from friends and family and their incessant questions about his war experience. He's not any more eager to talk about it now, he says. Nevertheless, he stays on the line, recalling events in a jumble of words, emotions, and disjointed scenes:

> I know we'd had a firefight battle. A lot of people got shot up and stuff like that. . . . I heard words out loud. Somebody higher up. I think it was a captain or something. . . . Some officer rounding people up. One officer walking around real pissed-off or something. Whoever gave him the word was from higher up. Somebody had a radio. Handed it to someone. Maybe a lieutenant. Said the man don't want to see nobody standing. . . . He was hollering, yelling, "You, you, you. Don't want to see nobody standing."

Bonilla says he didn't realize the intended victims were women and children until he had them in his sight. He swears he never pulled the trigger.

I saw children and women and was nuh-uh . . . There was one real old guy. Rest was women and children. I'd know if I'd fired that M-14[32] at someone, I know what it would do. M-14 at close range, mm-mm. It would do real damage. . . . I couldn't do it. . . . They said, "Get up there and get ready." They said, "Get that old man." I closed my eyes. I don't want to see small kids. A lot of guys thought that I had something to do with it because they saw me going up there. Nope. I just turned the other way. It was like this ain't happening. . . .

I seen something . . . One lady came out of one shack naked. . . . One guy had a .45 to her and asked her to do something stupid. I think that guy was from the mechanized [APC] unit. How old was she? Kind of young. To me like a kid. Maybe a teenager or something. They're a small people, so hard to tell. . . . Whatever they were doing to her inside, she was screaming. . . . They pushed her out. I remember seeing that. Then the shooting started and I closed my eyes. She might have been running. She might have been running to her family. . . .

I just stood there. So fast it was over. . . . I remember sitting down with my head between my knees. Is that for real? Someone said, "Keep your mouth shut or you're not going home." . . . I said, "If you're going to do it just do it." He was complaining, "You didn't fire a shot. Gotta keep your mouth shut or you ain't gonna go home alive. You'll go home in a body bag. And when you go home you better shut up."

He says he can't remember who else took part. He blames a mild stroke in 1996 for his forgetfulness. I think that whoever told him to shut up made a lifetime impression.

I call back a couple weeks later. He seems relieved to hear from me again. He adds a few more details: He remembers that he lost his best friend and mentor during the sniper fight the day before the massacre. He carried the body back, he says. He remembers that Carter was the one who ordered the troops to open fire. He also remembers Carter crying, because he didn't want to do it, but someone "on the radio" ordered him to shoot them.

"His eyes were red and watery," Bonilla says.

He again repeats that he aimed his weapon but couldn't shoot.

An M-14 is not a subtle weapon. It has a heavy recoil and ejects a shower of thick casings as it fires. Men who witnessed the scene from different vantage points told investigators that Bonilla opened fire.[33] One recalled that Bonilla bragged afterward about killing the old man. Still, I find myself believing him, or perhaps not wanting to believe that an ordinary man could stare at the face of a helpless child through a rifle sight and pull the trigger.

---

I call Carter again a couple months after our first unsuccessful attempt.

"Mr. Carter, you don't have to talk to me," I say quickly. "I'd just like to read to you what members of B Company told investigators about the massacre and your role in it, so you know what we're going to write about you. You can comment or not. That's up to you."

He doesn't hang up this time. I read excerpts from statements of a half-dozen men. When I finish, I wait for the same denial that he gave investigators. So his response surprises me.

"I don't doubt it," he says of the accounts. "But I don't remember."

He says that he has lost all memory of his time in Vietnam.

"I guess I've wiped Vietnam and all that out of my mind. I don't remember shooting anyone or ordering anyone to shoot."

"Do you remember getting an order from Reh to shoot the civilians?"

"It could've happened," he says.

"Did it?"

He says he doesn't know. I try working the edges. I ask how he got into the army. He says he was drafted and opted for officer candidate school. He was commissioned in 1967 and sent to Vietnam as a second lieutenant. He won promotion to first lieutenant while there and to captain when he returned to the States in 1968. He left active duty just weeks before CID contacted him in March 1970.

"I remember talking to them in March of '70," he says. "I never heard anything else."

Carter says he remained under military obligation on inactive status for another year. In theory, the army could have recalled him to active duty to face charges. In practice, the army rarely did that, for reasons that would become increasingly clear as Nick and I dug deeper. Carter confirms that he was not charged or even summoned to a hearing.

After his discharge, Carter says, he spent thirty-two years in the U.S. Postal Service. He is retired now. As the call draws to a close, I return to his Vietnam experience. What set off the massacre? I ask. Why those people and that day?

"Sometimes people just snap," he says.

When I press him to elaborate, he retreats. Sorry, Vietnam is just a "vague recollection."

On a chilly winter night, Nick and I drive to Stuart Lee's house in Pasadena, Maryland, on the western shore of the Chesapeake Bay.

The final report named him as a suspect, not in the massacre but in a separate killing the same day. Lee confessed to shooting an unarmed old man, according to the report.[34] He was still in the army at the time of his alleged admission. If he wasn't charged, likely no one else had been.

Members of B Company described Lee as a fearless medic in combat and an intimidating presence among his own ranks. So I am surprised when a diminutive, baby-faced man opens the door. I wonder if we have the wrong address. I introduce Nick and myself, my words turning to white puffs of condensation in the cold.

"We've been looking through declassified army investigation files from the Vietnam War and came across your name—"

"I'm not interested," he says and closes the door, but slowly enough for me to blurt, "We're not after you. We're interested in the higher-ups."

Lee opens the door wide. "In that case, I have a lot to say."

We sit on stools around a serving island in his kitchen. Although it's late, he starts a fresh pot of coffee. He is railing against Congress for losing the Vietnam War. They are not the higher-ups I had in mind; I meant military leaders in my desperate doorstep pitch. We discuss the role of politicians for about ten minutes before turning to the files Nick and I have set on his counter. I hand him the investigators' statement on his 1972 interview.

> After repeated questioning, S. LEE stated that at the time in
> question, he was under a great deal of pressure from battle

and that he did not kill the man in cold blood . . . S. LEE
was asked the specific question, "What caused you to shoot
the man, did he move?" to which S. LEE replied "he might
have." . . . When questioned as to the circumstances surrounding the shooting, S. LEE related that he believed the
incident occurred on 8 Feb. 68 . . . S. LEE continued by saying that his unit was going thru a village rapidly, not running but walking fast. He was carrying an M-16, a .45 pistol
and his pack. As he walked through the village, he could
hear shooting but did not know where it was coming from
or why there was shooting going on. S. LEE indicated that
he came upon the victim suddenly and shot him with his
M-16 although the man was not armed and did not appear
to be a combatant. S. LEE placed his hands over his chest
area to indicate where he had shot the victim.

Lee reads the document silently. When he finishes, he abruptly
leaves the room. Nick and I watch as he slowly mounts a staircase in the next room. He descends a few minutes later with a
scrapbook that he drops gently on the counter. He opens it to a
page with a commendation affixed, a medal of valor for risking
his life to reach the wounded in the firefight that killed five members of his company.

"This is February 7."

Then he turns the page. There is another commendation, a
Purple Heart for assisting fallen soldiers in another battle, even
after he was wounded.

"This is February 9."

I ask about February 8.

"What was going on that led—"

"I had a lot of stress. Everybody was under a lot of stress. We were just trying to stay alive. This was the same period of time when we lost a lot of the company. So a lot of things were going on."

He searches for the right words to describe their state of mind.

"We were out of control," he says. "We were all very trigger-happy and everything else. Shoot anything that moves or don't move or anything that's in our way. You have to be in that kind of—you've got to be in that environment to really understand what goes through the soldiers' mind at the time."

Not everyone was trigger-happy, I think to myself. The files revealed scores of men who didn't participate but watched in horror. I ask about the unarmed old man.

"Like I explained to them, during February 7th through the 9th, it was a very horrendous time for our company at the time," he says. "I felt that whatever I did that day was part of my duties and just for self-preservation, for me staying alive. I guess I was, I would say it was best for me to stay alive rather than be dead so I could help my other soldiers. That was my job."

Lee says he didn't witness the massacre. He also says he didn't see an APC run over a man, although other members of the company placed him at the scene.

"It's a big blur right now. I think even in those days it was a big blur for me."

We talk about the investigation. CID investigators suddenly appeared on his doorstep at West Point five years after the fact. He believes two others waited in his backyard to make sure he didn't try to escape. They led him to their car "like I was a criminal." The interview took place in an office outside West Point and extended into the evening. He grew fatigued, so they agreed to finish the next day. That night, he received orders to pack. He was being transferred to Fort Ord in Monterey, California, effective immediately. His wife had just gotten home with their newborn.

"The explanation they gave was they didn't want the publicity."

The investigation notes say Lee refused to meet with investigators again. Lee contends he never heard from them again. The army kept him in suspense for more than a year, before he received a surprise phone call at the Fort Ord infirmary.

"They call me into the orderly room and this colonel gets on the horn with me, told me who he was and stuff." Lee can't recall the name, only that he was from Washington, D.C. "He says, 'We want to apologize and let you know that you've been cleared' of whatever the investigation. . . . He actually said something like I was the wrong person. The investigation was over."

Lee says he remained in the army and retired in 1988 after twenty-two years of service. It's time to go and, as we prepare to leave, Lee shifts the discussion to Iraq. The enemy once again is mixed in with the civilian populace, he says. That puts U.S. troops in a treacherous situation.

"We're after war crimes all the time or whatever. You've got to remember, our government is the one that sends us there."

We talk again by phone several weeks later. He has thought more about the massacre and wants to make sure I understand that just because they were women and children didn't mean they weren't a threat. The Vietnamese were quick-change artists, he explains; they would sell soda to troops in the day and lay booby traps at night.

"It doesn't matter if they're little tiny children or not. They might be strapped with explosives," he says. "In Vietnam everyone was a combatant."

Among the "higher-ups" on our contact list is Taylor, the battalion commander who kept tabs on his companies in a helicopter. Two men, Bennett and Ambeau, gave conflicting accounts of his orders on the day of the massacre.

According to Bennett's version, Reh asked Taylor what to do with the civilians. Taylor replied with his standing order to "search and destroy." Bennett did not believe the order meant to kill civilians. He also denied knowledge of a massacre and refused to provide a sworn statement.[35]

In Ambeau's sworn statement, the battalion commander said, "If they move, shoot them." The captain verified the order and passed it on to Carter moments before the massacre.[36]

Nick has a brief phone conversation with Bennett, who lives in Towanda, Pennsylvania, an old lumber town.

"I'm not getting involved. I had nothing to do with it, and it's over with," Bennett says. "There was nothing really there."

I call Ambeau, who lives in Little Rock, Arkansas. He is willing to listen as I read his sworn statement to him. I read Bennett's too. Ambeau says he is sure of what he heard. He adds that he is glad I called. The massacre was the worst of many ugly incidents, most of which were never reported, he says. His memories of Vietnam have begun to bother him again, and he recently saw a doctor about it.

"The firefighting you could handle. It's all that other stuff that plays on your mind," he says. "We just basically search and destroy with no rhyme or reason. . . . How in the hell do you go in there, completely destroy everything they have, beat up their family members, rape their wives, and burn down their houses?"

The search-and-destroy missions drove Vietnamese to the enemy and robbed U.S. soldiers of any sense of purpose.

"There was one case where someone beat up this old man. I said, 'You're real tough to go out and beat up a seventy-three-year-old man.' I thought of my grandpa. He [the soldier] said, 'Oh, you gook-lover,'" Ambeau says. "At least I know I left the country with a good conscience. I never shot no innocent person. I can leave with a clear conscience. But there are many others who didn't."

He is worried about his son and son-in-law, who have enlisted and are leaving for Iraq.

"I got a feeling this situation in Iraq is going to end up the same way. . . . I told them just do the right thing and listen to your conscience."

---

Taylor joined the army in 1943, served in three wars, and retired a full colonel in 1977. His awards and decorations included a Bronze Star in Korea and an Air Medal for Heroism in Vietnam.[37] He now lives in Alexandria, Virginia. Before paying him a visit, I review his two interviews with CID. The first took place within a week of Henry's going public. The investigator mistakenly asked him about the events of "9 Feb. 68" instead of February 8. Taylor obliged by recounting the fierce battle his battalion won and denying knowledge of a massacre.[38] More than three years later, a CID investigator re-interviewed him, this time about the correct date. Taylor said he had no memory of the day. He reiterated that he had never at any time ordered the killing of civilians. He declined to provide a sworn statement, citing a "pressing engagement." So I have only the investigator's abbreviated summary of their conversation.[39]

I park on the street in front of Taylor's house. He is working outside in the side yard and eyes me warily as I approach. When I identify myself as a reporter and mention the Henry allegation, his jaw tightens.

"I'm not going to talk to you," he says through clenched teeth. "Why don't you get an honest job? What possible reason is there for bringing this up now?"

After a battery of insults, he reveals that his most urgent concern is the impact a story might have on an upcoming battalion reunion. For years, the men of his battalion have avoided reunions, he says. Thanks to the media, they are ashamed of their service in Vietnam. He has worked hard to fire up enthusiasm for the next gathering. An article that resurrects the massacre will scare them away.

"Why open old wounds?" he demands angrily. "Why don't you get an honest job?"

"Didn't the attacks on Kerry in the presidential campaign show the wounds never really closed?" I ask. "These declassified records can help set the record straight."

"What purpose will it serve?" he says. "Why don't you get a respectable job?"

The conversation continues in this way, with my questions met with his, my responses rejected with angry derision. I check the time and am surprised that more than an hour has elapsed. Taylor has not budged on his refusal to discuss the investigation or to read his men's sworn statements. He reluctantly accepts my offer to call him before a story runs, and I take leave. When I get to my car, I pull out a notebook and quickly jot down the most memorable lines from our conversation. It doesn't take long. He'd recoiled every time I steered the conversation back to the massacre. But he supplied one important missing fact. I place a star next to the quote:

"The matter was fully investigated, and everyone was cleared. That's all I'm going to say about it."

---

I mail a letter to Reh with one last appeal for an interview. He ends his long silence with an e-mail on April 29, 2008. He acknowledges giving Carter an order just before the massacre. Reh says he does not recall his exact words. He remembers being worried they might be taken literally. He insists he called Carter back to clarify:

I did take up the phone to the 3rd platoon a second time, as Henry said he observed . . . just a few minutes after the first phone call ended, because I felt a sudden anxiety that the 3rd platoon leader would take my previous order too literally. The 3rd platoon leader and I then had a detailed phone call about the specific, sequential actions he could use to stop any detainee from attempting to leave the area, from initial voice warnings to increasing levels of physical force, if a detainee persisted in his attempt to leave. I do not recall that I told him during that call to kill anyone attempting to leave. I think that we also discussed that a man would more likely attempt to leave than a woman or child, and if he were stopped, then no one else would attempt to leave, so such force would not be necessary against women or children. I believed that he completely understood our plan and intended to follow it. We ended the call, and I resumed doing whatever I was doing with another platoon.

Some minutes after that phone call ended, I heard some gun fire coming from the 3rd platoon's direction, and I got back on the phone with the 3rd platoon leader to find out what it was about. As soon as I understood his situation, I ordered him to cease the firing. . . .

As the Company Commander, I took responsibility for the actions and lives of my men. Most followed directions, and in this shooting event I believe I gave my 3rd platoon leader a good and clear set of directions as the situation evolved. . . . If they had been followed, what happened might not have happened.

In Reh's version of events, Carter shoulders all the blame. But Reh's recollection of an extended second conversation with his lieutenant is not corroborated by the record. It is not mentioned in the statements of ten men who overheard the transmissions, including Carter's RTO, Reh's RTO, Henry, or Ambeau, who was standing near Reh. They told CID that Carter and others opened fire within minutes of receiving Reh's instruction. Also at odds with numerous witness statements is Reh's recollection of an Armored Personnel Carrier crushing a Vietnamese man. Reh says he witnessed an incident in which an APC ran over a man accidentally not intentionally.

"As I remember, the man was breathing and alive after the track was off of him."

He says I'm wrong to suggest that he did not pay a price for the massacre: "Aside from the physical and emotional damage combat inflicted on me, I lost jobs and promotions during the four to five years that the U.S. Army conducted its investigation of me in relation to the shooting referred to in your article."

In a series of brief e-mail exchanges over the next week, I ask Reh about the discrepancies between his accounts and those of his men, and why he did not report the massacre or take action against Carter.

"After forty years, I'm not sure why I did not report the shooting," he writes back, and leaves the other questions unanswered.

There are other massacres in the files.

In September 1969, in a hamlet on the border of Quang Nam and Quang Tin provinces, a reconnaissance squad from the 196th Light Infantry Brigade came upon at least nine unarmed women and children during a search-and-destroy operation. Several of the soldiers lined up outside a hut, counted to three, and opened fire on the people inside, according to army records. The men then turned their M-16s on an infant in the arms of an old woman, who held up her hand as if to stop the bullets. All perished. They were counted as enemy kills.[40]

Pvt. Davey V. Hoag, a member of the squad, refused to take part. He reported the massacre to CID at Fort Lewis, Washington, in 1972. At least five other members of the unit reported that they had witnessed the attack, and several more corroborated other rapes and killings. Some told investigators that their 1st lieutenant, later promoted to captain, knew about the massacre and other incidents but did nothing. The final report confirmed the massacre and identified seven suspects. The army charged only one, a private. The private's division commander exercised his authority under the military code to withdraw the murder charges and discharged him instead.[41]

Lundblad can't find a current address or phone number for Hoag. An investigator's notes from 1973 say Hoag had entered a psychiatric unit at the VA hospital in Oklahoma City. His attending physician told the agent that the former private "has brought up war crimes since being a patient in the hospital" and that he would need long-term treatment.[42]

I query an Internet database of Oklahoma newspapers for any mention of Hoag since then. There's just one, in the September 23, 1996, *Daily Oklahoman*:

"HOAG, Davey, 50. Prayer service today; services Tuesday."

A search of online phone books leads me to relatives and eventually a cousin, Marylyn Toyekoyah, in Anadarko, Oklahoma. She recalls him as a friendly jokester before he left for Vietnam, and deeply troubled when he returned.

"He wasn't like his normal self. He started drinking a lot and having nightmares," she says. "I know he was kind of disturbed and not well in the mind."

He never mentioned the massacre to her, she says. In fact, he rarely talked about the war. She says she lost touch with him and didn't know how he died.

Nick and I count seven confirmed massacres in the Army Staff's archive, not including My Lai, and thirty-four accounts of mass slayings that CID investigators didn't substantiate. More than 124 deaths were confirmed and hundreds more alleged. Later, we will come across evidence of massacres that never made it into the files at all.

| PLACE Washington, DC | DATE 23 Jun 71 | TIME | FILE NUMBER 70-CID121-00811 |
|---|---|---|---|

| LAST NAME, FIRST NAME, MIDDLE NAME ███████████ | SOCIAL SECURITY ACCOUNT NO. ███████ | GRADE CPT |
|---|---|---|

ORGANIZATION OR ADDRESS
Stu Det, 4th US Army, Ft Sam Houston, TX

**SWORN STATEMENT**

I, ███████████████████, WANT TO MAKE THE FOLLOWING STATEMENT UNDER OATH:

During the approximate period Aug 68 through 10 Apr 69, I was assigned as the S-2, 2d Bn, 503d Inf, 173d Abn Bde in Vietnam.

Shortly after a contact which our unit had in an area referred to as the rockpile, I had a conversation with ██████████ in which he was concerned with photographs taken by a SGT ██████████ of Military Intelligence. Apparently, ████████ had positioned the bodies of a woman and a child in such a way as to appear that they were innocent civilians killed by friendly fire. ████████ was concerned over these photographs and wanted them repossessed. He stated that if ████ did not turn over the photographs, that he had enough information on some of ████████ interrogation techniques to do ████ considerable harm. One thing he specifically stated was that he observed ████ using water torture on a prisoner. ████████ further stated that he was going to inform ████████ that if he did not turn over the photographs, he would report his use of the water torture to higher headquarters.

Q: Can you clarify when ████████ mentioned the water-torture incident to you?
A: Within two days after the contact at the rockpile.

Q: Did ████████ indicate when the water-torture incident had taken place?
A: The impression I had was that it had occurred while ████ was on an operation with ████████ and that it possibly occurred at the rockpile. It was definitely on a mission with our unit.

Q: Did ████████ name anyone else who was present at the water torture?
A: No, he did not, but normally his radio operator, SGT ████████ accompanied him wherever he went and in all probability, he was with him.

Q: As to the location of the water-torture incident, you are not certain where it occurred but believe that it did occur at about the time of the action at the rockpile, is that correct?
A: That's correct. ████████ primary concern after the rockpile contact was these alleged photographs that were taken, and it was during this time that he mentioned this lever on ████████ if he did not deliver.

Q: Do you know whether or not ████████ ever did report the water torture incident?
A: I don't think he did immediately, and I also do not think he reported it just prior to his relief when body counts and weapon counts were being questioned by Bde. At a later time, in May 69, I returned to Vietnam to attend a court-martial, ████████ conveyed to me the impression that he was more or less openening everything up. I had the distinct feeling that he

| EXHIBIT Y | INITIALS OF PERSON MAKING STATEMENT ████████ | PAGE 1 OF 3 PAGES |
|---|---|---|

ADDITIONAL PAGES MUST CONTAIN THE HEADING "STATEMENT OF___ TAKEN AT___ DATED___ CONTINUED." THE BOTTOM OF EACH ADDITIONAL PAGE MUST BEAR THE INITIALS OF THE PERSON MAKING THE STATEMENT AND BE INITIALED AS "PAGE___OF___PAGES." WHEN ADDITIONAL PAGES ARE UTILIZED, THE BACK OF PAGE 1 WILL BE LINED OUT, AND THE STATEMENT WILL BE CONCLUDED ON THE REVERSE SIDE OF ANOTHER COPY OF THIS FORM.

DA FORM 2823 1 JAN 68     FOR OFFICIAL USE ONLY     b6,7C     71

One of dozens of sworn statements the army collected in an effort to discredit a whistle-blower that instead produced evidence of widespread detainee abuse in the 173rd Airborne Brigade.

## CHAPTER TWO

# STICKS AND PHONES

When the sounds of night in Vietnam come back to him, it isn't the boom of artillery he remembers first. It's the intermittent wail of pain from the building next to his sleeping tent.

"You could hear the *screams*," he says.

Robert B. Stemme Jr. is in a softly lit room off the garden of his townhouse high on a San Francisco hill. He has white hair, wire-rimmed glasses, rosy cheeks, and a strong chin. He dresses in loose-fitting denim, the wardrobe of retirement after a lifelong career as an investigator for the public defender's office.

In 1968 and 1969, he was serving in the 172nd Military Intelligence Detachment at a base camp in Binh Dinh province on the central coast. While there, he witnessed the torture of detainees by U.S. interrogators. He reported the abuse while in Vietnam, and again as a veteran in 1970. Having failed to stir much interest then, he is surprised at my interest so many years later.

In truth, I almost passed him by. His case appeared on a one-page case summary in a fat stack of cases that CID closed as "unsubstantiated." Nick and I had our hands full with the three hundred–plus allegations from cases that CID confirmed, such as those of Jamie Henry and Davey Hoag. We didn't plan to pursue the unproven cases, at least not for our first set of stories. However, I was keeping track of them in a simple spreadsheet. So when I came to a case summary labeled "51. Stemme-Brown-Martinsen Allegation," I paused for a minute to skim the sheet for the data I needed. It listed three veterans who appeared at a news conference at the Los Angeles Press Club in the summer of 1970—Stemme, Frederick Brown, and Peter N. Martinsen. Their allegations "consisted generally of the use of electrical devices and abusive treatment . . . of VN detainees during interrogation" by members of the 172nd MI. The entire summary ran just four paragraphs, and Stemme's account had been reduced to two opaque sentences:

> Mr. Stemme was contacted on 14 and 19 Aug 70. On both occasions, he declined to provide specific information regarding his allegation.[1]

The report was dated September 28, 1971. The status line read: "Investigation completed; unsubstantiated."

I would not have given the case a second look, if the writer had not tacked on this intriguing coda: "The Stemme-Brown portion of this allegation has been incorporated into Case #58, the Herbert Allegation."

Anthony B. Herbert's was a notorious case. He had been a hard-charging, highly decorated Korean War hero, the cover boy on a Rangers training manual, who led a battalion from the 173rd Airborne Brigade in Vietnam from February to April 1969. His superiors abruptly stripped him of his command, a fatal blow for a career officer. After losing two appeals, he met with CID investigators in September 1970 to accuse his superiors of retaliating against him for reporting atrocities that they didn't want to investigate.[2] The accused included the deputy brigade commander, Col. J. Ross Franklin, who had gone on to serve on the Peers Commission inquiry into the My Lai massacre. Gen. William Westmoreland moved swiftly to contain the scandal with a high-level internal investigation into Herbert's allegations.[3] Nonetheless, Herbert took his case to the public in a series of news articles and appearances on network television.

The publicity changed the rules of engagement. The army's problems were the army's business, to be dealt with internally—and certainly not aired publicly by an active-duty officer. Now army leaders returned fire. News stories reported that Herbert's commanders considered him a "keg of dynamite" and "completely oriented to killing mercilessly."[4] Franklin asserted that Herbert had lost his command because of performance deficiencies and never tried to report atrocities in Vietnam. The army released a series of fact sheets on the investigation that called Herbert's credibility into question: Investigators could not confirm fourteen of twenty-one atrocities that he said he witnessed or heard about; only two of the reports warranted action; they could find no evidence that he told Franklin about war crimes or suffered retaliation as a result.[5] *Army* magazine printed the findings in February 1972; the article pointed out the unsubstantiated charges and declared "this eminence is undeserved."[6] By then,

Herbert's appeal had reached the secretary of the army, who removed the unfavorable efficiency report from the besieged officer's personnel file and ordered his promotion. Herbert retired
soon afterward.

The controversy's finale was a 60 Minutes exposé in February
1973 that painted him as a liar and an exaggerator.[7] He sued the
show in what became a landmark Supreme Court case, establishing that libel plaintiffs could probe the editorial decision-
making process to establish actual malice.[8] Though Herbert won
the battle over evidence, he lost the trial and retreated from the
public spotlight.

Herbert's case lay in our "confirmed" pile, flagged by Nick for
special attention. An internal army memo showed the public affairs office had leaked damaging information about Herbert to
60 Minutes producer Barry Lando shortly before the piece aired.[9]
Other records showed that army personnel had been ordered to
scrub every sentence Herbert wrote or spoke in public for discrepancies, major or minor.[10] CID chief Henry Tufts sent the results to newly confirmed Chief of Staff Creighton W. Abrams Jr.
in early 1973 with a cover letter that reflected the depth of the
army's antipathy:

> This package . . . provides sufficient material to impeach
> this man's credibility; should this need arise, I volunteer for
> the task.[11]

Yet a closer look at the army's fact sheets revealed that, while
only a handful of allegations had been confirmed, they were egregious. One involved the execution of eight detainees by South
Vietnamese soldiers under the watch of a U.S. adviser. Herbert

said he arrived as they slit the throat of a woman whose child clung to her leg. Four other incidents involved torture of detainees using water, electric shock, and sticks. The most significant finding did not appear in the fact sheets but rather as a three-sentence aside in a twenty-two-page report on the Herbert affair that Tufts prepared in July 1971 for a briefing with Secretary of Defense Melvin Laird.[12] The passage noted that CID agents investigating Herbert's allegations had come across evidence that interrogators from the 172nd MI used field telephones, water torture, and sticks "on various occasions" in addition to the instances that Herbert reported. Twenty U.S. and three South Vietnamese suspects had been identified, the notation said, providing the only hint of how widespread the practices had been.[13] Another clue is embedded in a memorandum for the chief of staff. The writer noted that the army's fact sheets omitted mention of "the determination by commanders to take no action" against three suspects still on active duty.[14]

A Freedom of Information Act request produced several heavily redacted records indicating the torture took place over an eighteen-month period from 1968–1969—overlapping allegations from the Stemme-Brown-Martinsen press conference. I moved the case summary from the stack destined for my filing cabinet to the top of the "hot pursuit" pile.

---

In 1967, Nobel Prize–winning philosopher Bertrand Russell convened a citizens' tribunal in Stockholm, Sweden, and Copenhagen, Denmark, to investigate U.S. war crimes in Vietnam. The proceedings were preserved in various archives, and

I found Peter N. Martinsen's name on the witness list in Denmark. At the forum, Martinsen testified that he took part in beatings and watched others torture detainees while serving as an interrogator with the 541st MI from September 1966 to June 1967:

> I interrogated one and I had no data on where he was captured or what he was doing. He was just presented to me. I started to question him and he kept saying that he was not a Viet Cong, that he didn't know where the Viet Cong was, etc. I was quite sure that he was lying. I was not certain if he belonged to the Viet Cong, but I was quite sure he was lying about not knowing where they were. I decided to beat him. This did not help. I struck him with my hand. This did not produce anything except a long string of "I don't knows" . . . and then—as was often the case—another interrogator took my place, an interrogation officer. I told the officer, a lieutenant, that I couldn't get anything out of the prisoner. The lieutenant proceeded to do the same thing as I had been doing, finally beating the prisoner, and this did not work. The lieutenant had an army field telephone, which runs on batteries and a generator. You crank it and it gives a nasty shock, a very nasty shock, quite painful. The interrogation commenced with the prisoner being tortured by field telephone. The telephones were first placed on his hands and then the field telephone wires were placed on his sexual organs. I left, I could not watch it.[15]

Interrogations took an even darker turn when he began working with the 172nd MI, he testified.

I witnessed more torture than I had seen on any special operation in Vietnam. We were cooperating with the 172nd
Military Intelligence Detachment, which is attached to the
173rd Airborne Brigade. We received a large group of prisoners, and we had a "Chieu Hoi." A Chieu Hoi is a deserter
from the Viet Cong. He is generally used as an informer to
give information about his former comrades. A certain prisoner was pointed out by the Chieu Hoi as being some sort
of local cadre in the Iron Triangle. . . The prisoner was taken
into the tent in the afternoon. Our unit stopped interrogation in the evenings because our tents were so full of holes
from bullets and other things that our light seeped out and
attracted enemy fire. Anyway, another unit continued to in-
terrogate at night and all of a sudden an enlisted man from
that unit came over and said: "We just lost a prisoner." I said,
"What?" I couldn't believe it. And he said, "We have. The
captain was wiring him, and he just fell over and died." The
captain came over a little later and said: "Yes, I was wiring
him. He was just about to break. He was just on the verge of
telling me something when he died." There is a log which
must be kept in regard to the prisoners. It is a very informal
thing but you have to fill in the disposition of the prisoner. In
this case the prisoner was dead, so a doctor was called, a
brigade surgeon, as I recall, in the 173rd Airborne Brigade.
He diagnosed the cause of death of the prisoner as being
heart failure, which is logical. The man had been electrically
tortured to death. He probably had a weak heart.

On another occasion, Martinsen said, he received orders to in-
terrogate teenage girls who had been gassed by troops clearing

a tunnel. They were gasping for breath, and one grew increasingly ill.

> I kept calling the doctor to say, "Doctor, she has pneumo-
> nia." I knew that because I have had pneumonia. The doc-
> tor kept saying: "No, No. She'll get better," and she kept
> getting worse. She was finally evacuated to Lai Khe, to the
> 3rd Brigade, 1st Division field hospital, where I hear she
> died. I denounced the stupidity of the doctors and the stu-
> pidity of the commanders for trying to keep her there to in-
> terrogate her, and I almost got court-martialed for it. That
> was one of the most odious things I saw there.

The forum attracted little coverage in the United States. But
the army took notice. The case summary from the war-crime
archive indicates that CID agents interviewed him soon afterward. They questioned him again after the 1970 press conference
in Los Angeles with Stemme and Brown. Martinsen agreed to
talk if granted immunity. But CID declined "based on the general nature of the allegation, Mr. Martinsen's attitude and his
record," the case summary said.[16] The reference to lack of
specifics seemed odd, given his detailed remarks at the forum.

Janet Lundblad searches her databases for Martinsen's where-
abouts, but his trail has run cold. She finds too many Frederick
Browns to tease out the right one. I find crime stories quoting an
investigator named Robert Stemme in the San Francisco public
defender's office. Lundblad produces a home number, and I call.

In 1966, Stemme was sitting out a semester at the University of Hawaii when a letter from the draft board arrived. The war and the antiwar movement had been distant noises on opposite horizons until then. Adrift in the Pacific, "we were oblivious out there," he recalls. He enlisted, and he tried to view the development as an opportunity to kick-start his adulthood.

"I'd grown up in the military and gone to military schools. I was thinking about that as a career, because my father was an Air Force officer. So I took a battery of tests. They said I could do anything I wanted. I decided I wanted to be a combat photographer or spy—I'd seen too many James Bond movies—and I wound up getting interviewed by this military intelligence group in Hawaii."

After basic training at Fort Lewis in Tacoma, Washington, he attended intelligence school at Fort Holabird in Baltimore, Maryland. He finished in August 1967, and the army shipped him to the Presidio in San Francisco, where he quickly caught up on current events. It was the Summer of Love. A few blocks from his office, the peace torch was leaving Golden Gate Park for a massive antiwar protest in Washington, D.C. Tens of thousands of peaceniks, protesters, and flower children occupied the city. Inside the Presidio, soldiers who'd been to Vietnam painted an exceedingly bleak picture of the war. Stemme received his orders on his twenty-fifth birthday in June 1968.

"I was pretty well convinced this was not going to be a good thing. But because of my background, bugging out just would not have occurred to me."

His assignment sounded about as good as it could get under the circumstances. He was to be part of a covert intelligence group that operated out of villages along the South China Sea.

"But other forces intervened. I got to Vietnam, and somehow orders got changed from this little secret spy group to this military intelligence detachment to the 173rd Airborne Brigade in the Central Highlands, which was a little upsetting to me because the only uniform I had was the one I had on my back. I had a duffle bag full of seersucker suits."

He tried to persuade his superiors that there had been a mistake.

"They said, 'Well, it's going to take awhile to straighten out, so you'll have to go to jungle school.' So I did that, and it never got straightened out, and I was forwarded to LZ English, which was kind of my home for the rest of the year."

"LZ" stood for "landing zone," but English also served as a support area and base camp in Binh Dinh province. The installation occupied a rise overlooking a patchwork landscape of rice paddies on the central coast. Structures cobbled from sandbags, wood, and scrap metal sat on a floor of red dirt that turned to thick mud in the rain.

"I don't think we even had generators for lights at first. So what they were using for illumination was the same thing you shit in. It was a fifty-five-gallon drum that was cut off. They had like diesel fuel in it. It was just lit like a big torch."

One of his first memories is of a Buddhist monk, taken into custody, walking over to a burning drum and calmly sitting in the fire.

"He self-immolated," Stemme says. "It was horrific."

Stemme worked counterintelligence. He was assigned to cultivate friendly informants in nearby farming hamlets. He was expected to gather information on enemy movements and collect names of potential Vietcong cadre in the communities. It was a deceptively benign job description, a truth he learned quickly and dramatically. The soldier he relieved had passed along his sources, and one of them alerted Stemme to an infirmary run by the Vietcong on a mountain near the base. It was lightly guarded, an easy target for a raid. Stemme passed along the information, figuring that U.S. or Vietnamese forces would take out the guards and evacuate the sick and wounded.

A few days later, an acquaintance directed Stemme's attention to the mountain. "Look!" he shouted, pointing to the mountain.

Stemme turned to see C-130s dumping fuel at the location of the infirmary. He felt sick to his stomach. The planes released white phosphorous, and the fuel ignited. He later heard the patients inside the infirmary had suffocated or burned to death. This was Stemme's introduction to the Phoenix program, a secret CIA–South Vietnamese campaign to identify and eliminate suspected Vietcong supporters in South Vietnam by capturing or killing them. Estimates of lives lost range from twenty thousand upward, including an unknown but significant number of innocent civilians.[17] Stemme soon realized that many of the suspected Vietcong sympathizers he was expected to identify would be targeted.

"I wasn't interested in producing much actionable intelligence after that unless it posed an imminent threat to our troops," he says.

Stemme's counterintelligence assignment spared him from the grim job of questioning the detainees dragged onto the base from the surrounding countryside. But he couldn't escape the sight and sound of the interrogators' brutal techniques. The questioning often took place in a thin-walled structure, divided into stalls, just outside Stemme's sleeping tent.

"My bed was maybe thirty feet from where all this stuff was going on. So I could hear this shit all night long," he says. "It was pretty standard practice that people got slapped around or hit with things or guns pointed at them or whatever. Field telephones, all those things, were tools of the trade."

Interrogators also used the "water rag," a variation on today's controversial water-board torture. They would place a cloth over a detainee's face and pour water on it until he or she nearly drowned.

It's common to hear veterans talk about the harsh methods employed by Vietnamese army interrogators. But these were U.S. soldiers wielding the water, sticks, and wires. Most of their captives were local citizens suspected of aiding the enemy. They were as likely to be Vietcong as hapless farmers, and it was hard to tell from their screams whether resolve or ignorance kept them from spilling secrets. When a detainee died in the process, the official reports identified an underlying medical problem as the cause of death.

"I thought it was wrong. I'd lived all over, the U.S., Europe, and Japan. I didn't really differentiate between people. Everyone is a human being. Torturing people—I was appalled at the whole thing," Stemme says. He first appealed to the interrogators.

"I'd say, 'This shit is fucked up. You can't do that. It's producing negative results.' Had no effect."

He guesses about a dozen of the sixteen to eighteen men in the unit felt as he did. They struggled over how to respond. It seemed there was nowhere to turn. The unit's executive officer had been in the room when abuse occurred but did not intervene, according to Stemme and the statements of other men from the unit. The base commanders seemed to go out of their way to avoid knowing. They dropped in rarely and only when announced, so the sticks and wires could be hidden before their arrival.

"They were ticket punchers," Stemme says—career officers doing time in Vietnam to advance through the ranks.

Mistreatment of detainees extended beyond the intelligence unit. Stemme said he witnessed a brutal interrogation while in the field with members of a 173rd Airborne Brigade platoon.

"There was this young Vietnamese woman, probably a teenager. And there was this guy that was holding her from behind by her arms and this other guy who had her fingers and was just breaking them one after another as we were walking up. And I'm fucking freaking out. And I'm right there with her and [the commander's] RTO and my interpreter. And I said, 'You've got to stop that.' He said, 'They're Vietnamese,' and just turned around and went away, although they were with his people and their operation."[18]

In the fall of 1968, CID investigated a complaint that members of the 173rd Airborne Brigade support battalion abused detainees during interrogations. Witnesses called the abuse "common knowledge." Three soldiers admitted to participating in an interrogation in which the detainee was shocked with an electrical generator, dragged by his hair, kicked, and shoved. They faced courts-martial, but only one was convicted and he received no prison time.

With no serious repercussions, the torture and killing of Vietnamese went from tolerated to accepted to sport for an increasingly violent segment at LZ English. Two soldiers in the 173rd Airborne Brigade brazenly competed for the highest "body count"—military jargon for enemy kills. The winner got R&R in Qui Nhon, the nearest big town on the South China Sea. Many on the base suspected their numbers were padded with exaggerations and innocent farmers.

On February 25, 1969, Stemme was asleep on his cot, when a soldier shook him awake with an urgent message: Report to the military police shack immediately. He quickly snatched his fatigues off the ground, wiggled into them, and ran. Suddenly, he felt as if his skin had caught fire. He tore open his shirt to find his body covered in ants. He frantically slapped at them, shook out his clothes, and then continued to the shack. The assignment they handed him would permanently sear the flesh-crawling sensation of the ants with the gruesome scene that followed. Take an interpreter and get to the gate, he was told.

"So I grab an interpreter and go out to the gate and there's this group of very distraught peasant farmers at the gate. I say what's going on, and they take me to this area two hundred meters outside the village, easy walking distance of the perimeter of the LZ."

The bodies of two teenage boys and a man lay in the field, arranged like spokes of a wheel.

"They were just riddled with M-16s."

In the center, where their heads met, a grenade had blown a hole in the ground. Weapons were scattered near the bodies. Yet the villagers vehemently insisted they had been unarmed. They wanted to know why the Americans would kill children tending their flocks of ducks.

CID soon arrived on the scene to investigate and ascertained that members of a U.S. reconnaissance team had reported the three as enemy killed in action. The team was led by Platoon Sgt. Roy E. Bumgarner Jr., one of the two soldiers engaged in the body-count contest and the odds-on favorite to win. According to other members of the unit, he marched the three unarmed villagers to a secluded spot and shot them. He ordered one of his men to remove their civilian identification cards and valuables, detonate a grenade by their heads and drop weapons near their bodies. He kept a small cache of recovered enemy weapons in his bag for such occasions.[19]

"He called them in as KIA to get an in-country R&R," Stemme says.

I knew the case—it was one of only a handful in the declassified files that had resulted in a court-martial and guilty verdict. Bumgarner's conviction for unpremeditated murder cost him no more than a cut in pay and demotion. He remained in the army and, after a brief absence, returned to combat in Vietnam.[20]

"I just couldn't believe that went away after what happened to those people. I was really kind of shocked," Stemme says.

The wrist slap reflected the "mere gook rule," he says. U.S. soldiers learned in basic training to dehumanize the enemy and carried the lesson to its logical conclusion in the field. So when army leaders pressured the men at LZ English to produce more bodies and intelligence, the "mere gook" rule provided an easy solution.

"Nothing else mattered," Stemme says. "There was just a complete sense that there was nobody you could go to, nothing you could do."

In early spring 1969, the anti-torture contingent of the 172nd MI hatched a plan. They each wrote and signed a statement decrying the abuse. They gave the letters to a captain in their group who was going home. He promised to carry them out of Vietnam and deliver them to military authorities stateside. The men still had faith—or at least hope—that army leaders back in Washington would act if only they knew.

"We said don't give it to anyone in-country," Stemme says.

But instead of waiting, the captain handed the papers over to the army inspector general's office during a stopover in Saigon.

"Next thing we know we have this major coming up from the IG's office who's Mirandizing us and asks us if we're admitting to committing war crimes. . . . It was all about us, when this was de facto command policy," Stemme says. "They were interested in shutting the whole thing down. They wanted it to go away fast."

The men reconvened and made a new pact: They'd shut their mouths.

Stemme left LZ English in June 1969 for a domestic spying assignment back at the Presidio in San Francisco. His job involved transmitting information from agents in the field who had infiltrated antiwar groups in eight western states. He became an admirer of one of the targets, the Citizens Commission of Inquiry into War Crimes in Indochina (CCI), an American organization linked to Bertrand Russell's group. After Stemme left the service in January 1970, having lost his desire for a military career, he contacted CCI . On April 14, he joined Martinsen and Brown for their appearance at the Los Angeles Press Club.

The public airing created a rift with his father that lasted to his death. But Stemme felt he had to speak out. He thought the outcry might force the army to stop the abuse. The outcry never materialized. The *Los Angeles Times* placed the story on page 21.[21] Two months later, the *Washington Post* folded Stemme's account into a roundup of torture allegations that appeared inside the front section.[22] The pieces received little notice, except from CID. The army could not ignore war-crime allegations that appeared in the media or on a congressman's desk. After the *Post* article, a CID agent called Stemme and asked him to provide a statement.[23] He went to the Presidio, where he wrote out a lengthy account of his experiences. Then two CID agents from Washington, D.C., met with him. One was a nondescript older man and the other a young agent with a dark mustache, Stemme recalls. They drove him to a "tourist trap" motel just outside the gate of the Presidio. They entered a room with two beds and sat around a table.

"Somebody asked if I drank, and I said yeah. The lead guy said, 'You're in luck. I've got some white lightning with me.'"

The man walked to the closet to retrieve a brown bag and pulled out a one-pint Mason jar filled with clear liquid. He poured the homemade brew into three glasses and cut it with water. As they drank, Stemme says, the agents tried to persuade him that the things he'd witnessed really weren't a big deal.

"'It was war, these things happen,'" he recalls being told.

He went over everything he'd seen, the entire hellish year with names, dates, and details, he says. They talked for hours before the agents ran out of questions and Stemme told all he knew. When I read him the two-line synopsis from the case summary, he laughs in disbelief.

---

The Col. Henry Tufts Archive resides at the University of Michigan Special Collections Library. The archive is unusual in that it holds six linear feet of pirated internal investigative files that the colonel removed from his office when Abrams ousted him as CID chief in 1974. Tufts stored them at his house in Toledo until his death in 2002. As per his instructions, the papers then were donated to an academic institution. They cover several well-known cases, including the My Lai massacre and a corruption scandal involving the army's worldwide network of officers' clubs. Most notably, the archive contains the Tiger Force files, mined by the *Toledo Blade* for

an important, Pulitzer Prize–winning series in 2003 on an elite platoon's murderous, seven-month crime spree in the Central Highlands. Nick flies to Ann Arbor hoping to find something useful on
the cases we're investigating. On his first day there, he calls with
good news: There's a file on the 173rd Airborne Brigade investigation. He begins e-mailing the final report of the investigation to
me page by page. I set up a special e-mail account to handle the
volume. The attachments reveal the names, dates, and method of
torture for dozens of incidents, including those reported by
Stemme. Combined with the other records, we eventually count
more than one hundred allegations of torture and cover-up between March 1968 and October 1969[24]—the most extensive case of
detainee abuse by U.S. troops to emerge from the Vietnam War so
far. The problem certainly was even worse. The investigation covered neither Martinsen's earlier tour of duty nor a later documented case of detainee abuse at LZ English in December 1970.[25]

We glean the names of twenty U.S. suspects, at least eight of
whom had confessed to abuse. They spoke of the routine use of
field telephones to shock detainees, water rags "to impair breathing," sticks, boards, and fists. There's no indication that any of
them—even those who confessed—faced court-martial. A few
names stand out, and Staff Sgt. David Carmon is among them.[26]
He is mentioned more than any other suspect—using a field telephone, employing the water-rag technique, beating a detainee
with his fists. The people he questioned looked bruised and
swollen afterward, investigators were told. One of the most disturbing accounts involved the interrogation of Nguyen Cong.

Nguyen arrived at LZ English in August 1968; the records
don't say why. Carmon and two other interrogators were assigned to question him. Witnesses told investigators that Car-

mon poured a bucket of water on Nguyen's head, slapped him, and kicked him off his chair; all three interrogators kicked and beat him. He kept passing out, so Carmon summoned a doctor. The doctor examined Nguyen and declared him fit for questioning. The interrogation continued until Nguyen suddenly began convulsing—one bystander said his eyes rolled back into his head. The interrogators stopped work and moved him into a confinement cage. They returned later to find him dead.[27]

The body was transported to a nearby hospital, where an American pathologist performed the autopsy. When he opened Nguyen's abdomen, he could see what had killed him—a ruptured spleen. The rupture could have been caused by "external trauma," the pathologist said. But the man had malaria, so it may have ruptured as a natural complication of the disease. He settled on "natural causes" for his official ruling. The CID investigator cited the pathologist's report to explain why he didn't pursue the death as a homicide.[28]

Nick locates an e-mail address for Carmon. He runs a patriotic-supply business out of his home in Wheelersburg, Ohio. Nick sends a first round of questions to him, and Carmon responds several days later.

*Where did you learn . . . the field telephone and water rag techniques?*

"The Vietnamese interrupters [interrogators] and Vietnamese National Police."

*Were such methods confined to the 172d MI?*

"NO."

*Can you describe how an interrogation with a field telephone would proceed?*

"What I saw were leads hooked to the legs of a metal folding chair. It was primarily used with the mountain/country detainees that weren't familiar with electricity. They would [think] it would make [them] sterile or something to that nature. When you turned the phone crank a light tickle of electricity would generally scare them into talking."

*What happened as a result of the investigation?*

"I was interview a total of four (4) times. They were charged with getting some bodies for scrape-goats. They were not extremely professional and tried a lot of bluffing."

He signs off this way:

> I served proudly with the 173rd Airborne Brigade (Sep) for 26 months in Vietnam. I am not ashamed of anything I did, and I would most likely conduct myself in the same manner if placed in a Vietnam type situation again. War is Hell! I was awarded the purple heart for wounds and two bronze stars, one for heroism in Dakto, Vietnam and one for achievement as an interrogator. I served my country to the best of my ability, and I'm extremely proud of my service. AIRBORNE ALL THE WAY!
>
>    Dave Carmon

In the next e-mail, he describes the pressure troops were under: "I understand why things like civilians killings happened. Numbers were a big thing in the war. Units were under a lot of pressure to get prisoners and body counts. A huge percentage of the prisoners brought into the MI [military intelligence] section were classified IC, innocent civilians," he writes.

He also elaborated on the question of whether other units used torture: "These methods were used by all units . . . Officers, LTC [lieutenant colonels] and below witnessed many interrogations, and many encouraged the mistreatment of the PWs [prisoners of war] . . . It was a brutal war. There is no doubt in my mind that everyone had knowledge."

Carmon stops responding to Nick, so I take up the correspondence and request a phone interview. Carmon declines. He explains that he had a change of heart after attending a 173rd Airborne Brigade reunion, where he spoke with other men involved in incidents we're investigating.

"I'm not interested in talking to you again. You are creating problems for me as well as other soldiers who are and were willing to fight and die for what we believed was or is a just cause."

I ask him to elaborate. He sends a terse reply:

"I urge you not to print 40 year news. Concentrate on urging the public to support the president on the war in Iraq."

In our last e-mail exchange, in response to questions about the detainee who died in custody, Carmon says he didn't hurt Nguyen:

"He was not roughed up by us at all. My Vietnamese interrogator slapped the individual a few times and some water was used, but he was not in good shape when we received him from the bats [battalions]. The interrupter said he was of little value and was sent back to the cage."

Then he closed for the final time with a lengthy defense:

> I would be confident in saying most everyone was aware of interrogation practices. It was a war, and war changes people. I can honestly say, "I don't remember hurting a PW." I scared the "H" out of several with water or maybe a tingle from a field phone. Our intentions were never to hurt anyone, we simply wanted the information the held. This is the reason that we primarily used water. Water poured over a cloth gave a sensation of drowning that generally scared the PW into talking. I "Never" talked to an NVA [North

Vietnamese army] that was loyal to their cause. The NVA would generally tell on the grandparents for jaywalking. . . . I just wish you could just go back in time to see what we were up against. Have you ever listened to the song by Big & Rich, "8th of November." Look at what happened on Hill 875, November 1967, or what happened in June 1967 to the 173rd Airborne. Look at the Brigade as a whole. We were sent to every Hell Hole in South Vietnam and fought for our lives.

---

Carmon says everyone knew. The investigation report's list of suspects included the unit's executive officer, Capt. Norman L. Bowers. Stemme and five other witnesses told CID that Bowers had observed or authorized torture.[29] On one occasion, a former interrogator told investigators, "Bowers changed the wires on the field telephone because they were not hooked up correctly." Bowers himself declined to talk to investigators, the report says.

He stayed in the army until 1989 and retired a lieutenant colonel. I reach him at his home in St. Louis, Missouri. He says he remembers the investigation.

"This investigation took nineteen months. . . . At the end of the nineteen months, those individuals were exonerated."

He says that he didn't dodge CID; he answered the investigators' questions. He told them that he did not allow his men to use field phones or a water rag on detainees.

"Those were methods of interrogation that were abusive, and they were not used in our unit," he tells me.

I run through the list of men who said he authorized or allowed torture:[30]

*Brown said you were in the room when he used the field telephone and water rag on detainees "with your concurrence." He observed you and Carmon use the field telephone on a detainee.*

"I don't know anything in that regard," he says.

*Carmon said you were present while he was using a field telephone.*

"I did not observe that in any case. And to my knowledge it wasn't done."

*Carey said you "authorized maltreatment of detainees in order to get information" and specifically mentioned field telephones. He said he saw an interrogator use a field telephone on a detainee in your presence.*

"I never observed that being done and would not have been involved in it."

*The men said they could hear screams at night. Did you ever hear screams?*

"I can't recall that ever occurring. . . . The commander of the organization, Maj. [Michael] O'Kane, and I as executive officer for the detachment had a separate hooch. The Artillery battalion was right next to us. They were firing all the time. There was traffic going by. It was very difficult to hear."

O'Kane had been commander of the 172nd MI from December 1968 to December 1969. CID investigators interviewed him in 1970. He "denied any knowledge of detainees torture by electrical shock" but on his lawyer's advice declined to sign a sworn statement, according to the investigation report.[31]

O'Kane calls me back from a barrier island in the Outer Banks on the North Carolina coast. He is on his cell phone.

"When I took over that unit, I had my work cut out for me," he says right away.

He discovered that his men were operating an unauthorized bar and shut it down as his first order of business, he explains. Sometime afterward, he noticed that an inordinate number of detainees brought in for questioning turned out to be innocent civilians. The battalion field units would capture them and report them as "VC" or "suspects." Their commanders would earn credits that would reflect well in their efficiency ratings.

"They would be competing against each other. I thought that was a terrible idea."

He says he cracked down on the practice by refusing to accept detainees if the field units did not produce recovered weapons or other evidence of suspicious activity.

I ask about the evidence uncovered by CID that his own men repeatedly tortured detainees on his watch.

"I can honestly say I wasn't aware of it."

He says he once came across two interrogators slapping a detainee and made it clear that wasn't permitted. He also recalls the inspector general's visit in 1969 to investigate allegations of torture by his men. He says he assumed that a "disenchanted, recalcitrant officer" in his unit had made a false report to get back at him for banning beer and alcohol.

"An investigation ensued. They didn't find anything," he says.

I point out that CID later concluded the allegations were true.

"When I got back to the States, there was an ongoing investigation. When it came to my attention some of the things that happened, I wrote a letter recommending this be investigated fully. And a pretty substantial investigation followed," he says.

He was not informed of the outcome, he says, and is surprised to hear that so many of his interrogators admitted using torture. He says he is disappointed that none of his men brought their concerns about the practices to him while in Vietnam.

"If there were sworn statements and those sorts of things, whoever is guilty of wrongdoing needs to be punished severely. I don't have anything to hide. My unit didn't have anything to hide. If they did, shame on them."

———————

Retired Col. J. Ross Franklin is next in the chain of command. He served as deputy commander of the 173rd from December 1968 through June 1969. During his tour of duty, he clashed with Herbert and took away his batallion command. Herbert later contended that he lost his command after reporting war crimes to Franklin.[32] CID interviewed Franklin for the Herbert investigation but also for the broader investigation into systematic torture by the 172nd MI. The final report of the 172nd investigation said CID found no evidence that Herbert reported the war crimes to Franklin, but it was silent on whether Franklin knew through other means that detainees were routinely shocked and doused in the interrogation huts.[33] So Nick and I seek him out for answers.

He left the army in 1980 and now runs an export business in Pensacola, Florida, called Pachomius Co. The biography, posted on his company's Web site, boasts of his decorated military career and his starring role in the Herbert smack-down.[34] Without elaboration, the posting notes that Franklin lived in a Catholic monastery from 1995 to 2002 before starting Pachomius, named after a saint who led an order of hermit monks. The company sells scrap, urea, sugar, petroleum, and various other U.S. commodities to emerging countries—and supports overseas orphans, the site says.

News clippings show that Franklin also spent time in prison in the early 1990s for his part in a real estate scam that allegedly

bilked investors out of as much as $10 million.[35] There's a jailhouse
interview with a local paper in which he maintains his innocence.[36]

When Nick and I reach Franklin on the phone, he is more than
willing to talk to us. He assumes we want to talk about Herbert
and begins to rail at his "cock and bull on war crimes." I tell him
we want to talk about the CID investigation into torture by the
172nd MI. He recalls the investigation but says he never saw the
final report. I say that CID documented more than one hundred
allegations of abuse and cover-up.

"If the army found it, I'd say it probably happened," he says.
"Interrogators obviously are under pressure and encouraged to
get information, and some of these guys are sadistic at heart."

I ask if he saw U.S. soldiers torturing detainees while he served
at LZ English—or if he had heard of any incidents.

"Well, if I knew anything, I'd be guilty of a war crime," he says.
"Nobody told me. I didn't even know what water-boarding was.
Electric shocks I had heard about—hooking up somebody to a
field phone and giving it a couple cranks."

He adds that he heard about field-phone torture in Korea but
never personally witnessed it there or in Vietnam.

"I just knew it was possible."

(In a later e-mail, he recalls differently: "I only once observed a
field phone used by Vietnamese police on a woman, secured by my
US troops-82d Airborne-and not the 173rd. A Vietnamese man was
also held under water several times. As a result, we found 50 rockets, scheduled to shoot into Saigon, where women and children
likely would have been victims. I did not know at that time that I was
supposed to report and investigate. I am happy I did not.")

I note that that the army uncovered routine use of field-phone
and water-rag torture at LZ English. There were beatings and

other forms of abuse too. If the abuse was so extensive, I ask, how could he not know about it?

"I don't know what the word 'torture' means. If you put a lot of pressure on people to save the lives of American paratroopers, I probably would—in each specific case I'd have to decide whether it was right or wrong."

He retreats, when I probe for what sort of "pressure" would be warranted in those circumstances—and how he would deal with the fact that many detainees at LZ English turned out to be innocent civilians.

"Never did anybody bring to me a case of abused detainees at LZ English."

I tell him that the screams from the interrogation hut kept soldiers awake at night. He says he didn't hear them.

"Frankly, I had an air conditioner in my hooch, and I was grateful, and I really wouldn't hear much of anything other than friendly arty [artillery] shooting once in a while."

---

Stemme isn't so lucky.

"Anytime I hear someone screaming in pain, I think about it," he says. "Abu Ghraib called to mind certain situations; sometimes when I would take pictures of people who'd been beaten by the cops, especially if they were Asian."

I point out that he chose a career defending the accused and incarcerated.

"Yeah, the underdog," he says. "It's no coincidence."

25 May 1970

Dear General Westmoreland,

I am a US GI now in Germany, and I worry a (lot) about Vietnam, and the wrong we are doing there to (the) Vietnamese people, and to GIs like myself. I read in (the) magasines and newspapers every day about My Lay, (and) the general at West Point. I also read a lot about (the) 9th Division lieutenant who had the prisoner shot because of pressure on him for body count, and about a 9th Division doctor who wrote his congressman about firing up a village for target practice but nothing right seems to be done about it.

Then yesterday I saw in the paper that a platoon leader and CO from 2-39 being charged with murder over the death of just two Vietnamese in the target practice report.

I was in the 9th Division, as a "grunt" in the 1st Brigade, when we were in Dinh Tong province, the same one as Dong Tam is in. (1st Brigade used to be up to Tan _____ where 3rd Brigade is now, but I'm mostly talking about Dinh Tong.) I never saw any big killing like My Lay, and don't have any dates exact to tell you about a(ny) prisoneres getting shot, but I know I have information about things as bad as My Lay, and I don't want to tell any congr(essman) for fear I will hurt the Army. I also know I'd never make

NOTE: True copy by lines. Some words were cut off the Xerox copy and have been typed, in parentheses, in obvious places. Lines are left where the print was illegible.
Typed 27 Aug 71.

A letter from an anonymous soldier to Gen. William C. Westmoreland, army chief of staff, reporting civilian killings by the 9th Infantry Division. A member of the Army Staff retyped the handwritten correspondence and added the note on the right-hand side.

## CHAPTER THREE

# A My Lai a Month

A farmer shot on the way home from market, a man on his bicycle, three farmers in a field, teenage brothers fishing peacefully on a lake—there are hundreds of such reports in the war-crime archive, each one dutifully recorded, sometimes with no more than a passing sentence or two, as if the killing were as routine as the activity it interrupted.

Case No. 159: "On 16 Jun 69, SPf _____, with the aid of PVT _____, allegedly murdered an unidentified VN female."[1]

Measured against My Lai, the unexceptional deaths of one, two, or three Vietnamese at a time generally posed little danger of becoming national scandals, and they were treated accordingly by the Army Staff's office. That is, until an anonymous letter-writer did the math.

The "Concerned Sgt Allegation" is a slender file.[2] It holds three unsigned letters to Gen. William Westmoreland and other army leaders from a soldier in the 9th Division. They are interspersed with memos that reflect careful reading by Westmoreland and his superiors. The writer's first missive, dated May 25, 1970, began:

> Dear General Westmoreland,
>
>    I am a US GI now in Germany, and I worry a lot about Vietnam, and the wrong we are doing there to the Vietnamese people, and to GIs like myself. . . . I was in the 9th Divison' as a "grunt" in the 1st Brigade, when we were in Dinh Tong province. . . . I know I have information about things as bad as My Lay, and I don't want to tell any congressman for fear I will hurt the Army. I also know I'd never make rank in the Army if anyone knew I was writing you, let alone a congressman and I'm thinking about staying in . . . .[3]

His concern, he explained, was the intense pressure on troops "to get a big body count." He was referring to enemy kills; the army collected and assessed the numbers to measure military success. There was a growing perception in the press and even in military ranks that the figures were greatly inflated by commanders who wanted to win promotions and justify an unpopular war. In response, then secretary of defense Robert S. McNamara required actual bodies to be counted.[4] But exaggeration wasn't the anonymous soldier's concern. Worse than making up numbers, he wrote, troops were killing innocent civilians to meet the army's demand for bodies:

> Number one killer in the 9th Div, was the rule that said shoot if they run. Not just prisoners or suspects, or guys

with weapons, but anybody. I suppose it was ok if it had of
been the Arvins [Army of the Republic of Vietnam] surrounding a village to search and some guy had run away
from the blocking force. But this rule meant GIs were supposed to shoot any dude that run. And lots of them did.
Run from the GIs, run from the gunships, run from the
loaches [helicopters], the gunships and loaches would hover
over a guy in the fields till he got scared and run and they'd
zap him. GIs could see people in a field and start toward
them and they'd run and get killed.

We always had to report how many we killed and what
they were doing, and I know I heard "taking evasive action"
more than a hundred times. . . . Most all of the times we
never found weapons or nothing on them.

Number two killer was the snipers. There was a guy in
the 2nd Brigade (off the boats) that got a DSC [Distin-
guished Service Cross] for killing over a hundred Vietnamese as a sniper. I know guys in our sniper teams that
talked about medals like a bounty system. A bronze star for
so many gooks, and then a silver star for so many more. And
they got the medals too. One of them told me there was an
official Div[ision] letter out saying how many a guy had to
zap to get what medal. Sometimes our guys would go out
at nite with starlite scopes, but most of the time they just
shoot any Vietnamese they'd see at long range in the day
time, like at early morning. . . . No weapons, no VC [Viet-
cong] documents, just a dead Vietnamese at about 300 or
400 yards who is automaticaly a VC just as soon as he falls.
I heard the batalion commander laugh about the snipers
and say that pretty soon there wouldn't be any nice farmers

left because the snipers would kill them all. He didn't care if they shot VC or farmers, he just wanted a big body count.

Number three killer was VC booby traps. There were so many booby traps that we couldn't go around and the way we got around it was to "detain a suspect" and make them walk in front of the point man. . . . None of us wanted to get blown away, but it wasn't right to use the Arvins or civilians to set the mines off. They didn't want to get blown away either, but nobody cared about the Vietnamese. When a civilian hit a booby trap he'd most likely get called as a body count too.

Number four killer was "accidents" with gunships or artillery. If anybody ever got sniper fire from a tree line we'd use gunships and artillery on the villages and go in later. Sure we got shot at from the village, but there was always a bunch of crying kids and women when we followed up the gunships. We'd be told that they were deserters from a free fire zone, but we'd always find civilians when we'd get to the hooches. It was there farm land, and they always looked like they didn't have any money to move. . . . So what could they do? I read all the time we never use artillery on villages, but I know different and its just like the "evasive action" and the snipers and the "suspect" ahead of the point-man. People (high officers) did not care about the Vietnamese so long as a big body count made them look good to the general. And in all these incidents, honestly hundreds of them there is some young officer or sgt who gave the order and some EM [enlisted man] who did it, and every one of them could be charged with murder if anyone ever reports it. But it wasn't their fault, it was the fault of the high officer who told them to do it that way.

The writer said "COL Hunt" was particularly demanding about body count. He would "holler and curse over the radio . . . and tell the gunships to shoot the sonofabitches, this is a free fire zone." Col. Ira A. "Jim" Hunt Jr. was the 1st Brigade commander in 1969. He also served as chief of staff of the 9th Infantry Division. He was well known in military circles for his body count fervor.

> He just wanted the most of everything, including body count. . . . I'm sure there are records somewhere that show how many the snipers killed, and how many "dead VC" were taking evasive action. . . . I know there are records that tell how many body counts we got and you can compare them with the number of weapons we got. Not the cashays' [caches] or the weapons we found after a big fight with the hard cores, but a dead VC with a weapon. . . . If we reported weapons we had to turn them in, so we would say that the weapons was destroyed by bullets or dropped in a canal or pady. In the dry season, before the moonsons, there was places where lots of the canals was dry and *all* the padys were. The General *must* have know this was made up. He wouldn't have been a General if he was that stupid.

"The General" was Gen. Creighton W. Abrams Jr., who succeeded Westmoreland in 1968 as commander of military operations in Vietnam.

> I read last week where we hung some Japan general after world war 2, not for killing people, but for failing to prevent his men from killing people, civilians and such.[5] Well, Sir, the 9th Division did nothing to prevent the killing, and by pushing the body count so hard, we were "told" to kill

many times more Vietnamese than at My Lay, and very few
per cents of them did we know were enemy. . . . In case you
don't think I mean *lots* of Vietnamese got killed this way, I
can give you some idea how many. A batalion would kill
maybe 15 to 20 a day. With 4 batalions in the Brigade that
would be maybe 40 to 50 a day or 1200 to 1500 a month,
easy. (One batalion claimed almost 1000 body counts one
month!) If I am only 10% right, and believe me its lots more,
then I am trying to tell you about 120–150 murders, or a My
Lay each month for over a year.

He closed the letter with this warning:

The Army needs to clean itself up before they throw a
bunch of young guys to the wolves. If the Army can't clean
up and find who was really at fault, then I guess I'll just have
to write some congressmen, and send them copys of this
letter plus all the names and dates and places I know of. . . .
I know this would be a real stink in public so I wanted to
write you first, and give the Army a chance before someone blows it to a Congressman or reporter.

Respectfully yours,

Army officials at the Pentagon took the threat seriously. Even
though most of the 9th had left Vietnam by August 1969, the
pressures and incentives for a high enemy body count remained.
Army Secretary Stanley Resor asked his general counsel's office
to review the letter and proffer an opinion on whether he should
take any action. The job landed on the desk of R. Kenly Webster,
a rising young civilian lawyer who served as the general counsel's

top deputy. Before rendering an opinion, Webster asked a Vietnam veteran to assess the letter. He concluded that the writer's concerns about body count were credible:

> It is common knowledge that an officer's career can be made or destroyed in Vietnam. A command tour there is much sought after and generally comes only once to an individual, who may have anywhere from six months to a year to prove himself in the "crucible of combat." The pressure to excel is inevitably tremendous; and it is my impression that a primary indication of such excellence has in the past been the unit's enemy body count. . . . Under such circumstances—and especially if such incentives as stand-downs, R&R allocations, and decorations are tied to body count figures—the pressure to kill indiscriminately, or at least to report every Vietnamese casualty as an enemy casualty, would seem to be practically irresistible.

Webster wrote a memorandum to Resor on June 16, 1970. He recommended against an investigation of the letter, because it was unsigned and lacked specific incidents.

"In reading the letter, however," he continued, "I was impressed by its forcefulness and by the sincerity of the feelings which give rise to the author's theory of command responsibility for the body count system, which is alleged to provide an incentive for unnecessary killings."

Webster urged Resor to determine what steps could be taken to ensure excessive pressure for body count "does not encourage the human tendency to inflate the count by violating established rules of engagement." His recommendation was a rare instance in which any of the wrenching accounts in the war-crime files moved someone to action. Resor immediately discussed the allegations with Abrams, then top commander in Vietnam, according to a memo that offered no details.[6]

Whatever came of their discussion apparently didn't satisfy the anonymous soldier. He wrote another letter, postmarked in Baltimore and dated March 30, 1971, the day after a military jury found 1st Lt. William Calley Jr. guilty of murder for the My Lai massacre. This time the soldier addressed his concerns to Maj. General Orwin C. Talbott, commanding general at Fort Benning, Georgia, where Calley's court-martial took place:

> I wrote to General Westmoreland about this Last year but
> he didnt do anything about it. I guess he is to busy.[7]

The ten-page, handwritten letter repeated much of what he had told Westmoreland and added this plea:

> The generals have got to do something about this pretty
> soon before anymore people get killed just to make some
> batalion comander look good.

A third, angrier letter followed, mailed on July 30 from Chicago to another figure in the My Lai case, Maj. Gen. William A. Enemark. As inspector general at the Pentagon, he oversaw the army's initial investigation into reports of a massacre at My Lai.

> I have been trying for a year now to tell somebody about
> a bunch of little things that add up to bad as My Lay or
> worse. . . . So I'm gonna try one last time to tell the Army

and see if anybody gives a "shit." I wrote to General Talbott at Fort Benning last spring and to General Westmoreland last summer, and now I am telling you to see if the Army will do anything about war crimes by high officers or just cover it up again. Cause if it gets covered up again Im gone write strate to Senator Dellums [U.S. Rep. Ron V. Dellums, D-Oakland, California][8] or Senator Kenedy [U.S. Sen. Ted Kennedy, D-Massachusetts] or the New York Time. With a election coming up you better honk they like to hear my shit. . . . And then all of you can explain why you got these letters and done nothing about the war crimes.[9]

The soldier signed the third letter, the last in the file, "Very truly yours, Concerned Sgt."

The second and third letters reached Westmoreland's office in late August. Two senior members of his staff briefed him on September 4, 1971. A meeting agenda in the file listed consideration of Kenly Webster's recommendations, discussion of the allegations against Hunt, and a status report on the effort to locate the writer "to prevent his complaints [from] reaching Mr. Dellums (Dem-CA)."[10] A follow-up memo reiterated the importance of finding the writer but reminded everyone that it would be illegal to "restrict any member of an armed force from communicating with a member of Congress" unless necessary for national security.[11]

I was puzzled by the commotion over three anonymous letters. They were powerful, without doubt. But Dellums had held hearings on war crimes in the House; John Kerry had testified about war crimes in the Senate; scores of veterans had given

firsthand accounts of war crimes at press conferences and antiwar forums. Why would army officials be so concerned over one
more soldier threatening to go public?

On September 7, 1971, Henry Tufts, the top commander of
the CID, had good news. His agents had "tentatively" identified
the Concerned Sgt as George Lewis, a specialist four who served
in Vietnam from June 1968 to June 1969. His awards included a
Purple Heart, Army Commendation Medal, Combat Infantry-
man Badge, Air Medal with two oak leaf clusters, and a Sharp-
shooter Badge with a rifle bar.[12] Efforts "are underway to
interview him," Tufts wrote.[13] The same day, Westmoreland informed his staff that the case would be closed. No further action
would be taken. No directives would be issued, on the advice of
Thaddeus R. Beal, an influential undersecretary.[14]

The file ends there. I make a trip to the National Archives to
make sure we didn't miss a follow-up report. I find nothing more.
No indication of whether Lewis met with CID and confirmed he
wrote the letters. If he was the Concerned Sgt, did the agents as-
sure him—or intimidate him—into silence?

Tufts has died, as have Westmoreland, Abrams, and Beal. Webster does not remember the case. The file contains Lewis's Social
Security number and a home address in Columbus, Ohio. But the
home address is outdated. Lewis sold the house several years earlier, property records show. The buyer of record is the Reverend
Grady Evans, whom I call. He's a gregarious man and apologetic
that he can't tell me more about Lewis.

"After we bought the house, I used to run into him on the
street," he says. "But I haven't seen him in three years."

Evans says Lewis lived in the house with his father, also named
George Lewis, until the elder man's death. The son was troubled.
He drank heavily, couldn't hold a job, and drifted in and out of jail

on petty crimes. He needed money, so he sold the house to Evans about ten years earlier. By 2000, Lewis had taken up residence in a nearby homeless shelter. I ask if Lewis ever talked to Evans about Vietnam. Not that he can recall, Evans says, but he remembers that Lewis kept a large American flag in the front picture window of the house when he lived there.

"He seemed to care a lot about that flag. Sometime after we bought the house, he came looking for it. But it was really filthy, and we'd disposed of it. He seemed really upset about that."

---

Talbott retired a lieutenant general and now resides in a quiet apartment complex for retired army officers along Rock Creek Park in northwest Washington, D.C. He reads the letter addressed to him, visibly moved by the soldier's words. But he insists he has never seen the document before this moment.

"A letter of that detail would be branded in your memory," he says.

He was aware of concerns over the 9th Division's body count. He commanded the 1st Division in 1969, and it was a matter of open discussion by senior ranks in Vietnam.

"The 9th Division insisted on a body count. They didn't care what body," he says. "I heard about Americal [responsible for My Lai] and 9th Division all the time. The 9th was worse, all on the body count basis."

Westmoreland could have intervened but didn't, Talbott says. Neither did Abrams, who succeeded him, he says. I ask, and Talbott says he didn't report his concerns to them. They had to have known, he explains.

"I can't believe the top headquarters in Vietnam could not have heard the gossip."

Talbott looks at the third letter, addressed to Maj. Gen. Enemark.

"I'm having cocktails with him this afternoon, after we're done here," Talbott says.

Nick and I had not been able to locate Enemark, and Talbott agrees to introduce us. He leads us a few doors down a carpeted hallway. Enemark is willing to sit down with us for a few minutes. He reads the letter addressed to him from beginning to end.

"I do not recall seeing this letter, and I think I would remember seeing it," he says when he finishes. "I remember stories about body counts. I remember once Gen. Abrams remarked that a sniper had been rewarded for one hundred hits. He got him right out of the country. He thought it was bad for the men and no man should have that sort of record."

I question the value of taking action against the soldier but not the commanders or policies that encouraged him. Enemark says he cannot offer any insights; he had his hands full at the time with My Lai.

"It was not investigated by my office," he says. "I can't help you on that."

Three years after Westmoreland closed the Concerned Sgt file, consigning it to the Army Staff's secret archive, the army published Col. Hunt's version of the same events in a monograph titled *Sharpening the Combat Edge: The Use of Analysis to Reinforce Military Judgment.*[15]

He coauthored the treatise with Lt. Gen. Julian J. Ewell, who commanded the 9th Infantry Division in the Mekong Delta from 1968 to 1969. Hunt served as his chief of staff, with periodic forays into the field to command brigades. They were tough taskmasters, who demanded results from their brigade and battalion leaders. On their watch, the monthly count of enemy losses rose 200 to 300 percent while U.S. losses dropped.[16] Ewell was rewarded with a promotion to commander of II Field Force, the largest army combat command in Vietnam.

The 1974 monograph is posted on the army Web site.[17] I print a copy and lay it side by side with the letters. Hunt and Ewell offered a starkly different perspective. They attributed the dramatic rise in enemy kills to superior military strategy. They responded to the Vietcong's guerrilla tactics by stressing "aggressive or even audacious small unit operations." They insisted on frequent night ambushes and daylight patrols, with aggressive air support. Their "15-second war" strategy fine-tuned shooting skills and emphasized beating the enemy to the draw:

> Each company, every third or fourth day during stand-down, would have the riflemen shoot at anything (tin cans, targets, whatever) until they could get a first round hit at 25 meters in 8 seconds. By repetition, this became an automatic reflex action. This one idea in combination with good night ambushes made it possible for our small rifle units to wreak heavy damage on the enemy with low friendly casualties.[18]

They measured success through an elaborate analysis based largely on enemy body count. Statistics on kills per month, kills per unit, kills per engagement, even rounds expended per kill were collected at the division headquarters to determine what strategies were working and which units were lagging and in need of a "visit." The results "were extraordinary," the treatise says.[19] The "analytic approach" was adopted not only by the 9th Infantry Division but also throughout II Field Force.[20]

They singled out sniper operations as shining examples of their success. They arranged to give seventy-two soldiers marksmanship training in the fall of 1968, on the theory that well-trained and properly deployed snipers could increase enemy kills while reducing American and civilian casualties. But the initiative got off to a slow start, producing only eight kills the first month and eleven in the second.

> This was clearly a dismal performance, considering the large number of men and the effort that had gone into the program. Therefore, we set about analyzing our equipment, personnel, methods, and tactics. We hit upon the flaw in the system, and while the solution was extremely simple, it had an immediate effect.[21]

Ewell and Hunt told battalion commanders they would be responsible for personally ensuring the snipers were properly utilized so they saw action and produced results—measured largely by the number of enemy kills they reported.

> Chart 12 shows the steady improvement in sniper results, culminating in 346 enemy killed in the month of April and leveling off at about 200 kills per month. It was a flat learning curve initially but it soon steepened up.[22]

They praised their leading sniper for "109 confirmed kills to his credit" and cited the Concerned Sgt's unit for showing initiative:

> They would insert snipers in the early morning along known trails and infiltration routes likely to be used by the enemy. They used sixman teams—highly trained individuals capable of remaining in the field for several hours without moving a muscle when the situation required.[23]

The Concerned Sgt had written that ambushes were especially treacherous for civilians "in the early morning when the Vietnamese might be going to work in the fields or to market."[24]

Where the two generals saw "matchless vision and expert marksmanship,"[25] the Concerned Sgt saw "dudes wasting any Vietnamese they seen and calling them VC cause they was dead but didnt have no weapon and no grenades."[26]

In another section of the monograph, Hunt and Ewell attributed a decrease in booby-trap deaths to a stepped-up safety program and use of specially trained Vietnamese Tiger Scouts.[27] The Concerned Sgt cited the increased use of Vietnamese civilians and soldiers to "walk point"—to walk just ahead of the unit through unsecured territory—"so none of the GIs would get blown away."[28]

The Concerned Sgt wrote his treatises years before Hunt and Ewell published theirs. Despite the overlap of topics, there is no indication in the file or the monograph that either of the senior officers had seen the Concerned Sgt's letters.

Ewell retired as a lieutenant general in 1973, and Hunt as a major general in 1978. Nick and I visit Ewell first. He lives in a gated retirement community for former officers in Alexandria,

Virginia. We finesse our way past guards and through security gates only to find we're no match for his wife. She blocks the door, says he's napping, and assures us that he has no interest in talking to reporters. I leave my number but never hear from him.

A day after our encounter with Mrs. Ewell, we appear unannounced on Hunt's doorstep in McLean, Virginia. He invites us inside. We sit on the living room couch, and he takes an armchair. After explaining the reason for our visit, I hand him copies of the Concerned Sgt's letters. This is the first time he has seen them, he says. He reads the first one and shakes his head.

"No one's going to say that innocent civilians aren't killed in wartime, but we try to keep it down to the absolute minimum. Innocent civilians are killed in Iraq every day, as you know," he says. "I find it unbelievable that people would go out and shoot innocent civilians just to increase a body count."

Nick flags the memo in the file from the general counsel's office, which says the Concerned Sgt's allegations about body count and civilian killings appear credible.

"I think there was definitely a pressure to make contact with the enemy." Hunt says. "You don't want your troops to go out and take a walk in the sun. There was pressure. But the pressure was not to kill innocent civilians; the pressure was to kill the enemy."

He says he had no reason to think the dramatic rise in body count was anything other than a sign that their military strategies were working. He took his commanders' word, saw no reason to investigate. They were operating in areas with large numbers of enemy combatants. He was more concerned if their body count numbers were low.

"One of the problems is Americans don't want to shoot anybody," he says.

Although he and Ewell pressed troops to engage the enemy, they also established strict rules for using firepower in populated areas to protect civilians, Hunt says.

"We had the regulation that you could not fire within five hundred yards of the village, and I was pretty adamant about that. The big question came when sometimes if these people were in the villages shooting at you, what would you do? That was a terrible dilemma that people would be in. But, understanding that, the rules of engagement were you would not do it. That was a division rule of engagement."

The Concerned Sgt letters described incidents in which battalion commanders overrode the rules and ordered artillery strikes on occupied hamlets.

"I don't know of any overriding of this," Hunt says. "Those sort of things can always happen. To deny something could happen in the pressure of warfare on what you're doing, things like that can happen. Whether it did happen or not, I don't know. But you can presume people would follow the regulations and do what is correct. Now, they don't always do that. The most egregious affair was the My Lai affair. . . . Nothing like that ever happened that I know of in the [Mekong] Delta when we were there."

Hunt says he has run out of time.

"I have a very important engagement here at noon. I'd be willing to talk to you further if you want to come back."

I drop Nick at the train station, and he heads back home to New Jersey. That night, I rifle through the files and look up old clips. A *Newsweek* article from 1972 estimated that "thousands of Vietnamese civilians" were "killed deliberately" by U.S. Forces.[29] The story dealt with Speedy Express, a six-month combat operation in 1968 to eradicate the National Liberation Front from

Kien Hoa, a key province in the Mekong Delta. The 9th Infantry Division reported 10,899 enemy killed—but only 748 weapons recovered. Investigative reporter Kevin P. Buckley interviewed residents, reviewed civilian hospital records, and consulted with military sources. He estimated as many as five thousand civilians had perished in the operation, a staggering sum that led him to the same conclusion as the Concerned Sgt. "The death toll there made the My Lai massacre look trifling by comparison," Buckley wrote.

Abrams refused to talk to Buckley. By then, the records show, the general had been apprised of the Concerned Sgt's allegations.[30] I ring Hunt's doorbell again the next day. He had given the Concerned Sgt's letters more thought overnight.

"I didn't want to get into it yesterday, but he [Concerned Sgt] was saying these snipers are war criminals. I said, oh, my God, the sniper program was a very effective program. It was effective. It was distributed to the other divisions in Vietnam. Now in Iraq you see in a guerrilla type of war that snipers are tremendous things."

Hunt also wants to reiterate the importance of body counts. There are only two ways to measure success in a counterinsurgency operation like Vietnam or Iraq, he says.

"You have combat operations and you have pacification, and one way of measuring pacification is how many villages are under the government and how many people. When you measure combat effectiveness, unfortunately, the measure at the time—and it's getting that way, if you haven't noticed, it's getting that way in Iraq—is the body count."

(The interview with Hunt took place before members of an elite army sniper unit in Iraq, under pressure to boost their "kill count," shot three Iraqis to death in 2007 and planted an AK-47 and command wire on their bodies. Three soldiers faced courts-martial. One was convicted of murder and sentenced to ten years in prison; two were acquitted of murder but found guilty of planting evidence to justify the killings.[31])

Was Hunt at all suspicious when the 9th Infantry Division's average monthly body count more than doubled without a similar surge in recovered weapons—and while the average monthly U.S. KIAs dropped 20 percent?[32] As he scrutinized the numbers coming in from the field and plugged them into his calculations, did it occur to him that they might point to a spike in civilian killings?

The disparity between kills and weapons was due to an increase in air support and night operations, and flooding due to the monsoons, all of which made recovery of weapons more difficult, he says. He knew that civilians were not involved, because the operations often took place at locations and at times when only enemy combatants would be out. For example, it was standard practice in Vietnam to designate large swaths of countryside as off-limits for civilians. Curfews kept civilians inside at night, Hunt says. U.S. troops could attack more aggressively at night with the confidence that only enemy combatants would be in harm's way, he says.

"You can almost bet that, I'm not going to say 100 percent of them, but a tremendous percent of them are enemy soldiers, are people, guerrillas, trying to carry ammunition, trying to do this."

I ask him about a rash of civilian killings in 1968–1970 by three of the II Field Force divisions that he and Ewell held out as success stories in *Sharpening the Combat Edge*.[33] Most of the incidents occurred northwest of Saigon, near the Cambodian border, where U.S. troops frequently clashed with Vietcong and North

Vietnamese forces. The attacks were the subject of repeated letters of alarm and concern from U.S. advisers, according to declassified records of the army inspector general.

Richard W. Parkinson, the U.S. senior adviser for Binh Long province, wrote to II Field Force headquarters in February 1969 after repeated assaults on civilians in Chon Thanh district, a heavily populated rural area of rubber-tree plantations:

> 1. Request command action be taken to reduce the number of casualties being caused to friendly personnel in Chon Thanh District. In 1968 the VC killed seven personnel in Chon Thanh District, while the US took a toll of over 10 lives. So far in 1969, the US has killed 10 and wounded at least [indecipherable]; the VC have not yet caused a casualty.
>
> 2. There has been several incidents of gunships killing personnel by rocket fire, LCH's [helicopters] chasing people off the road by flying at extremely low levels. . . .
>
> 3. The enemy is using these incidents to good advantage in their propaganda. What has been a very pro-GVN [South Vietnamese government] and pro-US area is fast becoming extremely antagonistic . . .[34]

On March 3, 1969, less than a month after Parkinson sent his letter, two Cobra gunships and two armed scout helicopters opened fire on a small crowd gathered around a pickup truck in an off-limits area. A crewmember radioed in the body count: Eight enemy killed in action. But when ground troops arrived to collect weapons, they found none, just the bodies of seven unarmed civilian woodcutters. They identified a woman, a young boy, and a middle-aged man. The other bodies were too badly disfigured to determine age or gender.[35]

Parkinson fired off another letter decrying the "wanton disregard for Vietnamese lives" and attached his earlier letter. The senior adviser for Chon Thanh district, Capt. Ralph Cruikshank, added his angry plea:

> This incident raises the death total to 12 people in one month with two missing.
>
> An extremely dangerous situation now exists in this district due to the killing and property damage. The people no longer can turn the other cheek because both sides have been slapped extremely hard. The once smiling people are now crying, even the [Vietnamese] District Chief thinks that perhaps the American Forces should leave the district. Something must be done. Units aren't stopping to think or check. I realize that when American troops are being shot at, killed and wounded, that people want to react; but not against helpless civilians. If they want to kill VC, we could tell them where if anyone ever bothered to ask our humble opinion.[36]

A subsequent investigation by the 1st Cavalry Division inspector general chalked the incident up to "poor judgement," and no action was taken.

Ewell took charge of II Field Force on April 2, 1969. He initiated a reward system for killing the Vietcong that further imperiled civilians. He allocated air support to divisions in large part on the basis of enemy kills, according to *Sharpening the Combat Edge*. Those getting the best result from their joint ground and airmobile operations earned a greater share of the air support. This "gave them incentive to try more imaginative ways to employ their assets."[37]

In the ensuing months, an assault helicopter crew killed two unarmed women and wounded seven other civilians; a light-fire team shot a child; troops in gunships dropped grenades on hamlets four times without provocation. On the ground, a Ranger squad shot an unarmed woman to death as she retrieved her bicycle in a restricted zone; a soldier used an automatic weapon to spray a boy fishing in a rice paddy, killing him instantly; soldiers pushed two schoolgirls under a moving truck, crushing them. A congressman inquired about "a contest in which totals of enemy personnel eliminated and materiel captured or destroyed determined which rifle platoon would win best in the Battalion." The 25th Infantry Division competition was attracting "much unfavorable publicity," an internal army memo noted.[38]

In September 1969, Ewell took notice of the civilian killings and ordered "indoctrination of all personnel as to the consequences of those acts and the fact that they will not be tolerated." He suggested that woodcutters wear light-colored clothing and paint a flag of the Republic of Vietnam on the roof of their trucks. Still the problems continued. The next month, Parkinson's successor, John Sylvester Jr., wrote another pleading memo:

> So far this year 31 civilians have been killed by American forces, a number by armed helicopters. To rectify a situation of discredit to the American armed forces we need at least stronger discipline or perhaps better troop information training for helicopter crews.[39]

A training session followed, but the inspector general concluded no disciplinary action was warranted.

Ewell departed in the spring of 1970, but the problems continued. On August 26 of that year, members of a 25th Infantry Division platoon reported killing "10 enemy soldiers . . . dressed in NVA uniforms" in an off-limits area of Chon Thanh district. The soldiers reported finding "booby trap wire" on one body and drawings of a military aircraft on another. The dearth of weapons caught the eye of the commanding general. He dispatched the division inspector general to the scene, where he found the bodies of two children, three women, and five men, all civilians and none wearing uniforms. Scattered on the ground were several bags of bamboos shoots, a dozen limes, and a wire tool for foraging.[40]

"The small drawing of a rifle and of an airplane on a book cover appears to be something a child would do," his report said.

They perished in a popular foraging area that had been designated a free-fire zone. The Vietnamese provincial chief told the inspector general that the people were "poor, uneducated and went wherever they could get food. He repeatedly stressed that he hoped US forces would be more careful in the future not to shoot unarmed civilians even in the 'off limits' area."[41] The report concluded that soldiers had not violated the rules of engagement by firing on the group in a free-fire zone. The platoon was "acting in consonance with legal orders and instructions which were its duty and obligation to obey."

Hunt nods his head thoughtfully.

"We had occasions where through a real boo-boo somebody killed ten to fifteen civilians," he says. "You're playing with hindsight. You're reading these things, but when you're there on the ground it's an entirely different story."

There are more substantiated allegations in the files: Gunships from the 9th Infantry Division reportedly fired into homes, killing a baby, two children, and a woman in Dinh Tuong province; a member of a Rangers team shot a duck farmer in Long An province as he returned home from market with his son.[42]

After finding a farmer at home in a free-fire zone, 1st Lt. James B. Duffy ordered his men to tie the man to a stake and execute him. At his court-martial, Duffy admitted the allegations but said he was following orders to eliminate all Vietnamese in the kill zone and bring back a body count. The defense swayed the court. He was convicted of involuntary manslaughter instead of premeditated murder and received a sentence of six months in confinement.[43]

I ask Hunt whether the body of evidence in the declassified files at least raises the possibility in his mind that some of their strategies encouraged civilian killings.

"If the reports had been coming through at that time, something would definitely have been done about it," Hunt says. "But now you're talking, as you said, thirty years later. There's not a hell of a lot that can be done."

He asks a question: "What is the focus of your research?"

I tell him we are trying to make sense of the declassified records: "How do they set the record straight from that time? And what can we learn from them for the future?"

"The future is now, what's going on in Iraq," Hunt says. "It's a real guerrilla war in Iraq, no matter what DoD says, it's a guerrilla war, the same as it was in Vietnam."

He retreats to a back room and returns with a copy of Gen. Abrams's remarks at the change-of-command ceremony for Ewell in April 1969, when he left the 9th Infantry Division to take over the II Field Force. Hunt says Abrams's unqualified praise proves that senior army officials did not harbor serious doubts about their record of success. He reads it aloud:

The performance of this division has been magnificent and I would say in the last three months has been an unparalleled and unequaled performance. . . . General Ewell, your division commander, over little more than a year has proven to be the brilliant and sensitive commander. His tactical concepts have been characterized by imagination, sensitivity to the kind of situation that you're all in, and he plays hard. General Ewell has been the epitome of the professional soldier, devoted to his country, devoted to his men, and devoted to his profession and the development of it. Thank you.

Lawrence B. Wilkerson wedges into a chair at the back of a busy Starbucks in northern Virginia. The former chief of staff for Secretary of State Colin L. Powell blends seamlessly into the retired military crowd at the noisy coffee house. But he has hardly faded from view in the year and a half since he left the White House. His decision to speak out against the Iraq war, which he once notably promoted, has given him a second wind of fame—or notoriety, depending on the audience.

Nick and I are meeting with him to talk not about Iraq but Vietnam. A source told me he ran into Wilkerson at a forum, that he knew about our project on Vietnam war crimes and expressed interest in the subject. Wilkerson says my source was mistaken—he hadn't in fact known about our research. But he notes that he had served as commander of a helicopter unit—with the 25th Infantry Division. With Hunt's interviews fresh in my mind, I'm curious about Wilkerson's experience. After a while, I ask him to talk about it. He leans forward to be heard over the whistle of the espresso machine.

"In the 25th Division, where I served for almost thirteen months in Vietnam, there was ample opportunity for me to observe things that I didn't like. I was a lieutenant, a 1st lieutenant and a captain in the course of that time. And I had responsibility initially for about fifty men and about, oh, I don't know, maybe $20 million worth of equipment and ten helicopters and a number of other things. By the time I finished my tour I had responsibility for about three hundred men and so forth. And it was a daily thing to keep—this was '69–'70, so this was late in the war—it was a daily thing to keep people from crossing the line with regard to the law of war, the law of armed conflict, the Geneva conventions and so forth. . . .

"I was a Scout pilot for the infantry battalions. So I knew what was happening with the infantry on the ground because I was as close as you almost. Oftentimes I was below the trees, flying between them, flying under bridges and down rivers and very slow, because you can't see unless you fly real slow. So I saw a lot of infantry action. . . .

"And, no question, you had to be on your guard all the time— especially when you just had a colleague wounded or killed, or you just had a group of colleagues wounded or killed, or your platoon or your company had or wherever, those are the critical times. It was also very critical when you had a situation that I think happens almost every day in Iraq now . . . where you don't see the light at the end of the tunnel. You don't, you know, you're just killing. That's it. There's no objective to it. Year after year, week after week, month after month, whatever. You don't see. And I served with guys in Vietnam, one of my men was on his third tour. . . . Several of them were on their second. . . . I had people

who volunteered from the 75th Rangers. Now, these are people
who had been on long-range patrols, some of whom had been to
Cambodia and to North Vietnam. So they had seen the bloodiest
part of war up close and personal and they volunteered to come
over and serve another year in my unit. So I had some people who
had been there for a long time and that adds to this sort of, you
know, momentum towards being other than a lawful warrior.
That plus the fact, as I said, you don't see the light at the end of the
tunnel. There is no, there's no victory. You can't see the victory
clearly, you can't see an end coming, you can't see when you will
go home other than your rotation date. And you know your rotation date is subject to change."

That's the sort of baggage men carried into the helicopters.
High above the ground, far from the people they were shooting,
under pressure to produce results, facing constant danger—it's a
testament to most of the pilots that there weren't more atrocities, he says. He has two personal experiences to relate.

"One was where an infantry battalion commander had declared an entire area south of Tay Ninh as a free-fire zone. And
you probably, if you've done this research, you've come across
that term before. And most of us treated that as, 'Uh-huh,
right'—that is, to say, 'I'm not shooting anything unless I can identify that it's enemy or it's shooting at me.' But some people, some
people—Cobra pilots and some of my colleagues in the Loach
[light observation helicopter] fraternity treated that as a license to
shoot anything that moved—wild boar, tigers, elephants, people—
it didn't matter. And so, in this particular instance, just south of
Tay Ninh, they declared it as a free-fire zone. And the battalion
commander for whom I was working on the ground wanted me
to treat it as a free-fire zone, and we got into an argument on the
FM radio, the ground-to-air radio, with me telling him—he's a

lieutenant colonel, I'm a lieutenant, and I'm telling him, '. . . I'm in charge of my crew, and we're not shooting anything unless it shoots back at us or we can clearly identify it as an enemy, and to hell with your free-fire zone,' were my words. And I got, shall we say, chewed out over the radio. And my Cobra pilot, who happened to be one of the people who was a little more trigger-happy in our unit, he was covering me up high. He got into it. And he wanted to shoot. . . . I told him to shut up, and he decided that he was going to go off and fire his rockets anyway at this particular area the battalion commander wanted some recon by fire into. So I just flew my helicopter in the area, and I said, 'You shoot and you're going to hit me. And if you hit me, buddy, I'm going to turn my guns up and shoot you.'"

Wilkerson laughs at the memory.

"So we, he hollered at me to get out of the area. And I wouldn't get out of the area. Plus I was looking at it, and I looked at it really closely and my crew chief got pretty scared cuz we were going so slow. And there was nothing there but a hooch and a man probably about seventy, an old lady probably about the same age, and two young children. That is it. And so I reported that to both the battalion commander and the Cobra up above. That did it. That calmed everybody down, because they realized if they had shot rockets at that house they probably would have killed all those people.

"The other instance was not so successful. The other instance was over near Dau Tieng, and I was working with a crew in my own helicopter that I knew was, let's say, a little bit trigger-happy. One of the reasons I had them in my helicopter was because I didn't want them in somebody else's helicopter. They were good soldiers. But they were a little bit, they were sometimes—I'd had an instance where my crew chief had actually fired his machine gun before I gave him permission to. And I landed the helicopter right in the middle of the jungle and I told him I was going to leave him there if he ever did that again. And he was so scared and he said, 'Oh, lieutenant, please put me back in the helicopter,' because we were in the middle of enemy country.

"And this day again an infantry battalion commander on the ground declared the area a free-fire zone. And, you know—my fault, and I fault myself for this to this day—I did not immediately say to my crew, 'Disregard that radio transmission,' because they listened to the radio just like I did. So we're flying along and maybe about fifteen minutes later or so, there's this—you'd have to see it to understand it. It's sort of like an ox-driven cart with a cover on it, not unlike a Conestoga wagon but much shorter and squatter. It's got a canvas cover on top of it. And there's obviously, driving the cart—that is, with the reins on the ox—a man who very well could have been an enemy. He was of the age. And so we made a pass down the road and suddenly came out of the jungle and over the road and there it was. And before I said anything, my crew chief let off a burst of machine-gun ammunition. And he was a very good shot. It went right into the wagon. And all he got was a burst of six, because I was on the radio immediately, and I said, essentially, 'If you shoot again I'll turn around and cut your head off. You don't shoot unless I tell you to shoot.' Well, the long and the short of it was there was a little girl in the wagon, and we killed her. And that'll be with me for the rest of my life."

Under the rules of engagement in a free-fire zone, the shooting was justified, he says. The only violation on the part of the gunner was failing to wait until he got Wilkerson's clearance.

"You can shoot anything that moved. *Anything.* Which was, you know, in my view—as an officer responsible for my men and responsible for conducting the war in the way I thought was the American way—that was ridiculous. It was ridiculous! I mean, free-fire zone? God. How do you know what's in this vast realm of territory you just declared a free-fire zone?"

According to procedure, the ground commanders were supposed to give notice to regional officials, who would alert citizens. Even when that happened, it wasn't enough.

"We think, okay, if we tell everybody to leave they will leave. And then anybody left is enemy," Wilkerson says. "Hell . . . in *this* country with the Internet, TV, and everything else, you still have people waiting for [Hurricane] Katrina to hit, right?"

The higher-ups had to know that civilians were being killed, he says, and that warning troops to be careful wasn't adequate.

"Once the evidence turns clearly the other way, you would think that they'd stop doing it. If you ask me directly, do I think free-fire zones are idiocy, yes. Are they an implicit recognition of the fact that you're authorizing people to do things they shouldn't? Yes."

The army's reliance on body count was another mistake, he says. It's "a miserable measure of success or even measure of effectiveness" with little value in a counterinsurgency, where winning depends on gaining local support, political control, and stability. He teaches a model that measures success against accomplishment of mission goals rather than counting dead bodies. If the goal is to support and protect sympathetic local officials and one of them is killed, the enemy wins, no matter how many dead insurgents are on the other side of the ledger, he says.

"If you understand clearly your full mission—your task *and* purpose—you know that killing the enemy, when the enemy is virtually infinite, is not a good measure of whether or not you are accomplishing your mission."

---

Resor served as secretary of the army from 1965 to 1971. He was a World War II veteran and corporate lawyer, appointed by President Lyndon B. Johnson and retained by Richard Nixon. Nick and I reach him by phone at his home in Washington, D.C. Now eighty-nine, he says he can recall only a handful of well-publicized atrocities besides My Lai. In public statements at the time, he portrayed atrocities as isolated incidents. We ask him about the Army Staff's collection of war-crime reports, but he says he doesn't know about them. He doesn't recall the Concerned Sgt letters or the body-count debate.

Resor was succeeded by Robert F. Froehlke, a longtime insurance executive, World War II veteran, and childhood friend of Defense Secretary Melvin R. Laird, who first tapped Froehlke in 1969 to be assistant secretary of defense for administration. Nixon appointed Froehlke secretary of the army in July 1971, and he served for two years. Retired and living in Scottsdale, Arizona, he does not remember the Concerned Sgt letters, but he recalls walking into a robust, ongoing debate over body count when he became secretary.

"A number of memos came in on body count," he says. "I wasn't there when we started the body count, but I've come to the conclusion that it resulted from frustration with the war. We wanted to have winners and losers. In this war, we weren't taking land, and the enemy was everywhere. You'd move forward, and the enemy would be right behind you. You didn't base winning and losing on taking land. Someone decided the only way to do it was how many people did we kill today. From a PR [public relations] standpoint in the U.S., that was not acceptable."

The use of enemy kills to measure success encouraged lying and exaggeration, he says. I ask whether he was aware of the more sinister implications—that civilians were being killed to bolster the numbers.

"Yes, it was raised and almost out of frustration there was never anything done. Other than orders, stating the obvious: In body count you will not take civilian lives. But it was hard to follow through. I know [Defense Secretary] Mel Laird in particular was concerned with his PR hat on."

Then why not eliminate body count as the official yardstick?

"We kept it up because we didn't have anything else to determine if we were winning or losing," Froehlke says. "We never got a solution to that problem."

I ask about war crimes. Like Resor, he immediately cites My Lai. Beyond that, he says, there were inherent risks in a war in which the enemy often dressed like civilians. I ask about the cases compiled by the Army Staff—few were cases of mistaken identity. He expresses surprise. He says he had no idea that Westmoreland had assembled a team of officers to collect atrocity allegations.

"To my knowledge, he did nothing about them," he says. "By 'to my knowledge' I mean he took no action."

―――――――――――

The *Times* researcher, Janet Lundblad, calls to say she has identified a Corpus Christi address linked to George Lewis's Social Security number. It has no phone number. I look at a satellite photo on the Internet. The house number tracks to a short block in a run-down part of town. There are a couple houses surrounded by empty lots. I call three phone numbers linked to the street. No one recognizes his name or description. I know from the files that he was a five-foot-eleven African American born in 1948. I mail a letter to the address. It reappears in my mailbox with "return to sender" stamped in red ink. Much later, I call the Department of Veterans Affairs to see if it has his address and would be willing to forward a letter to him. The representative places me on hold while she looks for his file. As I wait, I call up the VA Web site on my computer and notice a link to the Nationwide Gravesite Locator. I type in Lewis's name and date of birth and click. A new screen opens. My heart sinks. He is there. Date of death: April 24, 2004. Buried at: Ft. Sam Houston National Cemetery.[44]

The counselor comes back on the line, and I tell her that I think I've found him in the cemetery database. She's relieved not to have to break the news.

The Nueces County Medical Examiner's office sends a copy of the autopsy report. It lists the cause of death as cocaine intoxication with heart disease as a contributing factor. His military discharge papers, crumpled and almost illegible, were stuffed in his pocket. No family could be located.

The receptionist at the Fort Sam Houston National Cemetery refers me to Johnnie Barrientes, who schedules the ceremonies. He checks his records. Lewis was buried May 10, 2004, with full military honors, he says. A squad of volunteer riflemen draped his coffin in a flag and gave a twenty-one-gun salute.

## FOR OFFICIAL USE ONLY

(As of 13 Jul 71)

### 147. BUMGARNER INCIDENT

ALLEGATION: Murder.

SUBJECT/SUSPECTS:
1. PSG Roy E. Bumgarner, HHC, 173d Abn Bde.
2. SP4 James C. Rodarte, Co E/2/503d Inf, 173d Abn Bde.

VICTIMS:
1. Nguyen Dinh.
2. Nguyen Kich.
3. Phan Tho.
(all residents of Hoi Duc Hamlet, Hoai Tan Village, Hoai Nhon District, Binh Dinh Province)

COMPLAINANT: (Assumed) relatives of victims.

BACKGROUND: On 14 Feb 89, during a recon patrol in the vicinity of LZ English, Tuy Phuoc District, Binh Dinh Province, PSG Bumgarner and SP4 Rodarte came upon three VN males (see VICTIMS) whom they detained and then shot at close range using M-16 automatic fire. PSG Bumgarner then arranged the bodies on the ground so that their heads were close together. A fragmentation grenade was dropped next to the heads of the bodies. PSG Bumgarner then planted weapons on the bodies to support his claim that they were VC. SP4 Rodarte said in his statement that he did not think the three VN were VC.

STATUS/PROGNOSIS: Investigation completed; substantiated.

A command investigation was conducted. Solatium payment was made to the next of kin. PSG Bumgarner and SP4 Rodarte were charged with violation of Art 118, UCMJ, Premeditated Murder, and tried by GCM. Bumgarner was convicted of manslaughter and sentenced to reduction to E-1 and forfeiture of $97.00 a month for six months. Rodarte was found not guilty.

WITNESSES:
1. SSG ███████
2. SP4 ███████
3. SP4 ███████
(all of Co E/2/503d Inf, 173d Abn Bde)

INITIATED BY WHOM: N/A.

RESPONSE TO INITIATOR: N/A.

## FOR OFFICIAL USE ONLY

One of 246 case summaries written by the Army Staff in the 1970s. The summaries described a total of more than 800 war-crime allegations.

## CHAPTER FOUR

# BODY COUNT

When the winter monsoon season in Vietnam gives way to a patch of dry weather, our investigation moves from the men who reported war crimes to the places where they occurred. I hire a driving service in Saigon recommended by a former war correspondent. The driver is a gregarious chain-smoker who served in the South Vietnamese army. Our interpreter is a clean-cut and effervescent young man from the government press office in Hanoi. They make an odd couple but give me and Nick the benefit of two very different perspectives as we cross the country.

On March 6, 2006, we are in a gray Mercedes van heading into Hoai Tan village, deep in the rice paddies of Binh Dinh province on the south-central coast of Vietnam. We travel down a narrow country road lined with coconut trees. In the distance is a low mountain range. In between are viridian fields of ripening rice. We stop in front of a one-room house of terra cotta bricks and whitewashed concrete. A dirt path meanders to an open door. Huynh Thi Nay is expecting us. She is seventy-six and frail, with a short, square face and generous ears. She wears a purple jacket over loose black pants. She gestures for Nick and me to sit on two wooden chairs, as she seats herself.

I ask her to tell us about the events of February 25, 1969. They aren't distant memories; she has thought about them every day since. Guided by my questions, she begins her account with dawn and moves cautiously through the rest of the morning. At 7 a.m., she says, she set out on foot to buy food at a market in a neighboring hamlet. As she left, she passed her sixteen-year-old son, Pham Tho, who sat on the ground outside the door weaving a bamboo screen. She hoped to get back in time to make a hearty lunch for him. The eldest of four children still at home, Pham Tho had dropped out of school after ninth grade to help his parents with their farmwork. He harrowed and planted, and, twice a day, he took their flock of ducklings to feed in the rice paddies. As Huynh headed toward town, her son probably said something to make her smile—he often did—but their last exchange has been forgotten.

At the market, she traded a chicken for fish and produce. She walked home, balancing a basket of provisions. Halfway back, a young woman from the hamlet ran to meet her, shouting with unusual urgency.

"She said, 'Aunt, hurry back, two duck-herders were detained, the Americans detained two duck-herders . . . together with one irrigator.'"

(It is customary to address nonrelatives as "aunt," "uncle," "brother," or "sister," depending on age.)

Huynh ran home, dropping her basket as she passed her house, and continued running toward the field where Pham Tho would have taken the ducks.

"I rushed toward the cotton tree by the inner field. When I reached here I found a pair of bamboo cages—my son's—with a flock of young ducks on one side, a group of baby ducklings also on one side. I called out, 'Tho, Tho,' about three times, but no one replied," she says. "Then I just followed the road on foot, by myself, without anyone accompanying me. When I reached there, I saw a big jackfruit tree. There I found two hats, a duck-herding stick, a displaced hoe, and my son's hat, flown all the way up on the tree. I did not know what happened. I came—When I saw, I fell back, scared out of my wits."

She doesn't say, so I don't ask what she saw. I know from the declassified files that she found the bodies of her son and two others. Their legs and torsos were riddled with bullets, their heads blasted away by a grenade.[1]

"I rushed back to inform the community here. I was running back, crying all the way. My eyes were so full of tears that I could not see my way."

She made her way home, and stayed there with her young infant, while her husband spoke with authorities. When he returned, he told her that U.S. soldiers had taken the bodies away for an investigation. The army eventually brought them back in metal caskets and paid each of the families a small amount of money.

"He was a gentle, responsible son who cared for his parents," she explains. "I so regret that he died."

After Pham Tho's death, her younger son joined the revolutionary forces, she says. She later lost a daughter during a bombardment

that destroyed their house and left a crater "as large as a pond."
She points to the spot as we leave. It was backfilled and now is
covered by a garden of cassava.

―――――――――

By the time he crossed paths with her son, Platoon Sgt. Roy E.
Bumgarner Jr. had spent more than two decades in the military.[2]
He joined the Marines in 1948. He served in the Korean War
and received a Purple Heart among other honors and decorations. He also was court-martialed and confined in the Philippines, in Japan, and at Camp Pendleton, California, according to
his personnel file. (The documents provide no further details.)
He left the Marines in 1958 and joined the army. In 1961, he
pleaded guilty to assault and disorderly conduct. He was sentenced to three months in confinement. Four years later, he
shipped to Vietnam in the first wave of deployments. He
worked his way up from squad leader to platoon sergeant. In
1969, he was based at LZ English with the 173rd Airborne
Brigade. There he fostered a reputation as a prolific killer, competing openly with a buddy for the highest body count. Bob
Stemme had told us about the contest. When angry residents
from Hoai Tan hamlet gathered outside the gate of LZ English
on February 25 of that year, Stemme had been dispatched with
an interpreter to find out why. He followed them to the three
bodies. The army's ensuing investigation led to another court-
martial for Bumgarner.

According to the investigation report and testimony at his 1969
trial in Nha Trang, Bumgarner detained the three Vietnamese
while on patrol with a reconnaissance team. He knew they

weren't armed yet opened fire anyway. James C. Rodarte, a twenty-year-old team member, gave this account to a CID investigator, according to an official transcript of their conversation:

> BUMGARNER told the VN's to sit down. Then he asked me if I was ready, and I said, "Yeh, I guess so" and about that time he started firing. I started firing down at the ground. I was about 6 feet from the VN's and BUMGARNER was a little closer and to my right. Then he turned to me and hollered for me to put some more fire power out there, and when he said that, I thought that he was going to hit me from the tone of his voice. I put another magazine in my weapon, and fired into the ground again, and then over the heads of the VN's, who were laying on the ground at that time. Then BUMGARNER said for me to put some fire out to the flanks, so I fired the remainder of that magazine out to the flanks. Then I reached down and took the stuff out of one of the bodies pockets and put it on the ground, while BUMGARNER took care of the other 2 bodies. Then BUMGARNER told me to put all the stuff in my pocket, which I did. Then I fired a few more rounds toward the flanks, while BUMGARNER arranged the bodies in a half circle so that all the heads were close together. Then he took my rifle and told me to drop a grenade right next to the heads. Then he went over and got into a little ditch. After I dropped the grenade, I ran over to where he was and got down also. . . . [3]

Bumgarner retrieved several weapons from his carrying case and planted them near the bodies. He radioed in the deaths as enemy KIA, thereby raising his body count by three.

"I gave BUMGARNER all the papers and things from the bodies except for a ring and a watch," Rodarte told the investigator. "I am now wearing the ring, and I gave the watch to a friend."

The investigator asked, "Did BUMGARNER advise you in any way as to what to say concerning this incident if you were questioned by anyone?"

"He said not to say anything other than that we made contact and saw them running, and fired on them," Rodarte said. "He said don't make a statement, that we had everybody on our side and we could get out of it."

The investigator asked, "Do you feel that what was done out there by your patrol was right?"

"No, I don't."

"Can you give any reason explaining why the incident occurred?"

"I guess SGT. BUMGARNER is out of his mind or something."

"Is there anything else you wish to say at this time?"

"That I am sorry it happened, and wish that there was some way we could get it corrected."

Both Rodarte and Bumgarner were tried for murder in May 1969. Rodarte's lawyer successfully argued that the young soldier acted on Bumgarner's orders. A jury of officers acquitted him. (Rodarte declined to talk to us about the case.) In a separate proceeding, another jury of officers found Bumgarner guilty of unpremeditated murder. He received no prison time, only a reduction in rank and a $582 fine.[4]

———

Huynh Thi Nay serves us drinks of fresh coconut. I am surprised at her graciousness toward us, given her past experience with

Americans. Many returning U.S. veterans have remarked on the surprising hospitality of the Vietnamese.

We walk down a footpath to the home of Phan Thi Dan, the widow of the irrigation worker. She is a short woman with cropped silver hair, wearing a black jacket and lilac pants. Now seventy-nine, she sits cross-legged on a low table and lunges into a spirited account that spares none of the delicate details.

She says she last saw Nguyen Dinh alive at 7 a.m. the day he died. After breakfast, he grabbed his hoe and headed for the fields. As an irrigator, he was responsible for opening and closing the dirt dams that controlled the flow of water into the community's rice paddies. On his way out the door, she handed him her wedding ring for safekeeping. She planned to go fishing for shrimp that morning and feared she might drop it in the pond. The ring was her most valuable possession. They could not afford one when they married at fifteen. They waited three years, until the birth of their first child. Then they raised and sold a pig to pay for the long-awaited memento. She had cherished it over twenty years and nine more children.

About 9 a.m. on the day Nguyen died, she heard shots and an explosion in the distance. Shortly afterward, a neighbor ran to the pond, shouting at her to follow him.

"He said, 'Uncle Hai has been shot by the Americans.' Frankly speaking, I didn't believe it at first. I asked him if he was serious, was he telling the truth. He then asked how I could stand there. He told me to hurry up. He urged me to put down the fishing net. At that point, I burst into fear, sprang up, and ran, leaving everything behind."

A crowd had gathered at the site of the shootings.

"I saw they fired a mortar here, with an obvious crater about the size of a bamboo rice-drying basket. And there lay three of them—he was the oldest one—shot dead with guns. . . . Everyone was badly smashed up. No heads remained on the bodies."

An American and a Vietnamese interpreter arrived at the scene, she says. An investigator followed soon afterward, and U.S. soldiers began to collect evidence.

"I held three huge rocks, intending to hurl them, but they stopped me," Phan says. "Later on, when I get flashbacks, that fit of fury still arises in me. He died just in his early forties—let me see—when he was just forty-one years old."

She traveled to the nearby city of Nha Trang for the courts-martial. She was nervous about leaving her hamlet and afraid of Americans but determined to face the soldiers who killed her husband, she says. The fear turned to fury when she walked into the courtroom and spied her wedding ring on the evidence table. Once again, she had to be physically restrained, this time from throwing a chair.

"I still feel my eyes piercing them, and I had the temptation to beat them to death."

She kept her composure during her testimony. The lawyers could find no discrepancies between what she had told investigators and her responses to their questions in court, she says. No, her husband was not a member of the resistance. No, he owned no guns. He was an irrigation worker who carried only a hoe.

At the end of one of the trials—she doesn't recall which—the defense attorney asked her forgiveness.

"He said that the American on an operation had mistakenly shot innocent people and now was begging the court, beseeching my pardon. He apologized. I said I did not accept the apology, that I wanted my husband back . . . to go home to work and feed his wife and children, a big flock of children awaiting him in hunger and thirst. Let him go home to collect firewood and sell coal to feed me. I said so. Then the interpreter translated to the Americans. Then the American lawyer stood up . . . and said the soldiers had caused his death by mistake. They were on an operation for too long."

When the trial ended, the army returned her wedding ring.

"After he was dead for one year and two months, I sold it," she says. "I sold it and bought rice and clothes for my children; otherwise I had nothing for them to eat and go to school."

Bumgarner's tour of duty ended six months after his conviction.[5] The army allowed him to reenlist, despite the seriousness of the crime.

In 1972, the *New York Times* published an article on U.S. soldiers reluctant to leave Vietnam. The piece featured Bumgarner—misspelling his name—without mention of his murder conviction:

> The only time Sergeant Baumgarner went home was when he was so badly wounded that he had to be evacuated by air. A wiry, grizzled man with steely eyes and a crew cut, he has been wounded six times in Vietnam.
>
> "I've stayed because I like my work," said the sergeant, a native of Hickory, North Carolina. . . . "I've been a soldier too long to worry about the purpose of the war. We do what the President orders us to do. I'd fight the Eskimos if he told us to."
>
> Sergeant Baumgarner, whose left forearm is covered with a large tattoo of a naked woman, said that he had done

everything he could think of to try to extend his stay in Vietnam but that there simply are no more jobs.

"There ain't nothing you can do," he added in his soft drawl. "No sir, they're getting us out of Vietnam."[6]

A photograph showed him with his arm around a Vietnamese child. The picture caught the attention of Peter Berenbak in New Jersey. He had been a first lieutenant in the 41st Civil Affairs Co. at LZ English when the killings occurred. He fired off a letter to the editor and sent a copy to his congressman.

"Sgt. Bumgarner is a convicted murderer," he wrote. "So I feel a responsibility to speak for Sgt. Bumgarner's victims and ask the Army why this man is still in Vietnam?"[7]

He copied his U.S. representative, who forwarded it to the army for a response. Records show that a senior official from the Army Staff fielded the inquiry. He explained the army needed infantrymen in Vietnam; Bumgarner was experienced and willing.

"The type of court martial or the offense for which he was court-martialed does not automatically restrict his eligibility for reenlistment," the official wrote. "Thus, SGT Bumgarner, although convicted by a court-martial, for which he paid a debt, is contributing positively in his chosen profession."[8]

Records show that Bumgarner remained in the army after the war, serving in Korea and as an instructor at Fort Jackson, South Carolina, before his retirement in January 1981. He died January 26, 2005, at age seventy-four, in Hickory, North Carolina, and received a military burial at Arlington National Cemetery.[9]

We contacted Berenbak and he told us that he had been assigned to deal with distraught family members after the killings.

He arranged for them to keep a vigil near the bodies, which were stored on the base overnight before being flown to Qui Nhon for autopsies. When he initially saw the carnage, he said, he was convinced the North Vietnamese had mutilated them to "make us look bad." The investigation proved otherwise, and the revelation "changed my life and especially my attitude on the Vietnam War," he said.

He confided another reason for his fury. He produced a memorandum dated March 1968, a full year before the triple slaying, on an investigation into allegations that Bumgarner was killing unarmed Vietnamese farmers and planting weapons on them. According to the investigator's typewritten notes, a private claimed he had seen Bumgarner kill a total of five civilians on four occasions. In each instance, Bumgarner placed ordnance on them "to make things look right." Although classified as a war-crime allegation, the report does not appear in the Army Staff's war-crime compilation. (I later confirm the document's authenticity with the officer who signed it.) The notes include the private's description of one of the alleged incidents:

> We came upon two men working in a rice paddy about 30 meters from the trail. He took careful aim and shot one man in the shoulder. The man had held up his arms to surrender, but the Sergeant fired anyway. The second man began crying and they both called out something that I could not understand. I think they wanted him to stop shooting. The second man began crying and moved to his friend's side to keep him from falling. Sgt Baumgardner continued firing slowly until they were dead. The men never tried to run and never could be considered anything but unarmed farmers

working in a paddy. I told Sgt Baumgardner that it was murder and nothing else. He told me that I could just hate him,
but that these men were of military age and he had to kill
them. . . . He is just dangerous and his mind is twisted. I
don't care if the killings are ever proven but I do think he
should be stopped.[10]

Bumgarner and other members of his unit denied the allegations, the memorandum states. The platoon sergeant noted that
the private had been court-martialed (on unspecified charges) and
was out to get Bumgarner for it. A colonel called the private "a
disciplinary problem." He praised Bumgarner as one of the
"finest and most dedicated soldiers" in his brigade,[11] and the case
was not pursued further.

---

Our list of cases takes us from province to province across central
and south Vietnam. We stand on the shore of a glittering lake in
Quang Ngai province, where in 1967 a staff sergeant executed
two unarmed teenage brothers and reported "two VC KIA." We
find no members of the family in the hamlet, just the boys'
graves. In Binh Duong province, north of Saigon, we traverse the
perimeter of a dense rubber plantation, where U.S. troops shot
villagers collecting wood in 1969 and foraging for food in 1970.
The army claimed large patches of this countryside as free-fire
zones, essentially declaring open season on civilians who wan-
dered across the invisible line in search of food or fuel. We interview residents who say they too were captured by U.S. troops,
one of them in her family's garden, which had become off-limits.

They are living evidence that many U.S. soldiers resisted the pressure to shoot first and ask questions later.

We arrange a stop in the Mekong Delta, where the Concerned Sgt reported that 9th Infantry Division troops regularly killed civilians to meet the army's demands for a high enemy body count. Our driver heads west from Saigon to Long An province, a fertile region of mango and coconut groves, watermelon patches, and rice fields. Our destination is Hamlet 5, An Nhut Tan village.

In December 1969, U.S. troops were in the midst of an aggressive push to eradicate the Vietcong and defeat the North Vietnamese army in the region. Gen. Julian Ewell was in charge of II Field Force and keeping close tabs on the stats. By his accounting, they killed 3,130 enemy combatants that month. Only 130 Americans perished—an extraordinary ratio of 24:1.[12] Ngo Van Thong, a farmer from Hamlet 5, would have been included in the enemy body count.

According to army investigation records, a helicopter landed in his community on December 21. A Ranger team from the 9th Infantry Division disembarked and moved from house to house in search of Vietcong suspects. They came up empty. Then they spotted Ngo and his young son walking toward them from across a field. The soldiers went out to meet them. The Vietnamese interpreter demanded Ngo's identification papers and shooed the young boy away. One of the Rangers then opened fire, killing Ngo. They left the body in the field, chased away distraught family members, and reported the death as one KIA.[13]

Their victim was a popular and relatively prosperous member of the community. His death made the local newspaper. At the insistence of village officials, the army opened an investigation two

months later, on February 2, 1970. Authorities arranged a lineup,
so villagers could identify the shooter—but one of the soldiers
was missing. Army records say that Specialist 4 Jerry R. Mooradian was taken to a field hospital in Saigon on February 5 for treatment of "acute anxiety" and then flown to a U.S. Army hospital
in Japan.[14] He declined to provide investigators with a statement.
His fellow team members told CID they did not see who pulled
the trigger—but that Mooradian afterward insisted he alone had
killed the man.[15] There was an early move to blame the Vietnamese interpreter, and Mooradian wanted to make sure the man
did not take the fall. The interpreter told investigators that he was
standing next to Mooradian when the soldier shot Ngo, referred
to below by his given name, Thong:

> When we walked a few steps, SGT MOORADIAN raised
> his weapon and fired a burst. I saw THONG fall down, got
> up and jumped ahead. SGT MOORADIAN fired another
> burst at him. We both went over to him and saw that the
> man was already dead. SGT MOORADIAN again fired an-
> other burst right in the man's head. . . . After that an old
> woman came over to us and asked for THONG's body. I in-
> terpreted what she wanted to SGT MOORADIAN, but he
> would not let her do so, and said that if she went close to the
> body he would kill her.[16]

The investigation report concludes that Mooradian had killed
the man but was "lacking mental responsibility and capacity."[17]
No one was prosecuted.

Before our trip to Vietnam, I drove two hours south of Chicago
to Mooradian's house in the rural community of Rutland. He

wasn't home, but his wife answered the door and gave me his cell phone number. When I reached him, I explained the reason for my call. He told me he didn't remember killing Ngo.

"There was a lot of things that happened," he said. "I'm not going to go into it."

I asked if he remembered his stay at a hospital in Japan.

"I remember that," he said. "I went back to Vietnam right after that."

I told him about the Concerned Sgt's letter. Mooradian said he knew a soldier who wrote to higher-ups to complain about the body count—a "whiny baby" later killed in action. He said the body count did, in fact, put undue pressure on the troops, but he blamed the politicians, not his commanders.

"The soldier on the ground had to come up with a body count to get to people in Washington so they could justify being there," he said.

I asked if that might have been a factor in Ngo's killing. He said he had nothing more to say and hung up.

Two weeks later, I walk into an airy, sunlit house overlooking a grassy field in Hamlet 5 and greet the victim's son, Ngo Van Ba-Nho, a slight fifty-three-year-old man with thick black hair and a wispy mustache. He wears a white polo shirt and dark blue pants. He is joined by his wife, two grown children, a grandchild, and an aunt who also witnessed the shooting. He tells us that he was the second of seven children and very close to his father.

"When I was a child, my dad would take me everywhere he went. He carried me on his back when I was little. Even when I grew up, I would follow him everywhere."

His father had built his duck farm into a thriving enterprise with hundreds of birds in his flock. He would buy them as ducklings, raise them, and sell them to traders in the city. He often took Ngo Ba-Nho along on his rounds. He was fifteen in the winter of 1969, when they set off together to purchase a brood of ducks in a neighboring district two hours away. When they arrived, they learned the birds had not yet hatched. So they headed back empty-handed. On the way home, they stopped at a relative's house. It was late afternoon by the time they neared their hamlet. They were stopped by friends who urged them not to go any farther. "Painted-face Americans" had landed and were going house to house. U.S. troops frequently swept through their hamlet, but the Rangers with camouflaged faces were the most frightening.

"Everyone would panic just to hear that the painted-face American troops were coming to the neighborhood," Ngo Ba-Nho says.

His dad did not want to wait. He was tired and thought his civilian identification papers would protect them. As they crossed the field for the final hundred meters to their house, the Americans and a Vietnamese interpreter came out to meet them. "A tall American" reached into the open pocket of his father's white shirt, removing his ID card and a wallet with a large wad of cash intended to pay for the ducklings, Ngo Ba-Nho says.

"My dad looked helplessly small," he recalls. "They held me by my neck and pushed me, shouting, 'You go back home.' . . . I ran from the site, all the way here. I just kept running, panic-stricken, speaking in tears to my grandma that my dad was ar-rested by the American troops."

They watched from the house as the soldiers marched his dad down a footpath. Then he heard the "rattle" of a weapon firing and saw his father fall.

"I saw Dad jerk up in his white clothes then. He jerked up, then one of them walked up right by his side and shot, making a big hole on his tummy. So Dad fell down. After falling down, he still tried to get up, calling out, then the weapon fired once more, so Dad immediately collapsed on the field's edge."

He started to run toward his father, but his grandmother held him tight. The soldiers stopped his aunt, who also tried to reach his father, and they searched her too. No one was allowed to retrieve the body from the field for burial until the next day.

After the elder Ngo's death, his ducks had to be sold off to support the family. They never regained their financial footing. Ngo Ba-Nho gave up school to help his mother. He harvested wild rush from his neighbors' land that she weaved into mats to sell at the market. His mother supplemented that income by working in the fields for other farmers.

They never learned what came of the investigation into his father's death. Several weeks after the shooting, he was asked to view a lineup of American soldiers to see if he could identify them. But he couldn't tell. The men who had stopped his father had beards and painted faces. These men were clean-shaven and scrubbed. He is surprised to learn that investigators identified the soldier suspected of shooting his father but not that the army declined to prosecute him.

Ngo Ba-Nho needs to return to work. We walk to the spot in the field outside the house where his father died and stop at his burial mound before we go.

---

We set aside extra time to find the hamlet in Quang Nam province where the massacre reported by Jamie Henry took place. When asked by investigators, members of B Company could recall the thatch-roofed hooches, the slight depression where the women and children huddled, and the red hue of the dirt—but not the name of the town or its geographic coordinates. They hadn't lingered long enough to find out.

An unsourced notation in the file indicated the hamlet was roughly fifteen miles west of Hoi An, an ancient trading port on the central coast. We have few options except to drop our luggage at a hotel there and drive in a westerly direction. The van rattles alongside the slow, brown water of the Thu Bon River. We pass through a vast green patchwork of rice paddies, cut into neat squares by earthen dikes that double as footpaths. Every few miles a congregation of brightly painted concrete houses breaks the monotony. Our interpreter, Le Minh Tuan, makes some inquiries for us and identifies a hamlet roughly fifteen miles west of Hoi An where a massacre took place in early 1968. We stop at a farmhouse there and talk to a seventy-four-year-old farmer who lost his wife and a child in the attack. But he says Korean soldiers killed them and no Americans were involved. He leads us down a footpath to a shrine and a small, concrete memorial dedicated to those who died in the massacre. The inscription clearly indicates they were killed by South Koreans. They fought with U.S. and South Vietnamese forces during the war and had a reputation for brutality. Our next stop is a nearby hamlet with a memorial, this one a large stone in the middle of a communal garden. The inscription commemorates the slaying of thirty-two people from two villages by U.S. and South Korean troops in August 1968. Several elderly survivors tell us the inscription is wrong—only South Korean troops took part in the massacre. Our interpreter is out of leads.

Not ready to give up, I ask the villagers if they've heard of any massacres committed by Americans. An old man nods and directs our driver to My Luoc, a hamlet in a neighboring district of Duy Xuyen. The man says we will find a memorial near the marketplace.

We follow a column of farmers into town. They carry long poles across their shoulders with a basket dangling from each end. We pass stalls with sweet buns and steaming pots of rice noodles to park by a small plaza with a statue of a flame roughly ten feet tall. A gold-lettered inscription says the 5th Marine Regiment and the Army of the Republic of Vietnam massacred thirty-three residents and wounded sixteen in three separate attacks between 1967 and 1970—none of them the right date.

A crowd gathers around us. Cars are an unusual sight in the countryside, and westerners even rarer. The interpreter and driver tell them we are Americans with questions about the massacres. They tell us about the first attack, the worst of the three, which claimed nearly half the victims. An old man in a worn green jacket introduces himself as seventy-four-year-old Le Tuan. He says the Marines swept through the hamlet after a battle with local resistance fighters outside town.

"They came from An Hoa," he says, pointing in the direction of a former Marine combat base several miles away.

The Marines, in fact, had lead responsibility for securing the region in the late 1960s. Records show they conducted thousands of operations in a bloody and ultimately unsuccessful effort to defeat the Vietcong, the North Vietnamese army, and an ever-growing throng of local resistance fighters.

In the hours leading up to the massacre, Le Tuan says, he fled with the rest of the men to avoid being killed or taken captive.

They didn't think the Americans would harm the women, children, or old people, as troops had searched the town in the past and left them alone. But this time he returned to find his house burned and his five-year-old daughter dying of a bullet wound, he says. His wife and four other children were safe in a bunker.

We also are approached by a tiny one-eyed woman and her companion, a taller, branch-thin lady with lips stained bright red from chewing betel nuts. The one-eyed woman is seventy-seven-year-old Le Thi Xuan. She tells us that soldiers came into her home demanding to know where the guerrillas were hiding. Her father-in-law didn't know, so they shot him, she says. A soldier demanded the information from her and jammed his elbow into her eye to try to force her to tell them, she says.

"I didn't know!" Le Xuan insists, as if we too doubted her.

When the soldiers left, she says, she grabbed her two young sons and ran to the bunker of the tall woman now standing beside her. The woman is eighty-year-old Pham Thi Cuc, who explains that neighbors often hid in her bunker during attacks, because it was fortified with steel scavenged from railroad tracks. She says she grabbed two toddlers and was about to follow Pham into the shelter when a bullet grazed her forehead and another tore into her thigh.

"One white American shot me, and one black American came and stopped him," she says. She gathers the folds of her long, brown skirt to bare a hard oval lump on her lower thigh.

"The bullet," she says.

The black man reached into his pocket—she thought for a bandage, but he pulled out a grenade and tossed it into the bunker. The blast killed her mother and sister. Le Xuan's twelve-year-old son also perished, and her five-year-old boy was seriously wounded.

Altogether, sixteen died that day, the villagers say. I ask about the memorial. They say they took up a collection in the hamlet to pay for materials and applied for approval from the provincial history museum. They erected the monument in 2004.[18]

After we finish our interviews and take pictures, I ask the crowd whether anyone knows of another massacre in the area. I tell them we are looking for the hamlet where a massacre by the army took place on February 8, 1968, and am struck by how absurd my question sounds. But Le Tuan, the man in the green jacket who lost a daughter, gestures west down the road that follows the river.

───────────

We drive into Vinh Cuong Hamlet No. 3 and pull to the side of the road by a sweet potato patch. Rising ghostlike behind a shirtless gardener is a white tablet roughly ten feet tall. We follow a footpath to read the inscription:

> Here at 16.00 on the 15 of August, 1968, the 5th Regiment of the U.S. troops conducting a mopping operation, burnt the houses and forced people to gather in lines. They barbarously opened fire to massacre 37 of our compatriots, among which were 16 elderly and 21 children. This is one of the savage manslaughters by the U.S. invader on our homeland.

The shirtless man stands, brushing soil from his hands, and introduces himself as fifty-six-year-old Ho Dong Giang. We ask, and he tells us the memorial marks the spot where the massacre took place. The villagers took up a collection to build the shrine to mark the thirtieth anniversary.

As in My Luoc, a curious crowd begins to gather. The light is fading, so we ask him if we may return the next day to speak with him alone. He agrees.

We arrive at his home as the morning mist lifts. Ho is dressed in a red and blue running suit, his thick dark hair neatly parted to one side. He offers tea, and we sit in a nook with a window. Neighbors occasionally appear in the opening to linger and listen. He tells us he was eighteen at the time of the massacre. There had been a fierce battle between local fighters and the Marines outside of town earlier in the day. The Marines brought in artillery, and able-bodied residents fled across the river to safety. He was among them.

"Only old folks, women, and young children remained," he says.

He thought they would be safe in the bunkers. But when he returned that evening in the rain, he found bodies piled outside the bunker on his land and at a neighbor's home. We ask about survivors. He says there were several. Ho Thi Van, a teenage girl who escaped out the back of his family's bunker, still lives in the hamlet, just down the road. He dispatches someone in the window to get her.

She is fifty-four, with long hair tied back in a ponytail. She is a beautiful woman, a grandmother now, with a graceful walk and unwavering gaze through her one good eye. A teenager at the time, she remembers a cold rain on the day of the massacre as her mother hurried her and her five siblings to the bunker. Soon after the shelling stopped, they heard Americans just outside the entrance.

"Mama-san, baby-san," she remembers them calling—slang terms for Vietnamese women and children that U.S. troops commonly used. As everyone else filed out the front, her mother shoved her toward a hidden back exit and told her to meet her uncle at the river. She slipped out and crawled into the tall reeds, glancing briefly over her shoulder to see her family line up outside the bunker, she says. Then she ran fast and quietly to her uncle's waiting arms. As they waded into the river, they heard the crack of weapons firing.

That evening, another uncle brought her back to the hamlet. As they emerged from the tall grass, they saw a pile of bodies outside the bunker.

"It was raining. Under the rain, they lay dead in cramped positions, some on top of each other. Dead bodies scattered all around."

She memorized the positions and the wounds of her family members as she helped separate the bodies: "I had a younger sister who was just three years old, and my mom fell on top of her. She died from being knocked down and crushed under others, not from shooting. And a brother of mine was carrying his younger brother on his back when they were shot, and one bullet hit both of them. They died exactly in the same posture, one on the other's back."

The only survivor, a younger brother, escaped by hiding in a dark corner of the bunker. They both joined the local resistance after the massacre as a means to avenge the deaths, she says. She served as a nurse and lost her eye in battle. Her brother died in a firefight.

I ask if anyone in the bunker thought the Americans would hurt them. She says only her mother, who warned that the Marines had massacred their neighbors in Phu Nhuan Hamlet 2 a year earlier. We get directions to Hamlet 2, which lies on the other end of a wide, flat field of grain. Before we leave, I ask if she is still angry.

"No, now we are at peace," she says. "But if the war returns and the Americans come back, I will try to shoot one round before I die as revenge for my family."

A narrow road takes us to a community center in Hamlet 2—and another monument. The inscription recalls a massacre by the French in 1947 that killed thirty-five people. Underneath is an account of another massacre, twenty years later, by U.S. and South Korean forces that "killed 52 persons and injured 13, most of them elderly, women and children. (There was one pregnant woman.)"

A woman in a Nike hat tells us she lost three relatives in the massacre. Others say both the Americans and South Koreans fired on people. The Americans were distinctive, they tell us. They were taller than the Koreans, and there were whites, blacks, and "Cubans" (Latinos) among them.

Seventy-six-year-old Ho Ngoc Phung says the pregnant woman was his cousin. He returned home after the massacre and found her in the smoldering remains of her home. The Marines came from "Duc Duc," he says, referring to a town near the An Hoa Combat Base. There was little question about where the community's loyalty lay after that day, he says.

"The Liberation Army gathered the surviving villagers and promised them revenge for those innocent villagers."

———

Nick and I had expected the search for Henry's hamlet to be difficult. But we thought we'd be looking for a needle in a haystack of hamlets, not a haystack of massacres. On our third and final day in Quang Nam province, we make a last attempt to find the place B Company decimated. Our interpreter, Le Minh Tuan, has made inquiries overnight, and he directs the driver to a community a few miles farther south. People there tell us that U.S. troops slew three elderly women and an elderly man at their farmhouse just outside an army base. We walk with them through an old minefield to the graves, thank them, and bid farewell. We stop for lunch at a roadside noodle stand and regroup. Our interpreter had been dubious about my practice of asking nearly everyone we meet whether they have heard of any massacres. Nevertheless, he turns to the man at the next table and poses the question. The man knows of a massacre site and directs us down a road that turns into a footpath, which leads us into Hamlet 1 Nghi Thuong, a community of several hundred people in the Que Son district. I look around and notice that the deep-red dirt and rows of thick hedges appear to match the descriptions in the Henry file. There is no memorial in sight, so we ask several villagers who have emerged from their homes. They lead us down a path to a gentle ravine. The opening to an old shelter is still visible in the hillside. That's where the massacre took place, they say. Americans raped a woman there and then shot her and fifteen others living in the shelter, they tell us. Three elderly farmers were killed in nearby fields. The similarity in the numbers, the rape, and the depression in the ground give me hope that we finally have found the place where B Company opened fire. Our interpreter asks for the date.

"October 26, 1969," a villager says, using the lunar date.

The western date would have been December 5, 1969, nearly two years after the massacre Henry reported. I press, ridiculously, but they are sure of the date. A young man speeds away on a bike. He returns a few minutes later with Pham Chi Tam. Villagers tell us he is the only member of his family who survived the massacre. Now forty-nine, he was twelve at the time and watching the water buffalo in the field when he heard weapons fire. He ran home to find burning bodies stacked "like a pyramid" outside the bunker his family shared with relatives. He explains that he later learned what happened from neighbors, who had watched events unfold from their bunkers. Seven Americans came through the community. One of them raped his sister. When members of the family intervened, another American shot all of them. Then the men stacked the bodies, detonated a grenade, and set a fire. In the pile of bodies was Pham's mother, his older sister and her five children, his older brother, a sister-in-law and her two children, and an aunt and four members of her family.

Until that day, he says, the Americans who passed through had been friendly and "loved children very much." They had played with him and given him treats. Another man in the crowd says this unit was different. They had rounded up and threatened villagers in a nearby hamlet before wreaking havoc here, he says.

Following the tragedy, the villagers took care of Pham. He now has five children, who thankfully have never experienced war. He says he has not forgotten his grief, and he is moved that Americans would remember. It's a sentiment we hear from others we encounter.

We leave Vietnam without finding the hamlet where members of B Company massacred nineteen people. Yet in three days, in a twenty-five kilometer stretch of countryside, we stumbled upon allegations of four other massacres by U.S. troops. After we return home, I have the recordings of our interviews re-translated and learn our government interpreter has done a scrupulously honest job. I ask the Marine public information office about the massacres. The press officer responds that they could neither confirm nor deny whether the allegations had been reported or investigated. The Marines did not keep a special file on war crimes, he claims. The cases were mixed in with all other types of criminal investigations. Nonetheless, I file a Freedom of Information Act request. I receive a response much later from Marine headquarters, Department of the Navy, that says the Marines routinely dispose of criminal investigations after twenty-five years.

"As such, any responsive criminal reports of investigation that may have been conducted into incidents pertaining to the murder of a Vietnamese noncombatant in all likelihood no longer exist in Department of the Navy files."

Some operational records still exist. The Vietnamese use a lunar calendar, so I track down an expert to convert them to western dates, and Nick then searches the Marines' command chronologies. They are sketchy at best. The same month the Hamlet 3 massacre occurred, the 5th Marine Regiment reported that operations in the An Hoa region had resulted in 278 enemy killed in action. Only eighteen weapons were recovered—a ratio that suggests the count may have included unarmed civilians.[19] A Combat After Action report shows members of the 1st Battalion, 7th Marines were in the same district as Hamlet 1 Nghi Thuong on the day of the massacre. They reported taking sixteen women and children into custody for questioning—the same number of people that villagers told us had perished at the bunker.[20] There is no way of telling from the records whether the report is referring to the same hamlet or people. Eleven weeks later, on February 19, 1970, a five-man patrol from the same battalion killed five unarmed women and eleven children in Son Thang-4, also in Quang Nam province. The case received news coverage at the time and later became the subject of a book, *Son Thang: An American War Crime,* by Gary D. Solis. Four men faced courts-martial and two were convicted. One received a life sentence, and the other five years. Both sentences were reduced by their commander to one year.[21]

I consult W. Hays Parks, senior prosecuting attorney with the 1st Marine Division, who served as a Marine infantry officer 1968–1969. He says he visited the An Hoa combat base twice on cases. He says that to his knowledge none of the massacres we came across were reported, although he adds that they would not have come to his attention if they had been classified as combat-related casualties. But he argues it's unlikely so many massacres could have been kept secret.

"I'm somewhat of a skeptic from my recollection of serving in that area and having prosecuted cases that this could've gone unnoticed," he says. "But I'm not about to say it couldn't have happened."

He suggests the villagers may be using the term "massacre" in a symbolic sense and that the numbers on the monuments represent all civilian wartime casualties. It's my turn to be skeptical. The numbers on the memorials would be significantly larger, if that had been the case. We had, in fact, collected information from the survivors about other wartime deaths—children and siblings who died in shellings, from illness, or, in the case of those who fought, in combat. They weren't counted in the numbers on the monuments.

I contact Solis, the author of the book on Son Thang-4, who served two tours of duty as a Marine in Vietnam and taught the law of war at West Point until his retirement in 2006.

"I'm confident that there were numerous unreported murders by U.S. personnel in South Vietnam that constituted war crimes," he says. "My extensive review of Vietnam-era records of trial and my interviews of many Marine judge advocates who were there indicates as much. There is no official record of those events, however, because such records neither were required nor were kept on an unofficial basis."

However, Solis says the unreported war crimes that came to his attention did not include massacres. Heonik Kwon, a social anthropologist at the University of Edinburgh in Scotland who has studied massacres in the Vietnam War, says he has come across credible evidence that many in fact did occur in Quang Nam province but escaped notice beyond the affected communities. The worst wave took place in the late 1960s, when the clash over control of the contested region intensified. The pressure on troops for tangible results—in the form of high enemy body counts—inevitably drew upon "the more accessible, stagnant pool of civilians."[22]

"I would disagree with [Parks] who speculates that civilian 'massacres' during the Vietnam conflict should stand largely as a metaphor," Kwon writes in an e-mail exchange.

The massacre memorials mark date-specific tragedies and are distinct from the "standardized memorials for the heroic revolutionary dead" that cropped up soon after the war ended, he says. Religious tradition differentiates combat and even accidental deaths from those caused by "gross injustice." The victims of unjust deaths, such as atrocities, are believed to "perpetually reexperience the agony of violent death."[23] The Vietnamese government initially discouraged commemoration of massacre victims, preferring to rally the recovering populace around more uplifting monuments to military martyrs.

The massacre memorials began appearing in greater numbers during the late 1980s and 1990s, when political liberalization allowed more grassroots control over local issues. An improved economy permitted families to raise money for remembrances and proper reburial of victims. "Commemorative fever" swept hard-hit provinces, such as Quang Nam and Quang Ngai, where the My Lai massacre took place.

"An Hoa was a quite chaotic place during the second half of the 1960s and the area suffered violence from both sides of the war," Kwon says.

Massacres were committed by U.S., Korean, and Vietnamese forces, he says. And although no individual massacre may have been as large as the one in My Lai, the cumulative losses were significant. Kwon notes that journalist Seymour Hersh wrote that My Lai was out of the ordinary but not isolated.

"He is right. And if we stop thinking of an extreme event such as village massacres in terms of the number of the dead bodies it resulted in—and I believe this is what the survivors of these events are asking us to do—we can even say that Hersh's judgment is somewhat too modest. What happened in My Lai was not terribly out of the ordinary in 1966–1969 in Quang Nam and Quang Ngai."

Moreover, the United States is under an international obligation to enact legislation punishing acts such as those alleged to have occurred. Under Article 146 of the Geneva Convention Relative to the Protection of Civilian Persons in Time of War (and a similar provision in the Prisoners of War convention), the United States undertook to enact legislation punishing "grave breaches" of the convention, as defined. The Executive Branch took the position (albeit prior to Toth), that its existing legislation was sufficient for this purpose. Hearings on the Geneva Conventions for the Protection of War Victims Before the Senate Committee on Foreign Relations, 84th Congress, 1st Session 24-29, 58-59 (1955). The Executive Branch has not yet proposed a statute to plug the gap left by Toth, although one is now pending in Congress (H.R. 4225). Given the status of our international obligations, there might be some difficulty about discarding our existing authority as worthless without even trying to invoke it.

## V.   Conclusion

There is statutory authority which would allow discharged servicemen to be tried for violations of the law of war which are alleged to have occurred at My Lai Hamlet. The statutory provisions have been upheld by the Supreme Court, albeit in situations not completely analogous to that involved here. Although there are court decisions indicating some constitutional difficulty about military trial of discharged servicemen, the fact that war crimes are involved may well provide a sufficient basis for the invocation of military jurisdiction in this particular case. Constitutional problems might, in fact, be mitigated by establishing a tribunal which would offer the accused most, if not all, of the protections they would receive in a civilian trial. Given the procedural flexibility available, at least if a military commission were used, any set of procedures compatible with Due Process of Law could be required under authority of a Presidential directive.

If you agree with this view of the law, I would suggest that we attempt to obtain Executive Branch agreement on the propriety of trial by military tribunal in this factual situation. I am ready to assist you in any way you think necessary. Mr. Ronald J. Greene of my staff can be reached on Code 11, extension 53305, to give any necessary assistance to anyone in your office working on this problem.

Robert E. Jordan, III
General Counsel

8

The last page of a 1969 memorandum by army
General Counsel Robert E. Jordan III seeking
Nixon administration approval to prosecute suspects
in the My Lai massacre who had left the service.

## CHAPTER FIVE

# DROWNING WITH CASES

Steven Chucala served as top legal adviser to Henry Tufts, chief of the Army Criminal Investigation Command during the Vietnam War. I had been told that Chucala would be frank, if unapologetic, and a window into decision-making at the highest levels.

The newspaper clips show that he retired as a lieutenant colonel in 1987 but still works at Fort Belvoir, Virginia, where he is the chief of client services in the legal assistance office.[1] I have to go through the army's press office to interview him. After weeks of wrangling, I am instructed to report to the base security checkpoint. An army public information officer escorts me to a compact car, which already holds a second army public information officer and, to my surprise, the Marine press officer who handled my inquiries on the Quang Nam massacres. It's a cramped ride on a warm spring day, but we soon debark outside a nondescript building that houses the legal services office, where soldiers go for help on wills, contracts, adoptions, and divorces.

Chucala leads us to a conference table in a hearing room and sits kitty-corner to me at one end, as the three public information officers align themselves on the other side. He is slim, no-nonsense, with a light fringe of hair and lively eyes behind windowpane glasses. He doesn't wait for questions. There are a few things I need to know about CID in the early 1970s, he tells me.

"This is where, I'm afraid, I'm the only one left that can talk about it. Henry Tufts is dead," he says. "The whole list of all these people are gone. I'm the only one left."

That's why I had pressed so hard to meet with him.

---

The military is bound by federal and international law to investigate reports of war crimes and prosecute the offenders. Broadly defined, war crimes include willful injury to noncombatants, prisoner abuse, wanton destruction of property, and mistreatment of corpses.

During the first four years of the war, the army didn't pursue many allegations. An internal memo claimed that only fifty were reported between 1965 and late 1969.[2] It was during this period that Jamie Henry, still in the army, and Bob Stemme, in Vietnam, made their first attempts to report atrocities—but were intimidated into silence by military investigators.

After the My Lai scandal broke, hundreds of allegations surfaced, and Gen. William Westmoreland issued directives reiterating the army's legal obligation to investigate them. His critics had seized on the fact that the massacre and cover-up occurred in 1968, while he was the top commander in Vietnam. There were calls for him to be held accountable,[3] and he didn't want to give his critics more ammunition. The quantity of investigations increased dramatically—but not necessarily the quality. The archive contains more than five hundred war-crime allegations that CID closed as unfounded/unsubstantiated or due to insufficient evidence. Many of the case summaries reflected paper-thin investigations. Some didn't go much beyond an interview with the soldier or veteran who reported the allegations and denials from the accused. The discard pile included allegations that women and children were massacred in Quang Ngai province in 1967 by a Tiger Force reconnaissance unit—the decorated platoon tied to a murder spree the army covered up and the *Toledo Blade* exposed in 2003.[4] Likewise, Stemme's torture allegations had been classified as "unsubstantiated" in 1970. Two years later, CID secretly confirmed his unit had repeatedly abused detainees. I count at least fifty-three incidents that CID had in fact confirmed but closed as unproven, in many cases because investigators decided they did not constitute a crime.[5] Many of the corpse mutilation cases fell into this group because investigators could not prove that the soldier in possession of an ear or skull was the same person who severed it from the body. In other cases, civilian killings were substantiated but classified as unproven because the investigation concluded they were accidents or combat-related. While the decision not to refer for prosecution may have been understandable in some cases, the misleading classifications contributed to the perception that many reports had been wholly fabricated.

Henry's case was rescued from the unconfirmed stack in 1972. An invisible hand intervened to kick it back to the San Francisco

CID office for further investigation to correct several "deficiencies." When prompted or allowed to do a more thorough investigation, agents established without a doubt that members of Henry's company had massacred nineteen people.[6] But Henry II was an anomaly. Many unconfirmed allegations never got a second look.

Henry's case illustrates another reality about war-crime investigations. Despite all the work investigators put into his case, nothing came of it, not a single court-martial. The spike in investigations after My Lai did not translate into a run on convictions. As of late 1972, CID had investigated 284 suspects in war crimes other than Mai Lai, according to an internal status report. Thirty were convicted—fifteen prior to My Lai. The army's statistics also reflected a disparity in the fates of commissioned officers and the rank and file. Officers represented roughly 30 percent of the suspects but just 14 percent of those convicted. They were more likely to have allegations against them closed as unfounded.[7]

The Army Staff debated what to do about the conspicuously low conviction numbers. Some wanted to fold in convictions for any crime against a Vietnamese citizen—a tactic that would at least push convictions above one hundred.[8] The proposal was rejected at the time, although the higher number has since found its way into some postwar histories.[9]

I mine our own database for a more nuanced look at the army's conviction record. I start by separating out the cases in the Army Staff archive that CID reported as founded. From those, I parse the most serious cases—violent crimes against persons—and count 191 suspects.[10] Fifty-two, 27 percent, were tried by courts-martial. Twenty-three were convicted, a 44 per-

cent success rate. There are too few war-crime prosecutions
for a rigorous comparison, but Justice Department statistics
offer some perspective: On average, more than 70 percent of violent crime prosecutions result in convictions.[11] The army's
own conviction rate for all types of crimes hovers around 90
percent.[12]

All twenty-three convictions involved egregious allegations
of murder, rape, or torture. Yet only fourteen men received
prison terms. And though the sentences ranged from six months
to twenty years, at least half spent less than a year in confinement. The harshest sentence in the war-crime archive[13] went to
a military intelligence interrogator accused of raping a thir-
teen-year-old girl in a prisoner-of-war compound. He was sentenced to twenty years' confinement at hard labor, total
forfeiture of pay, and dishonorable discharge. On appeal, his
punishment was reduced to one year's hard labor and partial
forfeiture of pay. He served seven months and sixteen days.

---

Chucala begins with a short course on how the military justice
system was supposed to work:

"The CID normally investigates felony-type offenses. What
happens is that they put together the outcome of what they've investigated. If it clears the person, that goes into the report.
They're not out to hang anyone. They're out to impartially develop the evidence in the case as best they can. Then they put together a report of investigation like you're holding here. Now,
they make findings and, you might say, conclusions of their own
because you have to make a conclusion. If you're going to say

this is an Article 128 [assault] or Article 121 [larceny] offense or 92 [failure to obey an order] or whatever, that means you have concluded that there is enough evidence in the investigator's mind that it fits in that area for someone to take an ultimate determination or disposition of it."

The suspect's commander generally makes that determination. Hardly disinterested parties, they are given tremendous deference by the military justice system.

"The CID has no control over a commander," Chucala points out.

He says he has just explained the way the system was supposed to work, but what I need to understand is that CID was a mess at the time.

"We had a very chaotic situation," he says, as the public relations officers shift uncomfortably in their seats. "We're talking about the establishment of the CID command that you know today."

Chucala is referring to the removal of CID in 1971 from control of the provost marshal general, who had served a dual role as military police chief and criminal investigation commander. That year Carl C. Turner, who held the post from 1964 to 1968, went to prison for stealing 136 guns intended for the federal government and selling them to private collectors, though he may have diverted three times that many. The charges stemmed from a three-year probe by the Senate Permanent Subcommittee on Investigations that also found widespread "corruption, criminality and moral compromise" in the operation of noncommissioned officers' clubs. Military personnel were taking kickbacks from suppliers and stealing from the army's multibillion-dollar network of officers' clubs and commissaries. The wrongdoing was brazen—there were shipments of diamonds and furs to clubs in combat zones in Vietnam. The hearings produced evidence that the provost marshal's office had known and covered up the problems. Defense Secretary Melvin Laird responded by ordering creation of a separate CID command that reported to the army chief of staff.[14]

"I was sent there on two days' notice to help put it together in 1971," Chucala says. "And part of that mission was to develop the individuals in the entire command of almost three thousand agents worldwide on how to properly investigate adequately and come up with the proper report. . . . So at the time all this hell is breaking loose, we're in the first stages of putting together a worldwide investigative force and trying to train people and trying to develop them and develop their expertise, which was totally lacking before."

The "hell" that broke loose was a tidal wave of war-crime allegations that followed My Lai, inundating agents already buckling under a heavy wartime caseload of larceny, drug, fragging, assault, and murder offenses.

"They were drowning with cases and these war-crimes things were superimposed on top of everything. . . . All of a sudden all of these people come out of the woodwork talking about offenses that allegedly occurred two years ago, five years ago, and six years ago. . . it really became a nightmare because the allegations would read something like, 'The radio telephone operator of Company A or something or other back in such and such and such valley in 1969 raped so-and-so.' 'Okay. So what was the name of the radio telephone operator?' 'I don't know.'

"In other words, we were confronted with a situation where any day of the week there were over five hundred thousand soldiers pouring in and out of Vietnam. Visualize trying to investigate and find out who this person was that he believes he saw commit this crime. . . . We couldn't even figure out the names of the people, or some of these 'Winter Soldiers' people wouldn't tell us the names," he says. "Now what do you do?"

The "Winter Soldier" war-crime forum in 1971 produced more than two hundred allegations, all of which CID was required to follow up on. But the sponsor, Vietnam Veterans Against the War, discouraged participants from cooperating. They were instructed to refer agents to their public testimony and not divulge details that would cause "trouble for the peons instead of the generals," in the words of one veteran that CID interviewed.[15]

The declassified papers showed that many of the men provided names, units, dates, and locations in their testimony or their interview with CID. Armed with the same information as Chucala's investigators, I tell him, we found men thirty-plus years later. While we have the benefit of the Internet, the army had the advantages of proximity and access to personnel files.

In many cases, it was too late anyway, Chucala says. The allegations were several years old, and the suspects had been discharged. They were civilians, out of the army's reach.

"They would leave the service and literally we would lose jurisdiction over them."

The army didn't court-martial many of the suspects who remained in the service, I say. Others got away because CID took so long to start and complete its investigation.

"I can only speak unofficially now. Let's get that straight," Chucala says. "When you have the news media and everybody else pounding on, 'This is not a just war, we shouldn't be there, blah,

blah, blah, our soldiers shouldn't be in there suffering' . . . I can understand why these agents felt that—don't push it any further, because everybody wants to lay it to rest."

The administration's handling of the My Lai investigation further demoralized CID ranks, he says. Thirty men were recommended for charges. Sixteen were charged, five tried, and Lt. William L. Calley Jr. alone was convicted. In April 1971, Nixon decreed that Calley be allowed to serve his sentence in home confinement.[16] How could anyone else be punished after that? The move effectively disarmed the military justice system. Commanders balked at pressing charges, lawyers didn't want to prosecute, juries were unwilling to convict, Chucala says.

"It's true. Everybody wanted Vietnam to go away. We were there how many years? Fifteen years. I can understand. That's not my philosophy, but I can understand. . . ." he says. "I'm not here to defend human beings. But with Jane Fonda and others running around and demeaning the military, and we're seeing that today, I hope somebody wakes up today. What the news media is even doing today in influencing the behavior of soldiers in the field—I don't mean against the government. What I mean is—and I've been around long enough to sense it—if you browbeat the whole purpose of us being there, if you demean the whole purpose of why we're there, what we're doing, why should we even be there, there will be a certain group of people in any society that will react against whom they're supposed to be freeing or taking care of. So the terms 'gook' and all these other terms that started—I think were fed even—by the news media creating more anger in these people for not wanting to be there. It is amazing."

When I counter that the army drilled the term "gook" into soldiers during boot camp, Chucala offers this defense:

"What I'm saying to you is, you're also dealing with another phenomenon. A soldier is trained to kill, not to be killed. I don't know soldiers who like killing. I don't know any. I was first trained as an infantry unit commander, Fort Benning. Nobody I know wants to kill anybody. Now, how do you get this individual to have the gumption to kill someone? You don't tell them hold hands and sing 'Kum Ba Yah.' You have to instill in them something that says he's really bad, and if it's you or him, it's him. That's where these terms come from. And in war, don't expect to call them 'friend' or 'comrade.' I mean, these are terms that psychologically come out because this person has to be geared towards killing the enemy. If not, he shouldn't be there. He's going to get himself killed and whoever's with him. It's unfortunate. Yes, you have to orient a person not to be ruthless, not to disobey the law. But these are the little things that the term 'Jap' and all these other terms came up to even during World War II. So it's nothing new. This is not race relations, by the way."

To the relief of the public relations officers, I steer the conversation back to the matters at hand. But it is a revealing tangent from one of the war's top law officers, who didn't connect the "gook" desensitization of basic training with the "mere gook" rule on the ground in Vietnam and the plethora of cases that swamped his office in the 1970s—although veterans we interviewed did.

I ask about Henry's case. If prospects for prosecution were so poor, why send it back to the CID office in San Francisco for a more thorough investigation? Chucala says he doesn't remember that specific case but that he sent many out for further investigation.

"We had the authority and we did send back many through the region headquarters," he says.

Even if he knew the suspects wouldn't be prosecuted, he wanted agents to learn how to conduct a proper investigation. He guesses that the Henry case was sent back for that reason.

"A teaching mission," he explains.

***

When Chucala tells me the government couldn't prosecute suspects once they left the service, he offers the prevailing and public stance of the U.S. military. I poll other military law experts, most of whom served as military lawyers in the Vietnam era. They too assert that the army lost jurisdiction upon separation. They point to a 1955 U.S. Supreme Court decision, *Toth v. Quarles*. The Court ruled on constitutional grounds that the military could not try ex-servicemen by court-martial for violations of the Uniform Code of Military Justice.[17]

But then a former army prosecutor in the My Lai cases calls back. He says he dug around in his files after we talked and found an internal army memorandum that addressed the question. He says he'll send it to me, that I ought to read it.

The memo is dated December 2, 1969, and is written by then army general counsel Robert E. Jordan III. Its purpose was to advise the U.S. attorney general's office on whether the government could prosecute My Lai suspects who had left the service. At the end of an eight-page legal analysis, Jordan drew this conclusion:

There is statutory authority which would allow discharged servicemen to be tried for violations of the law of war which are alleged to have occurred at My Lai Hamlet.[18]

He wrote that the *Toth* case involved an ordinary murder, while the My Lai killings were war crimes. War crimes violate not only the military code but also the law of war—an international legal authority rooted in treaties and custom that governs the conduct of wars. The law of war incorporates the Geneva and Hague conventions. The United States not only can but also is obligated to prosecute citizens who commit war crimes, regardless of their current military status, the memo argued. They could be tried through courts-martial, a special military commission, or a tribunal, as long as they were afforded similar rights and protections as in the federal courts.

The memo closed:

If you agree with this view of the law, I would suggest that we attempt to obtain Executive Branch agreement. . . . I am ready to assist you in any way you think necessary.

Jordan had been the Pentagon's legal point man on the My Lai massacre. He fielded reporter Seymour Hersh's initial inquiries and, after photographs of bodies appeared on the nightly news, was dispatched to provide the first high-level public acknowledgment of the case. At an hour-long press conference, he revealed that Calley would be charged and twenty-four current and former servicemen were under investigation. Asked whether the army could try ex-soldiers, according to news reports, he responded that the Supreme Court "has not been favorably disposed." Someone then asked whether the army retained jurisdiction if the offense was a war crime. He called the theory a "potential avenue against the civilians" but "uncharted legal waters."[19] Ten days later, he sent his memo on the question to the attorney general's office.

In the end, the army did not charge suspects who had been discharged. In 1971, Jordan left to join the Washington office of Steptoe & Johnson as a partner. He launched his postgovernment career by representing oil companies in their battle to build the Trans-Alaska Pipeline. He wrote a paper that year for an international law symposium arguing that some of the most controversial practices in the war—bombarding inhabited villages, designating free-fire zones, and relocating civilians—were not flatly illegal under The Hague and Geneva conventions.[20] Since then, he has enjoyed a long, successful run as a litigator for large commercial interests on antitrust, environmental, and whistle-blower matters. His is not the résumé of a radical. So his views on trying ex-servicemen should have carried some weight in the administration. I call to find out what came of his memorandum.

Jordan asks me to send a copy of the memorandum. He says his own set of documents from that period was accidentally destroyed when he submitted them to the declassification process. After he has a chance to review the memorandum, he follows up with an e-mail:

"I would be proud to stand behind this memo, which was an effort to provide a balanced analysis of the issues involved in trying discharged army personnel for alleged violations of the law of

war at My Lai," he writes. "In my judgment a very strong case
was available for trying the My Lai folks."

As we continue the discussion on the phone, he says he hammered out the legal issues with the future Supreme Court chief
justice.

"Bill Rehnquist and I worked on this," he says.

Before his contentious confirmation in 1971, William Rehnquist was the assistant attorney general in charge of the Office
of Legal Counsel—the top legal adviser to Attorney General John
Mitchell. In that role, Rehnquist defended government secrecy,
domestic surveillance, and the arrest of antiwar demonstrators.
He made the call to the *Washington Post* to ask the paper to stop
printing a top-secret Pentagon study on the Vietnam War or face
legal action.[21] Despite his strong public stands on those issues, he
was known for his ability to see both sides of a legal issue.[22]

Jordan says he also had the backing of his boss, then secretary
of the army Stanley Resor: "Resor was a very principled guy. He
thought what happened in My Lai was a horrible war crime and
that we couldn't go around talking about what the Nazis did and
the Japanese did in the Second World War and not do anything.
People said, 'Well, this was a different war. You can't tell who the
enemy was.' Bullshit."

Yet Jordan says he does not remember hearing back from Resor
or from Nixon administration officials after submitting his memorandum. (Resor, eighty-nine, later tells me he does not recall the
memorandum but says he has forgotten many details of his tenure.)
To Jordan's knowledge, the matter was not pursued further.

"We would have needed the president's support to proceed,"
he says. "We didn't have much support upstairs."

Resor may have decided not to push the matter. He was reeling from a public chastening just three months earlier over another notorious war-crime case. He took a strong stand on prosecuting eight Green Berets, including Col. Robert B. Rheault, then commander of the 5th Special Forces Group in Vietnam. They were charged with plotting to execute a Vietnamese spy and dump his body in the South China Sea. The decision to charge them drew protests from hundreds of Green Beret supporters. Worried about the political fallout, Nixon operatives worked "the rear guard" to sabotage the case, Jordan says. The CIA, which had promised to provide key evidence for the trials, abruptly changed course and refused to cooperate. The army's case quickly unraveled. Resor, red-faced, had no choice but to drop the charges.[23]

The question of whether the government could prosecute ex-soldiers for war crimes resurfaced in 1996. Then a Vietnam veteran and former POW persuaded Congressman Walter B. Jones, a freshman conservative Republican from North Carolina, to introduce legislation that would allow the U.S. government to prosecute former North Vietnamese soldiers for mistreatment of American servicemen. Jones said he wanted "to help protect the rights of Americans in foreign lands by giving federal courts the authority to try and prosecute the perpetrators of war crimes against Americans."[24] By the time the legislation passed—with overwhelming bipartisan approval—it also gave federal courts explicit authority to try former U.S. servicemen for committing war crimes.[25] A decade later, the War Crimes Act had yet to be used, for or against an American veteran.[26]

Chucala's grim depiction of CID in the early 1970s is underscored by our interview with the lead investigator and attorney on Henry's case. Jonathan Coulson retired after twenty-four years in the armed forces and now owns a gun shop in Alabama. Nick and I reach him by phone.

"I remember the case in some detail," he says. "I was a very young agent to get a case like this. I'd just made warrant officer."

He inherited the file in 1972 while assigned to CID's Los Angeles office, he says. The case was already two years old.

"The guys ahead of me diddled around with it. . . . Unfortunately, L.A. was pretty much a retirement office. The case was handed around to old guys on their way out."

They submitted the case to officials at headquarters, who kicked it back for further investigation. Coulson arranged for agents in various parts of the country to interview additional members of the unit. He interviewed medic Stuart Lee and re-interviewed the battalion commander, Lt. Col. William Taylor, among others.[27] Every Friday a senior officer in Washington would call to check on Coulson's progress.

"That is unusual to be monitored that closely," he says. "They wanted to make sure I was headed in the right direction."

But he adds that he was not pressured to produce a particular result. In the end, he confirmed the massacre, ten additional murders, a sexual assault, and a corpse mutilation. His report identified nine living suspects and one who had died in action. It appears that by the time he signed his name to the final report in December 1973, all but two suspects had left the army.[28]

"The biggest single problem is these allegations didn't come to our attention until so long after the fact," he says.

Even if they had, the prospects of courts-martial were slim, he says.

"Vietnam was a lost cause. We all knew it," he says. "You don't want to stir up a hornet's nest again. If you're a commander, you've been there."

Did that bother him as an investigator?

"There was frustration there, without doubt. I spent years doing this," he says. "Sometimes you just went through the motions for lessons learned."

And because the public wanted answers, he adds. But the army kept his findings a secret, I say. The information still is useful, he contends.

"Even if the public doesn't know about it, the army does," he says.

A few weeks later I call back. In the interim, revelations by *Time* that Marines killed twenty-four Iraqis, including women and children, in Haditha, Iraq, have received wide pickup in the media.[29] Coulson cuts me off.

"If your story came out now, people would connect the two, and I don't want to be part of that," he says and hangs up.

Robert Briney is the attorney who advised Coulson on his final report. He heads the Office of the Legal Defender in Maricopa County, Arizona. He recalls the Henry case. The thick file arrived just weeks before his three-year stint in the army ended. He was told there was interest "from high" in the case. So he threw himself into it, devoting full time to review of hundreds of witness statements, investigator notes, and photographs. The specifics of the case have grown fuzzy over the years, he says, but the images remain in sharp focus.

"There was a dead VC. He was propped up between two GIs wearing ears around their necks. Someone put a cigar in his mouth," Briney says. "I thought, when I was younger, that we were above that."

He worked with Coulson on charges that might stick against the few suspects who remained in the army. He left before any decisions were made. He never heard back and figured that the army had dropped the case. I tell him he's right.

"My feeling is they thought the war, if not over, was pretty much over, why bring this stuff up again."

———————

Cases like Henry's were not the only casualties of a deeply demoralized CID. On April 15, 1971, the officer leading the high-profile probe into Herbert's war-crime allegations committed suicide. Maj. Carl E. Hensley shot himself in the head in the bedroom of his home in Clinton, Maryland. Within twenty-four hours, CID chief Henry Tufts told reporters that he had "fully explored" the matter and that the suicide had "absolutely no connection" to Hensley's work.[30] By that time, unbeknownst to the press or public, the Herbert investigation had moved well beyond his handful of public allegations and uncovered widespread use of water, field phones, and beatings on detainees by the 172nd Military Intelligence Detachment. But the broader findings remained a closely held secret. So Tufts made no mention of them when he insisted repeatedly that Hensley's suicide had nothing to do with his job.

The declassified records contain a thin packet of documents on Hensley's suicide that directly contradict Tufts's public statements. There is a sworn statement, dated April 19, 1971, from an army psychiatrist who had been treating Hensley. Maj. Dr. William E. Legat wrote that Hensley began feeling depressed and anxious about work two months before his death. The feelings had grown so overwhelming that he could not stomach going to the office. He took a leave and sought counseling. Legat concluded that Hensley was suffering from a "depressive reaction" related to his work. "He gave no indication of any personal difficulties and talked in rather general, abstract terms about problems on the job," Legat wrote.

He made note that Hensley appeared lucid, not delusional, and had no prior history of depression. They met four times and scheduled a fifth session on April 15. Hensley killed himself several hours before the appointment.[31]

The second document is a sworn statement by his wife, Dolores "Ann" Hensley, a month after the suicide:

> In February Carl withdrew into a shell, stopped eating, did not talk to the children and did not or would not talk to me. At this time, he weighed about 205 pounds and at the time of his death he weighed about 175 pounds. Sometime in February he saw a doctor at Fort McNair for what he called "his nerves." Still working long hours and not eating—waking up around 3 or 4 each morning.[32]

He was referred to Legat and began taking medicine, but his symptoms continued to worsen. He rarely left their bedroom.

On April 13 he went into a deeper state of depression and kept saying the only way out was to shoot himself. I asked him "the way out of what?" "Everything" he replied. He kept, saying that he had suppressed information and could get four to ten years at Leavenworth for what he knew. I asked what did he know and he (Carl) kept saying, "Enough, enough, it goes all the way up to the highest." He kept saying the way out was to shoot himself over & over. . . .

On the 15th, he got up, walked around with the children, talked to them tried to act normal, but was very nervous. After the children left for school he wanted to take a short nap before going to see Dr. Legat. He asked me to take the baby downstairs so he could sleep an hour. I went downstairs and felt a strange feeling that something was wrong, the baby had not seemed to bother him one way or the other until this morning. I slipped my shoes off and went back upstairs. . . . I went down the hall, found him standing in the bedroom with a shotgun. I screamed "Carl give me the God-damned gun!" He pulled the trigger.

My search for Ann Hensley leads to another obituary. It lists the names of their six children, and I reach Karla Florhaug, the second-eldest, at her home in Austin, Texas. She says her mother often spoke about their father's mysterious allegations, and they spent their lives wondering what he meant.

"She said he kept saying, 'It was going to go all the way to the top.'"

Florhaug was thirteen when her father died. A neighbor picked her up from school early. They hurried home to a surreal scene:

U.S. Army officers had overrun the place. They rifled through drawers and searched trash cans. They flipped page by page through books on the shelves. Boxes of documents were carried out the door. No one knew what they were looking for or what they found.

"It has always haunted us," she says.

She gives me the number of Joanne Wright, the neighbor and her mother's best friend. She may know more, Florhaug says. Wright says she has no answers either. Hensley was devoted to his job and never disclosed the secrets that were bothering him.

"He withdrew and he stayed in his room a lot. He didn't know how to face the world with what he knew. He said it would blow the top off the army. He couldn't handle it."

There was no chance to search for clues after his death. She was surprised at how quickly the army arrived at the scene and began scouring the house for work-related documents. The questions dogged Ann to her grave, Wright says.

"She said one day they'll know the truth."

Nick and I visit Legat, the psychiatrist, at his home in Bethesda, Maryland, where he has a private practice. We sit on a couch in a room cluttered with books as he reads a copy of his statement. He says he has never forgotten Hensley.

"I remember that phenomenon of him being concerned about things on the job. But it was nothing specific. It was so odd. . . . He couldn't discuss his job," Legat says. "My impression was that it was because there was something big he was keeping secret."

Legat reads his statement again.

"I know what's not here. When CID came to talk to me, he [the agent] said they were concerned about some war-crimes incidents in Vietnam."

The agent didn't offer any specifics. Legat says he assumed it had something to do with My Lai, because that was the most prominent case in the news.

"They wanted to know what he was so upset about," he says. "I said I didn't know."

Kenneth Weinstein was the director of investigations for the CID command at the time of Hensley's suicide. We initially contact him at his home in Florida to talk about the Henry case and several other investigations carried out on his watch. He does not recall any of them. But he has not forgotten Hensley. He explains that he was Hensley's immediate supervisor, considered him a friend, and urged him to see a psychiatrist when he began showing signs of stress. Weinstein says he was dismayed by his suicide but believed it was related to depression and not a cover-up.

We ask what CID found in the search of the house.

"I don't know anything about that. It doesn't sound like us," he says.

The death didn't take place on military property, he explains. Local authorities would handle the investigation and cleanup. I tell him what Wright and Florhaug said.

"When he killed himself he created an incredible scene in the home in the manner he killed himself. Agents who were friends of his went to his house. They kept family out until they could clean it up. They cleaned up blood. They voluntarily went to the home. They also wanted to make sure there were no guns left."

The CID investigators were not at the house on official business, he says. They did not search the house for records or remove any documents, he insists. When I ask about the statements by Hensley's wife and his psychiatrist, Weinstein says he did not know about them and has no explanation.

"There's absolutely no foundation whatsoever to what he says about going to Leavenworth or hiding facts. None of it. Absolutely none of it."

1. Investigations now in progress:      1

2. Allegations unsubstantiated      161

3. Substantiated (Probable Cause):      70

     a. Courts-martial:      36

     b. (1. Convicted:      20*

        (2. Acquitted:      16

     b. Charges dismissed (Not tried):      19

     c. Nonjudicial punishment:      8

     d. Adverse admin action:      15

4. Total investigations:      241

Note: Of those convicted, confinement was adjudged for 7 persons before charges were preferred against Calley, and in two instances afterwards. There were 15 pre-Son My convictions: 6 murder, 3 rape, 3 assault on PW/detainees, and 3 mutilation; there were 5 post-Son My convictions: 3 murder and 2 mutilation. Because of the unique circumstances relating to the criminal allegations having to do with Calley and others at Son My, the investigation of these alleged offenses was treated separately. Many of the acquittals and other dismissal of charges had to do with problems of the rules of evidence and/or separation of the accused from military service (and UCMJ coverage).

15 Jan 75

Report on the status of war-crime investigations other than Son My (My Lai) compiled by the Army Staff.

## CHAPTER SIX

# The War Behind Them

The scarcity of war-crime prosecutions caught the eye of a key army official in late summer 1972.

Brig. Gen. Robert G. Gard Jr. was a bright star in the Office of the Deputy Chief of Staff for Personnel. He ran the directorate in charge of discipline and drug policies. His responsibilities included oversight of an internal task force of ten midlevel officers charged with keeping top brass apprised of war-crime allegations reported to CID, Congress, or the media.

A year into the job, he asked for a status report on war-crime prosecutions to pass on to the new chief of staff. Gen. William Westmoreland had retired; Creighton Abrams would soon take his place.

When Gard received the breakdown, he asked whether the legal staff might have missed some. A memo in response to his question said court-martial records had been searched for violations of the laws of war. Records from the 1960s had been combed twice. Although it was likely some of the more recent ones had been overlooked, the effort to find them would not be worth the result. Gard reluctantly approved the fact sheet with the original number. Still disbelieving the army's record could be that poor, he scribbled a note in thick black script at the bottom of the form: "But shouldn't we note in the future that there are undoubtedly a lot of trials for murder, rape, etc, that technically are 'war crimes'—but not reported as such."[1]

When I type Gard's name into an Internet search engine, I'm surprised at the results. He appears on the roster of retired generals who in 2005 signed letters urging withdrawal of U.S. troops from Iraq and supporting antitorture legislation. He sits on the boards of several think tanks, including the Center for Arms Control and Non-Proliferation. He has a desk and phone in the center's narrow row house on Capitol Hill. Nick and I bring a stack of documents bearing his signature.

"Sorry I am late," he says as he takes a seat in a glass-doored conference room.

Gard looks as trim and square-shouldered at seventy-eight as a young West Point graduate. According to his official biography, he was class of 1950. He fought in Korea and Vietnam, earning a PhD between wars from Harvard in political economy and government. He headed the discipline and drug policy directorate from 1971 to 1973—and persuaded the army to rename the office Human Resources Development "to communicate a more constructive approach to discipline." He eventually became president of National Defense University and retired from that post as a lieutenant general in 1981. Since then, he has worked as a national security consultant.

At our request, he walks us chronologically through his Vietnam War experience. He tells us he was military assistant to Secretary of Defense Robert McNamara from 1966 to 1968, when he was grasping for a more reliable system of measuring enemy losses than the inflated estimates pouring into his office from military leaders in Vietnam.

"He [McNamara] looked at all the data, because when you're in a conflict of that sort, while we refused to count civilian casualties—I think much to our detriment—we do report estimates of enemy killed. McNamara watched the reports and so on. And one day he said, 'If these reports were accurate we would have killed the North Vietnamese army twice.' So he said, 'I don't think we should be reporting enemy killed unless we have concrete evidence.' I think it was a mistake to do that, but you can understand his frustration. . . . So we got into the body-count business. When conducting an operation, for example, you may surround an enemy unit. We customarily fired artillery into the doughnut. Then at the end of it you go in and you look around and see a bunch of dead bodies. They used to say if you find somebody who's dead and he's got an AK-47, that's a pretty good indication that he was probably a bad guy. But the trouble is you found a lot of bodies that didn't have any AK-47s near them."

In some cases, the weapons were snatched by retreating combatants who escaped the doughnut. On other occasions, the dead were civilians. As artillery division commander in the Delta from 1968–1969, Gard says, he served with a leading apostle of body count—Gen. Ewell, then the 9th Infantry Division commander. Ewell pressed troops "big time" to deliver large body counts and rewarded those who complied.

"There was . . . a big deal about who gets the 'assets,' including the airlift. Ewell—this again is part of creating the environment—Ewell would give the assets to the commander who was getting the body count. So if you were getting body count you got the airlift. There wasn't enough airlift for everybody in the division. . . ."

Gard recalls clashing with Ewell over the use of firepower in civilian areas.

"My units had a total of ninety-six cannons. My responsibility was to coordinate fire support for the division, and I was quite aware of the tendency on the part—which still exists, as you can see in Iraq—of our commanders to use firepower excessively."

A small hamlet lay just outside 9th Division headquarters. On successive nights, U.S. forces at the base were subjected to a quick barrage of fire from a mortar inside the hamlet.

"But that mortar was doing damage! It was damaging aircraft. Blew the end of my trailer out. I was sitting at a little table in a tiny kitchen at the end of the trailer. I had just gone back and laid down in the rear of the trailer when a mortar round hit right outside my trailer and blew holes all through it. If I'd been sitting at the table I wouldn't be here talking to you today. . . .

"Well, typically when you have something like that, depending on where the target is, you return fire with field artillery. With countermortar radar, you have an immediate fix on its location and, boom, you've got immediate response."

Ewell leaned on him to let loose, Gard says, but he pointed out that the hamlet was filled with families.

"I told him I thought it was unwise to do that. We had a confrontation on the issue. But we went in on the ground, got the mortar, and we never had any more problems with the village."

By sending in troops instead of artillery fire, he accomplished the goal without sacrificing civilians, he says.

(In a subsequent conversation, I tell him that Col. Ira A. "Jim" Hunt Jr.—Ewell's chief of staff—claimed they enforced a ban on

firepower within five hundred yards of a village. Gard is per-
plexed. "Having served with Hunt in the 9th, I must share with
you my incredulity that there was some sort of prohibition
against use of firepower within five hundred yards of a village. In
fact, I'd bet a lot that there never was. . . . I never heard of it.")

Gard says he objected to Ewell's tactics on both ethical and
pragmatic grounds.

"I've always been a huge critic, especially in the tough conflict
that we had in Vietnam and are now having in Iraq, in killing innocent civilians—not only for humanitarian reasons, as important as that is. But operationally it's not very sensible, especially
when you have a tribal society such as we're dealing with in Iraq
where there's a tradition of getting revenge for people who kill
members of your family or your tribe or even humiliate them."

The indiscriminate firing incidents that killed Vietnamese civilians were among the many uncounted war crimes, he says. Yet
when we turn the conversation to the war-crime allegations that
did get counted—the ones collected under his supervision at the
Pentagon—he looks blankly at us.

"I don't remember much about it," he says.

Gard says he took over the directorate in July 1971 with one
clear mandate: Do something about the drug abuse scandal. President Richard Nixon had just declared drugs "public enemy No. 1,"
and a headline-grabbing congressional report claimed rampant
heroin addiction among U.S. troops. Gard's orders were to create
and implement a worldwide drug-abuse program for the army.
He set up a drug-education curriculum for commanders, a urine-
testing system, and a treatment program, all in record time.[2]

"We had to put treatment programs in every major installation
in the U.S. Army. Huge effort," he says. "So this [the war-crime

compilation] could have been going on right under my area of responsibility and I may not have known a lot about the details of what they were doing."

Records indicate that Gard inherited the war-crime task force, the vestige of an earlier media firestorm and presidential directive. The effort likely traced back to December 2, 1969. *Life* magazine had just run color photos of the My Lai massacre, and Nixon pointedly asked whether the Pentagon expected any more revelations about atrocities.[3] A few weeks later, Secretary of Defense Melvin Laird told Stanley Resor, the secretary of the army, that he wanted monthly status reports on war-crime investigations.[4] By 1970, an ad hoc working group had been assembled to produce the reports. Although Gard does not recall, he assumed responsibility for the monthly report upon his arrival in mid-summer 1971.

We show him several memoranda with his signature from the war-crime files. His memory is jogged by the name Murray Williams, which appears on many of the documents. Williams had been Gard's executive assistant and would have handled matters of that sort, he says. (We later learn Williams has died.) Reports would have passed across Gard's desk for a signature as a formality on the way to Westmoreland's office.

"It wasn't something that I personally devoted a lot of attention to other than the reports that apparently the chief of staff wanted. They would come through me to send forward. I'd look at them."

As we page through documents on which Gard's signature appears, he reacts as if he is seeing them for the first time. He does not remember the fact sheet on war-crime prosecutions[5] but recalls concern over the army's record: "I guess it was because at this time we were being accused of ignoring war crimes, and he

[Abrams] wanted to find out to what extent we in fact had dealt with things on that basis."

He reprises his outrage at the official numbers, still insistent that many cases must have been overlooked.

We show him the Concerned Sgt's letters, but he doesn't remember them.

"These sound fairly authentic," he says after he finishes reading them.

In fact, they reflect many of Gard's own views on body count and indiscriminate fire. We also walk through the investigations of the massacre Jamie Henry reported and of torture by the 172nd Military Intelligence Detachment, the mountains of evidence and absence of trials. He says he is surprised.

"I frankly did not know the extent to which there apparently were investigations that were conclusive and that no action had been taken," he says. "If they were going to whitewash it, why have the investigation in the first place?"

He is bothered by the torture case in particular, because of the strong public stance he has taken against torture in Iraq.

"I've signed some stuff that Human Rights First has written up, and I even did a press conference with them on that first memo that came out of the Justice Department on what constituted torture," he says. "I mean, some terrible stuff coming out of the executive department of our government. And it's disturbing to hear that in clear-cut cases of obvious war crimes [in Vietnam] that people weren't held accountable. . . .

"It's an endemic problem if this was going on. Commanders should have exercised their authority. There should have been action taken by the chief of staff and the secretary of the army to ensure that we were following the proper procedures. That's inexcusable."

He is not finger-pointing, he says. He shares responsibility.

"We could have court-martialed them but didn't," he says. "The whole thing is terribly disturbing."

---

The Army Staff's office had marshaled an unparalleled body of evidence on the commission of war crimes in Vietnam, clearly devoting hundreds of man hours and reams of paper to the task. Yet we were having a hard time finding anyone who remembered it with any clarity. Gard is not alone in his struggle to recall the war-crime project. We meet with his old boss, Ret. Gen. Walter Kerwin Jr., the former deputy chief of staff for personnel, who lives outside Washington, D.C.

"I didn't even know there was a war-crimes outfit," he says.

Resor and Robert F. Froehlke, the two former secretaries of the army, had responded with surprise when asked about the war-crimes files. Former secretary of defense Melvin R. Laird, who once privately shared his desire to cover up My Lai,[6] wrote this in a 2005 *Foreign Affairs* magazine article advocating U.S. withdrawal from Iraq:

> Vietnam, however, should be a cautionary tale when fight-
> ing guerrilla style, whether it be in the streets or in the jun-
> gle. Back then, frightened and untrained U.S. troops were
> ill equipped to govern their baser instincts and fears. Count-
> less innocent civilians were killed in the indiscriminate hunt
> for Vietcong among the South Vietnamese peasantry. Some
> of the worst historical memories of the Vietnam War stem

from those atrocities. . . . To stop abuses and mistakes by
the rank and file, whether in the prisons or on the streets,
heads must roll at much higher levels than they have thus
far. I well remember the unexpected public support for
Lieutenant William Calley, accused in the massacre of civilians in the village of My Lai. The massacre did not occur
on my watch, but Calley's trial did, and Americans flooded
the White House with letters of protest when it appeared
that Calley would be the scapegoat while his superiors
walked free. The best way to keep foot soldiers honest is to
make sure their commanders know that they themselves
will be held responsible for any breach of honor.[7]

But Laird is not available for an interview. So I don't know if his
view was informed by the war-crime files.

The name of John W. Dean III, the former counsel to the president, appears on the run of memoranda between the White
House and army following John Kerry's Senate testimony on
April 22, 1971. At Dean's request, the army provided a status report on war-crime investigations that contained confirmed examples of the atrocities delineated in Kerry's remarks. The memo
was in Dean's hands when the president and top aides encouraged attacks on Kerry's account of murder, rape, torture, and
mutilation as outlandish and disloyal. I send an inquiry to Dean
by e-mail and attach a copy of the memo. He replies with a vague
recollection:

"I do not specifically recall the memo you sent along," he
writes, "but I do remember that we monitored the situation so
there would be no surprises."

In a follow-up conversation, Dean says the administration's primary concern would have been damage control. He says he held the view that the president should not get involved in war-crime matters, that he should let the army address them without interference. Others in the White House wanted the president to intercede, Dean says. The interventionists scored notable victories when the army dropped murder charges against the Green Berets and Calley served his abbreviated sentence in home confinement instead of prison.

I try a few other names from the records but have no luck. With Westmoreland and Abrams both dead, we are running low on potential sources.

The town of Tahlequah lies halfway between Tulsa, Oklahoma, and Fayetteville, Arkansas, where flat farmland meets the wooded fringe of the Ozark Mountains. It is famous as the capital of the Cherokee Nation and end point of the Trail of Tears—the epic forced relocation of sixteen thousand tribal members from their traditional lands in the east. Boudinot Baptist Church rests at the foot of Boudinot Hill just outside of town. The preacher is Ret. Col. Jared B. Schopper, the highest-ranking staff officer with day-to-day responsibility for maintaining the war-crime files. His name appeared frequently in the documents. With so many other key players in Arlington National Cemetery or unable to recall, I had carefully combed directories and clips and found him quoted in the religion column of a local newspaper. The effort pays off. When Nick and I reach him by phone, he remembers the war-crime files and confirms his role. But he initially says he is not interested in talking. He kept close hold on the allegations for good reason and doesn't believe they should be disseminated even now.

"We did not believe that many of these allegations had a foundation," he says. "We believed they were probably planted by North Vietnam and Hanoi."

I let some time pass and call him again. He is more receptive, and we talk at length.

Schopper retired from the army in 1977 and moved back to Oklahoma, where he had grown up. He found a second wind as a preacher, when his church invited him to fill the pulpit on several occasions. He eventually agreed to pastor the congregation. He'd always been religious, thanks to a strict Baptist grandmother, who led him to the Lord at age nine. He enlisted in the army in 1945 and graduated from West Point the same year as Gard, 1950.

During the Korean War, Schopper led a platoon in the 187th Airborne Regimental Combat Team under then Brig. Gen. Westmoreland. They met face-to-face while attending chapel services at Camp Chickamauga in Japan, Schopper says. They crossed paths again in 1965, when Schopper served as a staff officer at the Military Assistance Command-Vietnam headquarters during Westmoreland's command. He became a lifelong admirer. He considered Westmoreland a brilliant military leader of great integrity—"a fine soldier in every sense of the word."

In 1969, after a stint as a battalion commander at Fort Dix, New Jersey, Schopper was transferred to the secretariat of the general staff at the Pentagon. By then Westmoreland had become army chief of staff, and Schopper looked forward to working more closely with him. When the My Lai massacre broke in November of that year, Schopper was handed the job of tracking war-crime allegations. He wrote or supervised the writing of hundreds of case summaries, most drawn from investigation and courts-martial reports. He made sure allegations in the media or forwarded by members of Congress were recorded and investigated. He periodically briefed Westmoreland on potentially troublesome cases.

"My main job was to make sure allegations were tallied, and reported, and assigned a number," he says. He speaks with a preacher's gait, in halting phrases and measured words.

"For what reason?" I ask.

"Probably because the Son My and My Lai allegations became items that occasionally made their way to the front page," he says. "It was President Nixon who uttered, 'Get the army off the front page.' I didn't hear him say it. I was told it. We were following the president's orders. The only way to get them off the front page is to say they are founded and appropriate action was taken, or that they are unfounded and propaganda tools."[8]

The news media gave bigger play to atrocities if a cover-up was suspected. Schopper's job was to make sure that whenever an allegation surfaced, the army could say it was under investigation or had been investigated and repudiated—a response that often muted interest in the case or moved the story to an inside page. He regularly briefed Westmoreland or the vice chief of staff so they would not be caught unprepared, as they were with the My Lai revelations.

I ask why the army never publicly acknowledged many of the cases in the files—or the results of investigations that confirmed allegations. He explains that the army released information only when necessary, usually to satisfy an inquiry from the media or a member of Congress about a particular allegation.

"I believe that the allegations that you have seen were for offi-cial use only. That means we were following the president's or-ders to keep the army off the front page. We can't ignore the allegations but at the same time we don't want them to receive undue, undeserved attention, or we'll be helping the enemy."

Schopper says he does not recall specific cases anymore, only his overall impression that most of the incidents he recorded were not true. He reiterates his comment from our first conversation that the Communists instigated many of the accusations.

"Scores of the allegations were unfounded—which leads one to conclude that North Vietnam and the Vietcong used allega-tions of war crimes against the allies as a tool of propaganda and to show that there were many My Lais or Son Mys."

Nonetheless, army leaders took pains to impress the impor-tance of the Geneva conventions on U.S. forces, he says. He trav-eled to Vietnam in March 1971 to ensure the division commands had the appropriate rules and procedures on file for preventing war crimes and reporting those that occurred.

"I published a rather extensive memo relating to orders and di-vision policy that any allegations of war crimes be reported and in-vestigated. The division headquarters that I checked—I don't remember the names. I brought back word that indeed all division headquarters have allegation of war crimes required to be reported and thoroughly examined and investigated. . . . This was taken se-riously by most commanders, an overwhelming majority of com-manders. Calley and [Capt. Ernest] Medina[9] were exceptions."

He adds: "The necessity of the Geneva conventions cannot be argued. Absolutely there have to be rules of war or we will re-turn to the most primitive condition of war. If we are going to maintain any respect for humanity as a creation of God, we can-not turn combat into a scene of mass murder."

I ask about the army's failure to hold many soldiers and officers accountable in the confirmed cases. The United States' obligations include not only investigating war crimes but also punishing perpetrators.

"I know there were considerably more allegations than convictions," he says, but the decisions to court-martial and convict are up to individual commanders and the jury. army leaders did what they could within their power to meet their obligations under the law and to repair the army's reputation, he says.

"We certainly tried to follow as nearly as we could what President Nixon said or directed not only for respecting the reputation of the army but the reputation of the United States to not be in continuing violation of the Geneva conventions. And we succeeded."

What did the army do with the cases after he had collected and numbered them and alerted higher-ups to potentially troublesome ones?

"Generally no action was taken," Schopper says. "What happened to the files then? I suppose they ended up in the reservoir of official documents that no longer have viability."

This, then, was what came of Henry's, Stemme's, and the Concerned Sgt's persistence, of Hoag's psychologically painful hospital interview, and of the hundreds of soldiers' accounts that had found their way to army headquarters—sometimes at considerable personal cost and emotional toll for the men who reported them. Only a few became action items, the subjects of high-level damage control rather than moral outrage. The rest were paper, pushed across the desks of distracted officers, and statistics sent up the chain of command to no discernible end. The only one really paying attention believed most were a Communist plot to undermine the war.

If the army's goal was obscurity, as Schopper suggests, he was right to claim success. Other than a relative handful of cases that received sustained front-page coverage, the reports had faded not just from the public countenance but from the army's own institutional memory as well.

———

Of all the other officers who played roles in the collection and suppression of the war-crime files at the Pentagon, the most intriguing to me is Ret. Brig. Gen. John Johns, a PhD who served in Vietnam and helped design the army's first course on counterinsurgency strategy. After the war, as chief of the Leadership Division in the army personnel office, Johns oversaw an overhaul of ethics training at army schools. He has spent the bulk of his career—forty years—instructing officers at West Point, the National Defense University, and elsewhere on making moral choices in war. He is an often-cited military ethicist and in the fraternity of retired officers who oppose the Iraq war.

His stint on war-crimes duty at the Pentagon is a little-known chapter in his life. As a lieutenant colonel in the early 1970s, he shared an office with Schopper. He helped the colonel review cases and decide which ones merited the attention of military leaders. He remained silent about what he saw as a member of the internal working group later dubbed the "Vietnam War Crimes Working Group (Unofficial)" on the box labels at the National Archives.

Nick and I meet with him at his house in the Virginia suburbs for the first of several interviews. There is little about him that betrays his seventy-nine years except the dusting of gray hair on his head. He sets a plate of cookies on the kitchen table and pours coffee before dropping into a chair. I slide the Concerned

Sgt letters and the Henry investigation file toward him. He skims them and shakes his head.

"When you have so many of these, you don't remember the specifics."

Johns can recite the general nature of the crimes—murders, rapes, torture with field phones, and the mutilation cases involving skulls and severed ears. He says he contacted Kerry's presidential campaign headquarters in 2004, after the Swift Boat Veterans for Truth launched their attacks on his 1971 testimony. He left messages for three weeks running that he could prove that Kerry was right. But no one returned his calls.

"I would have said, 'The Swift Boaters are totally inaccurate and here's why: I know, and you can confirm this in the National Archives . . . I was on this committee monitoring the war crimes and I knew all this."

The records on war-crime investigations were only the beginning, he says. Tens of thousands more Vietnamese civilians died in incidents that weren't investigated as war crimes but could have been, he says. These were officially sanctioned attacks in free-fire zones, indiscriminate firing on villages full of civilians, and the Phoenix Program, which permitted the execution of thousands of Vietnamese suspected of aiding the enemy.

"What the hell do you think the body count thing did in Vietnam? There is an official policy you cannot say was evil intended—but it dissolved into that. With the body count, almost everybody killed was a VC. Or we passively stood by while the Vietnamese took people up in helicopters and pushed them out. . . . You had systemic things like laxness and turning your head. Commanders see a situation where people lost it but they were good soldiers and Marines. They're reluctant to ruin their lives and put them in prison. They say, 'There but by the grace of God go I.' And a lot of that occurs."

He understood the reluctance to prosecute soldiers, and didn't consider it as egregious as sending them into a senseless war and placing them in untenable combat situations.

"You have to forgive me, but I have a reservation about blaming soldiers who are told to do something, and they let it get out of hand. I believe the chain of command should be disciplined and curbed. I don't think they [army leaders] did that."

By the time he was assigned to work on the war-crimes files, Johns already considered the Vietnam War a losing cause, one that would unavoidably lead to atrocities. He had served in Vietnam in 1962, where he saw firsthand the strength of the indigenous insurgency in the south, he says. He came to the conclusion then that the conflict required a political resolution rather than U.S. military intervention. The counterinsurgency course he cowrote emphasized the importance of winning hearts and minds rather than trying to kill off the enemy, and it reflected his fatalism about U.S. military involvement.

Later, as a staff officer on the Department of the Army Staff in the late 1960s, Johns wrote a study on the nation-building aspect of counterinsurgency. The study was distributed by the army secretary as policy guidance. However, Johns says the army rejected one important conclusion of his analysis, which looked at counterinsurgency operations from WWII onward: Foreign combat forces, such as the United States military in Vietnam, could not successfully conduct such wars. The most fundamental reason, he argued, was that the nature of such wars made atrocities inevitable, regardless of leadership and training of the troops. Fighting insurgents would place U.S. troops in populated areas, where the combatants were mixed in with civilians. That would give the insurgents a tremendous advantage, unless the U.S. forces were willing to accept a high level of civilian casualties. But killing civilians would only increase support for the insurgency. For those reasons, he strongly advised that U.S. military involvement not go beyond an advisory role.

"COIN operations are a different kettle of fish. The combatants are usually embedded in civilian populations, making it difficult to distinguish between friend, neutrals, and foe. Collateral damage is unavoidable. Moreover, it is impossible to prevent completely deliberate killing of innocent civilians such as My Lai, Tiger Force, and the November event in Iraq."

He is referring to the Nov. 19, 2005, attack on civilians by U.S. Marines that left twenty-four children, women and men dead in Haditha.

"When the enemy is difficult to separate from the population, troops lose their patience," Johns says. "Officials should not go into counterinsurgency operations without accepting the fact that atrocities will be committed, they will turn the people against us, and we will lose."

So he was not surprised in 1971, when the reports of atrocities began to cross his desk at the chief of staff's office.

"One question you should ask me, just talking about loyal dissent and whistle-blowing: 'John Johns, did you ever consider that you should have resigned, did what Kerry said? Made public all of the things that were occurring?' Do you want to ask me that question?"

"I was getting there," I say.

"'Didn't at least General Johns have the moral courage to resign and expose it?'" he continues. "I suspect there is an ambigu-

ity in my own mind. It's very easy to rationalize that you stay in
a system so that your voice can be heard internally versus resigning and getting out. And, as someone said, resigning in
protest and speaking out has no impact and it's better to stay
in. . . . I could have retired. I had twenty years of service, so it
wasn't to resign and give up all my benefits. I never really expected to be more than a lieutenant colonel anyway, so it wasn't
that. But I think it's because I consider these things more appro-
priately handled internally. I have some misgivings about airing
dirty laundry. I don't think it is good for people to just, every time
they see something they don't like, to go out to the public and
undermine confidence in the military. I don't like to undermine
confidence in the U.S. military because I consider a strong military
and the people's support of the military to be essential for national defense. I could even say to you, what are you accomplishing by digging up Vietnam? From a national defense
standpoint, and as a patriot, why are you doing this?"

Isn't that what critics say about his criticism of the Iraq war? Is
he trying to atone for his past silence by shouting from the
rooftop now?

"The Iraq war to me is one of the great blunders of history,"
he says, and a watershed in his own thinking. He had supported
dealing with atrocities internally. But the war in Iraq showed that
government and military leaders had forgotten the lessons from
Vietnam—or never learned them. He now believes the public
must be informed and enlisted to avoid another Vietnam in Iraq
and prevent similar mistakes in the future.

"We can't change current practices unless we acknowledge the
past. If we rationalize it as isolated acts, as we did in Vietnam and
as we're doing with Abu Ghraib and similar atrocities, we'll never

correct the problem. Counterinsurgency operations involving foreign military forces will inevitably result in such acts and we will
pay the costs in terms of moral legitimacy."

Johns says he feels freer to speak out now that he's outside the
army.

"I don't think the American people should be led blindly without
knowing what's happening. I justify that. Otherwise I wouldn't
even be meeting with you," he says. "The point I'm getting at is
that we cannot put our troops in these kinds of situations without having atrocities occur."

The Peers report on the My Lai massacre is the most widely cited
army report on Vietnam War atrocities. But the army produced
several other internal reports in the 1970s that addressed war
crimes other than My Lai. *Final Report of the Research Project: Conduct of the War in Vietnam,* a 163-page report bound in army
green, made the rounds at the Pentagon in May 1971. The document's purpose, according to the unnamed writer, was "to
show that General Westmoreland conducted the war in Vietnam
in a manner consistent with the requirements of international
law and that he fulfilled his obligation as a commander by re-
quiring the forces under his command to comply with the laws
of war."[10] The wording indicated a preordained conclusion, and
the report read like the defense document it was intended to be.
Westmoreland commissioned it from army lawyers after a spate
of news articles and broadcasts suggested he could be tried as a
war criminal for My Lai and other civilian killings that occurred
during his command in Vietnam from 1964 to 1968. The idea
gained currency when Telford Taylor made statements to that ef-

fect on the *Dick Cavett Show* on January 8, 1971.[11] Taylor had been the U.S. prosecutor at the Nuremberg war-crime trials following World War II. He surmised that Westmoreland might be found guilty under the legal standard that led to the conviction—and hanging—of Japanese Gen. Tomoyuki Yamashita for atrocities by his troops in the Philippines. Robert E. Jordan III, then the army general counsel, responded immediately that Westmoreland was not culpable, because he took "reasonable precautions" to prevent atrocities, while Yamashita did not.[12] Army lawyers produced the "Final Report" several months later to reinforce Jordan's defense. Over the course of seven chapters, they laid out the military justification for combat operations in which civilians died, the steps Westmoreland took to educate the forces about the laws of war, and the importance he placed on investigating war-crime violations. The report includes a rare reference to the Army Staff's still growing compilation of war-crime reports. The authors noted that CID conducted thirty-six war-crime investigations during Westmoreland's term as commander in Vietnam. Twenty of them could not be substantiated. The authors cited the statistics as proof he took his obligations under the Geneva conventions seriously and that war crimes were "an aberration and a violation of the policies established by General Westmoreland."[13]

The report concluded that the public would be better served by an investigation into the motives behind the proliferation of war-crime allegations:

> If there is to be an inquiry related to the Vietnam war, it
> should be into the reasons why enemy propaganda was so
> widespread in this country and why the enemy was able to
> condition the public to such an extent that the best educated

segments of our population have given credence to the
most incredible allegations, and, more like the children of
Hamelin than the most sophisticated members of our society, have fallen over themselves in their haste to follow
wherever they should be led.[14]

I find another reference to the Army Staff's war-crime compilation in a 1975 army monograph on lessons learned, written by
its top lawyer, Maj. Gen. George S. Prugh Jr., the judge advocate
general. *Law at War: Vietnam 1964–73* dealt largely with other legal
issues arising from the conflict. But in chapter 4, Prugh addressed
war crimes:

> On the American side, the sudden massive U.S. troop
> buildup in Vietnam that began in 1965 created many prob-
> lems for the U.S. command, and incidents of war crimes by
> U.S. troops began to be reported. For example, during the
> period between 1 January 1965 and 31 August 1973, there
> were 241[15] cases (excluding My Lai) which involved allega-
> tions of war crimes against United States Army troops. One
> hundred and sixty of these cases, upon investigation, were
> determined to be unsubstantiated . . . Violations commit-
> ted in Vietnam by personnel subject to the Uniform Code
> of Military Justice were prosecuted under the provisions of
> the code. From January 1965 through August 1973, 36 cases
> involving war crimes allegations against Army personnel
> were tried by court-martial. Sixteen cases involving thirty
> men resulted in acquittal or dismissal after arraignment.
> Twenty cases involving thirty-one Army servicemen re-
> sulted in conviction. . . . [16]

There is no evidence that Prugh's research went deeper than the most current two-page statistical summary available as of the date of his report. If it had, he would have found the 241 "cases" (as numbered by Schopper) represented more than 800 allegations, and a fourth of the "unsubstantiated" cases actually had been corroborated.

Prugh concluded that army leaders had done an admirable job of preventing and punishing war crimes:

> Despite laws and preventive education, war crimes were committed. Most were isolated incidents, offenses committed by individual U.S. soldiers or small groups. Investigations were conducted, and the records of courts-martial proceedings contain the cases of individuals who were tried and punished.[18]

He singled out army commanders for special praise:

> It is tragically true that troops on both sides committed atrocities; but had it not been for the genuine concern of commanders at the highest levels that U.S., Vietnamese, and allied forces conduct themselves humanely and in accordance with the laws of war, the Vietnam War probably would have been far more brutal.[19]

I forward the report to some of the veterans we interviewed. Jamie Henry takes a day to get his thoughts together and writes back.

"A total whitewash, but what do you expect from the Army. I would guess that there were hundreds if not thousands of allegations of various abuses. Not stealing bananas, but serious

abuses. The army could not possibly bring all of these problems
out into the open, (which court martial trials would do) without
admitting that they had failed in every aspect of training, tactics,
and command of the troops in Viet Nam and the ultimate responsibility and the corruption went from the rice paddies, all the
way to the Pentagon. It's sad in a way. There were many hard
fighting honorable troops in the war that deserved a better
legacy."

I ask for his own analysis of U.S. war crimes in Vietnam, the lessons learned that didn't make it into the army's report:

A large part of our problem in Vietnam was that officers
stood by and allowed, watched and participated in the murders and atrocities. When officers are out of control you
have NO HOPE of controlling the men. Well, some men.
Most of us were well behaved. It starts out with little di-
gressions that soon grow into large ones. When 1st Platoon
started cutting off ears and some of the other crap they did,
the captain should have court-martialed the lieutenant and
the men who participated and put a very public stop to it.
That lieutenant was West Point and career and a very aggressive fighter and it probably would not have been career
enhancing for a captain to try to bring him under control.
Vietnam should not have been the disaster that it was for B
co [Company]. We were almost always up against NVA
[North Vietnamese army] so there should not have been the
blurring of who the enemy was, but it soon turned into
everyone was the enemy and in reality that started in basic
training.

I don't know that there are or were massacres in Iraq yet. I would hope that the army had learned its lesson in Vietnam. That they acknowledge "The Henry Allegation" means that they know what happened over there and they probably know that it happened over and over again. I would hope that they have instituted a policy of NOT killing civilians and innocent people. Having it say so in the UCMJ [Uniform Code of Military Justice] is not enough. It has to be a policy that is started at the very beginning of Basic Training and is hammered home day after day after day. It doesn't seem to me that it would be that difficult to accomplish. Just don't kill people that are NOT shooting at you. How complicated can that concept be?

# ACKNOWLEDGMENTS

I am indebted to my husband, Tom Brune, an extraordinary journalist who has been my inspiration and enabler for twenty years. Kali Tal, founder of The Sixties Project, whose persistence shook the Army Staff's war-crime archive loose. Nick Turse, historian and author, recognized the significance of the records, spent the better part of two years as my reporting partner to bring their secrets to light, and is writing his own book, a history of war crimes in Indochina. Janet Lundblad, an amazing researcher, who could find Noah's Ark if given enough time. John Carroll and Dean Baquet, newspaper editors with grit, who gave me the initial resources to pursue this project. William Frucht, my book editor, for exceptional insight and direction. Gail Ross, my agent, for her vision and commitment, and Howard Yoon, for his writerly counsel. This book would not have happened without them. Alix Sleight and Meredith Smith for guiding me through production. Fellow journalist Peter Hardin and Karl Evahzz, author and researcher, who helped me get it right.

But most important, to Jamie Henry, Robert Stemme Jr., Robert D. Miller, Myran Ambeau, and many other Vietnam veterans who served their country a second time by coming to the phone and opening the door.

# NOTES

## Introduction

1. Seymour M. Hersh, "Lieutenant Accused of Murdering 109 Civilians," *St. Louis Post-Dispatch,* November 13, 1969. The *Post-Dispatch* and about two dozen other newspapers published the article, which was distributed by the Dispatch News Service.

2. Peers Inquiry, Report of the Department of the Army Review of the Preliminary Investigations into the My Lai Incident, Vol. 1, March 14, 1970, Library of Congress Call Number DS557.8.M9 U54 1974.

3. Records of the Army Staff, Office of the Deputy Chief of Staff for Personnel, Vietnam War Crimes Working Group, Records Group 319, National Archives and Records Administration (hereafter cited as Vietnam War Crimes Working Group, RG 319, NARA), College Park, Maryland.

4. *Viet Nam Generation Journal and Newsletter,* "Announcements, Notices and Reports," V-4, N1-2 (1992). http:www3.iath.virginia.edu/sixties/HTML_docs/Texts/ANR/VG_ANR_4&1_2_D.html.According to the posting, the records were made available at the National Archives and Records Administration

facility in Suitland, Maryland. The collection currently is housed at the Archives' campus in College Park, Maryland. Interestingly, the first scholarly foray into the records may have been by a German historian, Bernd Greiner, who directs the Research Unit: Theory and History of Violence at the Hamburg Institute for Social Research and is a history professor at the University of Hamburg. He recently published a German-language book on his research: *Krieg ohne Fronten: Die USA in Vietnam* (Hamburg: Hamburger Edition, 2007). The translated title is *War without a Front: The USA in Vietnam*. Among his conclusions, as described by his publishing house: "Just how many atrocities were committed in the course of the Vietnam War is a question to which there presumably will never be a definitive answer. But it is clear that such crimes were by no means singular occurrences, nor were they the acts of a few individual perpetrators of excessive violence."

5. Nick Turse is currently research director at the Nation Institute's Tom dispatch.com and author of The Complex: How the Military Invades Our Everyday Lives (Metropolitan Books/Henry Holt, 2008). He has a PhD in Sociomedical Sciences from Columbia University. He wrote his dissertation, "'Kill Anything That Moves': United States War Crimes and Atrocities in Vietnam, 1965–1973," on the doctrine of atrocity using the war-crime archive and other historical materials and texts. He is writing his own book, a history of U.S. war crimes in Indochina, for Metropolitan Books/Henry Holt.

6. Nick Turse and Deborah Nelson, "Vietnam Horrors: Darker Yet," *Los Angeles Times,* August 6, 2006; Deborah Nelson and Nick Turse, "A Tortured Past," *Los Angeles Times,* August 20, 2006.

7. Michael D. Sallah, Mitch Weiss, and Joe Mahr, "Buried Secrets, Brutal Truths," *Toledo Blade,* October 19–22, 2003.

8. War Crimes Allegations Case Files, Vietnam War Crimes Working Group, RG 319, NARA.

9. Analysis by Nelson and Turse of data collected from case summaries and investigation files, War Crimes Allegations Case Files, Vietnam War Crimes Working Group, RG 319, NARA.

10. 71-S381-18 Testimony No. 8, Congressional Record (92nd Congress, 1st Session) for Thursday, April 22, 1971, pp. 179–210.

11. Memorandum from John W. Dean III, counsel to the president, to the judge advocate general, May 10, 1971, Central File, Vietnam War Crimes Working Group, RG 319, NARA.

12. Memorandum from Maj. Gen. Kenneth J. Hodson, judge advocate general, to John W. Dean III, counsel to the president, May 21, 1971, Central File, Vietnam War Crimes Working Group, RG 319, NARA.

13. Ken W. Clawson, "'Veterans for a Just Peace' Formed to Offset Kerry Unit," *Washington Post*, June 2, 1971; Jerry Schwartz, "Vietnam Vet Questions Kerry on War Record," Associated Press Online, August 26, 2004; Michael Dobbs, "After Decades, Renewed War on Old Conflict," *Washington Post*, August 28, 2004.

14. Bruce Kesler, "The Revolt of the Vietnam Veterans," *San Diego Union-Tribune*, December 19, 2004.

15. For example, Maj. Gen. George S. Prugh, Vietnam Studies: *Law at War: Vietnam 1964–73* (Washington, D.C.: Department of the Army, 1975), pp. 61–78; Guenter Lewy, *America in Vietnam* (Oxford: Oxford University Press, 1978), pp. 307–373; B. G. Burkett and Glenna Whitley, *Stolen Valor: How the Vietnam Generation Was Robbed of Its Heroes and Its History* (Dallas, Tex.: Verity Press, 1998), pp. 111–138; William Thomas Allison, *Military Justice in Vietnam: The Rule of Law in an American War* (Lawrence: University Press of Kansas, 2007), p. 92.

16. Timothy Egan, "Wounds Opened Anew as Vietnam Resurfaces," *New York Times*, August 26, 2004; Thomas B. Edsall, "Swift Boat Group's Tally: $6.7 Million," *Washington Post*, September 11, 2004; Jodi Wilgoren, "Truth Be Told, the Vietnam Crossfire Hurts Kerry More," *New York Times*, September 24, 2004.

17. Concerned Sgt Allegation, Vietnam War Crimes Working Group, RG 319, Box 1, NARA.

## Chapter One

1. Henry Allegation, Vietnam War Crimes Working Group, RG 319, Box 5, NARA.

2. Military service record, James Henry, National Personnel Records Center, St. Louis.

3. Capt. Shelby L. Stanton, *Vietnam Order of Battle: A Complete Illustrated Reference to U.S. Army Combat and Support Forces in Vietnam 1961–1973* (Mechanicsburg, Pa.: Stackpole Books, 2003), p. 333.

4. Ibid., p. 349.

5. Michael P. Kelley, *Where We Were in Vietnam: A Comprehensive Guide to the Firebases, Military Installations and Naval Vessels of the Vietnam War 1945–75*, (Ashland, Ore.: Hellgate Press, 2002), p. B-19.

6. Henry's accounts of the killings and massacre in this chapter are corroborated by the Final Report of Investigation, as well as by sworn statements by other former members of B Company, Henry Allegation, Vietnam War Crimes Working Group, RG 319, Box 5, NARA.

7. Taylor's description of the fight may be found at www.cacti35th .org/regiment/history/aars/aar_135_020968.htm.

8. James Henry, sworn statement, February 28, 1970, and Final Report of Investigation, Henry Allegation, Vietnam War Crimes Working Group, RG 319, Box 5, NARA.

9. The Criminal Investigation Division became the Criminal Investigation Command on September 17, 1971, but has continued to use the acronym CID.

10. James D. Henry as told to Donald Duncan, "The Men of 'B' Company," *Scanlan's Monthly*, March 1970, pp. 26–31.

11. Investigator's Statement re Donald C. Reh, March 13, 1970, and Final Report of Investigation, Henry Allegation, Vietnam War Crimes Working Group, RG 319, Box 5, NARA.

12. "Goodell Asks New 'Activities' Probe," *Washington Evening Star*, February 26, 1970.

13. "Horrors of War Recounted," *Detroit Free Press*, February 3, 1971; Jerry M. Flint, "Veterans Assess Atrocity Blame," *New York Times*, February 7, 1971.

14. Congressional Record (92nd Congress, 1st Session) for Thursday, April 22, 1971, pp. 179–210.

15. "Vietnam Veteran Posed as Captain," *Washington Post*, April 24, 1971; William Overend, "Who Is Al Hubbard?" *National Review*, June 1, 1971; http:www.nationalreview.com/flashback/overend200404230901.asp. Record of hearing before the U.S. Senate Select Committee to Study Governmental Operations with Respect to Intelligence Activities, December 2, 1975; FBI files on surveillance of Veterans Against the War and other antiwar groups, released by the FBI in June 2004 in response to Freedom of Information Act requests.

16. Ken W. Clawson, "'Veterans for a Just Peace' Formed to Offset Kerry Unit," *Washington Post*, June 2, 1971; Jerry Schwartz, "Vietnam Vet Questions Kerry on War Record," Associated Press Online, August 26, 2004; Michael Dobbs, "After Decades, Renewed War on Old Conflict," *Washington Post*, August 28, 2004.

17. Burkett and Whitley, *Stolen Valor,* p. 131.

18. Statements of former members of B Company and Final Report of Investigation, Henry Allegation, Vietnam War Crimes Working Group, RG 319, Box 5, NARA.

19. Wilson Bullock, sworn statement, November 16, 1972, and Final Report of Investigation, Henry Allegation, Vietnam War Crimes Working Group, RG 319, Box 5, NARA.

20. Robert D. Miller, sworn statement, August 5, 1972, and Final Report of Investigation, Henry Allegation, Vietnam War Crimes Working Group, RG 319, Box 5, NARA.

21. Gregory Newman, sworn statements, September 21 and October 3, 1972, and Final Report of Investigation, Henry Allegation, Vietnam War Crimes Working Group, RG 319, Box 5, NARA.

22. Agent statement on interview with Jose Victor Davila-Falu, February 2, 1973, and Final Report of Investigation, Henry Allegation, Vietnam War Crimes Working Group, RG 319, Box 5, NARA.

23. Myran Ambeau, sworn statement, August 18, 1973, and Final Report of Investigation, Henry Allegation, Vietnam War Crimes Working Group, RG 319, Box 5, NARA.

24. Agent statement on interview with Gary Bennett, July 27, 1973, and Final Report of Investigation, Henry Allegation, Vietnam War Crimes Working Group, RG 319, Box 5, NARA.

25. Final Report of Investigation, Henry Allegation, January 16, 1974, Vietnam War Crimes Working Group, RG 319, Box 5, NARA.

26. Agent statement, Final Report of Investigation, Henry Allegation, December 31, 1973, Vietnam War Crimes Working Group, RG 319, Box 5, NARA.

27. "Cacti Vietnam Photos—Don Reh, 1967–68," www.cacti35th.org/photos/phpslideshow.php?directory=reh.

28. "1/35th February 9, 1968," www.cacti35th.org/regiment/history/aars/aar_135_020968.htm.

29. Johnny Carter, sworn statement, March 3, 1970, and Final Report of Investigation, Henry Allegation, Vietnam War Crimes Working Group, RG 319, Box 5, NARA.

30. Robert D. Miller, sworn statement, August 5, 1972, and Final Report of Investigation, Henry Allegation, Vietnam War Crimes Working Group, RG 319, Box 5, NARA.

31. Agent statement re Frank Bonilla, February 5, 1973, and Final Report of Investigation, Henry Allegation, Vietnam War Crimes Working Group, RG 319, Box 5, NARA.

32. Another witness reported that Bonilla held an M-16 assault rifle, but Bonilla said it was an M-14. Both models were used in the war.

33. Former B Company members, sworn statements, and Final Report of Investigation, Henry Allegation, Vietnam War Crimes Working Group, RG 319, Box 5, NARA.

34. Final Report of Investigation, Henry Allegation, Vietnam War Crimes Working Group, RG 319, Box 5, NARA.

35. Agent statement on interview with Gary Bennett, July 27, 1973, and Final Report of Investigation, Henry Allegation, Vietnam War Crimes Working Group, RG 319, Box 5, NARA.

36. Myran Ambeau, sworn statement, August 18, 1973, and Final Report of Investigation, Henry Allegation, Vietnam War Crimes Working Group, RG 319, Box 5, NARA.

37. Military service record, William Taylor, National Personnel Records Center.

38. William Taylor, sworn statement, February 23, 1970, and Final Report of Investigation, Henry Allegation, Vietnam War Crimes Working Group, RG 319, Box 5, NARA.

39. Agent statement of interview with William Taylor, September 27, 1973, and Final Report of Investigation, Henry Allegation, Vietnam War Crimes Working Group, RG 319, Box 5, NARA.

40. Sworn statements of Hoag and five other members of his company, May 2, 1972, to October 15, 1973, Final Report of Investigation, October 30, 1973, and case summary, March 11, 1974, Hoag Allegation, Vietnam War Crimes Working Group, RG 319, Box 20, NARA.

41. Ibid.

42. Investigator's statement re interview with a physician at the VA Hospital, Oklahoma City, on June 15, 1973, Hoag Allegation, Vietnam War Crimes Working Group, RG 319, Box 20, NARA.

## Chapter Two

1. Stemme-Brown-Martinsen Allegation, Vietnam War Crimes Working Group, RG 319, NARA.

2. Herbert Papers, Vietnam War Crimes Working Group, RG 319, Box 8, NARA; Col. Henry Tufts Archive, Labadie Collection, University of Michigan Special Collections Library, Ann Arbor.

3. Memorandum for Commanding Officer, "Directive for Investigation," November 13, 1970, CID Agency, Department of the Army, Office of the Chief of Staff, Herbert Papers, Vietnam War Crimes Working Group, RG 319, Box 8, NARA.

4. Fred Farrar, "Army Tells Why It Removed Col. Herbert from Command Job," *Chicago Tribune,* November 17, 1971.

5. "Fact Sheet: Lieutenant Colonel Anthony B. Herbert," November 5, November 17, and December 7, 1971, and January 10, 1972, Department of the Army, Herbert Papers, Vietnam War Crimes Working Group, RG 319, Box 8, NARA.

6. "Front and Center: The Herbert Case and the Record," *Army* magazine, February 1972, pp. 6–11.

7. *60 Minutes* 5, no. 9, first broadcast February 4, 1973, by CBS.

8. *Herbert v. Lando,* 441 U.S. 153 (1979).

9. Memorandum for Robert W. Berry, Army General Counsel, "Request for Information on Release of Investigative Matter to Mr. Lando," July 11, 1974, Department of the Army, Criminal Investigation Command, Col. Henry Tufts Archive.

10. In addition to his media appearances in print and broadcast, Herbert published an autobiography: Anthony B. Herbert, Lt. Col. Ret., with James T. Wooten, *Soldier* (Englewood, Colo.: Cloverleaf Books, 1973).

11. Memorandum for Chief of Staff, U.S. Army, "Herbert's *Soldier*," undated, Department of the Army, Criminal Investigation Command, Herbert Papers, Vietnam War Crimes Working Group, RG 319, Box 8, NARA.

12. Memorandum for Chief of Staff, U.S. Army, "Task Force 70–512," July 2, 1971, Herbert Papers, Vietnam War Crimes Working Group, RG 319, Box 8, NARA.

13. Final Report of Investigation, 70-CID-121-00802, Carmon et al., August 23, 1971, Final Report of Investigation, 70-CID-121-00811, Col. Henry Tufts Archive, July 30, 1971.

14. Memorandum for Chief of Staff, U.S. Army, "'Soldier,' by Anthony Herbert," January 29, 1973, Herbert Papers, Vietnam War Crimes Working Group, RG 319, NARA.

15. John Duffett, ed., *Against the Crime of Silence: Proceedings of the Russell International War Crimes Tribunal* (New York: Bertrand Russell Peace Foundation, 1968).

16. Stemme-Brown-Martinsen Allegation, Vietnam War Crimes Working Group, RG 319, NARA.

17. Hearings on U.S. Operations in Vietnam including Operation Phoenix, Senate Committee on Foreign Relations, Congressional Record (91st Congress, 2nd Session) for February 18 and 20, 1970, pp. 87–162 and 257–444. "House Panel Criticizes Pentagon on Political Killings in Vietnam," *New York Times,* United Press International, October 4, 1972; "General 'Shocked' at Vietnam Assassinations," *Washington Post,* August 2, 1983; Mark Moyar, *Phoenix and the Birds of Prey: The CIA's Secret Campaign to Destroy the Viet Cong* (Annapolis, Md.: Naval Institute Press, 1997).

18. Stemme identified Herbert as the commander at the scene; Herbert said he was not present.

19. Case summary, sworn statements, Bumgarner Incident, Vietnam War Crimes Working Group, RG 319, Box 15, NARA; sworn statements of witnesses; records of courts-martial of Roy E. Bumgarner, May 26, 1969; army response to Peter Berenbak's Freedom of Information Act request; military service record, Roy Edward Bumgarner Jr., National Personnel Records Center, St. Louis, Missouri.

20. Ibid.

21. Jim Stingley, "Ex-GIs Charge Viet Prisoners Were Tortured," *Los Angeles Times,* April 15, 1970.

22. William Greider, "Ex-GIs Tell of Torturing Prisoners," *Washington Post,* July 19, 1970.

23. Case summary, Stemme-Brown-Martinsen Allegation, Vietnam War Crimes Working Group, RG 319, NARA.

24. Final Report of Investigation, 70-CID-121-00802, Carmon et al., August 23, 1971, Final Report of Investigation, 70-CID-121-00811, Col. Henry Tufts Archive.

25. Ambrose Incident, Vietnam War Crimes Working Group, RG 319, Box 16, NARA.

26. Final Report of Investigation, 70-CID-121-00802, Carmon et al., August 23, 1971, Final Report of Investigation, 70-CID-121-00811, July 30, 1971, Col. Henry Tufts Archive; agent and witness statements, U.S. Army Criminal Investigation Command, released through the Freedom of Information Act.

27. Ibid.

28. Ibid.

29. Ibid.

30. Ibid.

31. Ibid.

32. Herbert Papers, Vietnam War Crimes Working Group, RG 319, Box 8, NARA.

33. Final Report of Investigation, 70-CID-121-00802, Carmon et al., August 23, 1971, Col. Henry Tufts Archive.

34. http:www.pachomius.com/founder.html.

35. "Destin Developer Charged with Securities Violations," Office of Comptroller, State of Florida, PR Newswire, February 15, 1989; Associated Press, "War Hero Sentenced in Scam," *St. Petersburg Times*, August 2, 1991.

36. Associated Press, "Decorated Officer Awaits New Battle—Behind Bars," *St. Petersburg Times*, August 15, 1991.

## Chapter Three

1. Case Summary, Alvarado Incident, Vietnam War Crimes Working Group, RG 319, Box 16, NARA.

2. Concerned Sgt Allegation, Vietnam War Crimes Working Group, War Crime Allegations Case Files, RG 319, Box 1, NARA.

3. The file did not contain a copy of the original handwritten correspondence to Westmoreland, substituting a typed replica with grammatical and spelling errors intact. The second and third letters in the file were copies of the originals and also are excerpted verbatim.

4. Charles Mohr, "Washington Talk: McNamara on Record, Reluctantly, on Vietnam," *New York Times*, May 16, 1984; Charles Mohr, "War and Misinformation: American Briefing Officers in Saigon Give Accounts Unsubstantiated in the Field," *New York Times*, November 26, 1965; "U.S. Concedes Toll of Foe Is Inexact," *New York Times*, January 28, 1968; Lewy, *America in Vietnam*, pp. 78–82; Lewis Sorley, ed., *Vietnam Chronicles: The Abrams Tapes 1968–1972* (Lubbock: Texas Tech University Press, 2004), pp. 420–421.

5. Japanese Gen. Tomoyuki Yamashita was tried by a U.S. military commission in 1945 and hung for atrocities committed by troops under his command in the Philippines.

6. Letter to General Westmoreland from an Anonymous Enlisted Man Concerning Body Count Pressures in Vietnam, June 16, 1970, Concerned Sgt

Allegation, Vietnam War Crimes Working Group, War Crime Allegations Case Files, RG 319, Box 1, NARA.

7. Letter from an anonymous enlisted man to Maj. Gen. Talbott, March 30, 1971, Concerned Sgt Allegation, Vietnam War Crimes Working Group, War Crime Allegations Case Files, RG 319, Box 1, NARA.

8. Dellums held hearings on U.S. war crimes in April 1971. William Greider, "Atrocities Hearings Ended by Dellums," *Washington Post,* April 30, 1971.

9. Letter from an anonymous enlisted man to Maj. Gen. Enemark, July 30, 1971, Concerned Sgt Allegation, Vietnam War Crimes Working Group, War Crime Allegations Case Files, RG 319, Box 1, NARA.

10. See Me: "'Concerned Sergeant' Allegation," August 30, 1971, Concerned Sgt Allegation, Vietnam War Crimes Working Group, War Crime Allegations Case Files, RG 319, Box 1, NARA.

11. Disposition form, "Concerned Sergeant Allegation," Concerned Sgt Allegation, Vietnam War Crimes Working Group, War Crime Allegations Case Files, RG 319, Box 1, NARA.

12. Military service record, George Lewis, U.S. Army, January 4, 1968 to January 1, 1974, National Personnel Records Center.

13. Memorandum and ID data sheet, "Concerned Sergeant Allegation," September 7, 1971, Concerned Sgt Allegation, Vietnam War Crimes Working Group, War Crime Allegations Case Files, RG 319, Box 1, NARA.

14. "SEE ME, 'Concerned Sergeant' Case" and referral slip canceling action, September 7, 1971, Concerned Sgt Allegation, Vietnam War Crimes Working Group, War Crime Allegations Case Files, RG 319, Box 1, NARA.

15. Lt. Gen. Julian J. Ewell and Maj. Gen. Ira A. Hunt Jr., *Sharpening the Combat Edge: The Use of Analysis to Reinforce Military Judgment* (Washington, D.C.: Department of the Army, 1974). Ewell and Hunt wrote the monograph in 1973. The army first printed it in 1974 and republished it in 1995.

16. Ibid.

17. www.history.army.mil/books/Vietnam/Sharpen/index.htm.

18. Ewell and Hunt, *Sharpening the Combat Edge,* Chapter 6, "Tactical Refinements and Innovations," p. 125.

19. Ibid., p. 122.

20. Ibid., Chapter 10, "Corps Level Operations," p. 191.

21. Ibid., Chapter 6, "Tactical Refinements and Innovations," p. 121.

22. Ibid., p. 122.

23. Ibid., p. 123.

24. Letter to Gen. Talbott, March 30, 1971, Concerned Sgt Allegation, Vietnam War Crimes Working Group, War Crime Allegations Case Files, RG 319, Box 1, NARA.

25. Ewell and Hunt, *Sharpening the Combat Edge*, p. 123.

26. Letter to Gen. Enemark, July 30, 1971, Concerned Sgt Allegation, Vietnam War Crimes Working Group, War Crime Allegations Case Files, RG 319, Box 1, NARA.

27. Ewell and Hunt, *Sharpening the Combat Edge*, p. 145.

28. Letter to Gen. Westmoreland, May 25, 1970, Concerned Sgt Allegation, Vietnam War Crimes Working Group, War Crime Allegations Case Files, RG 319, Box 1, NARA.

29. Kevin Buckley, "Pacification's Deadly Price," *Newsweek*, June 19, 1972, pp. 42–43.

30. See Me: "'Concerned Sergeant' Allegation," September 4, 1971, Concerned Sgt Allegation, Vietnam War Crimes Working Group, War Crime Allegations Case Files, RG 319, Box 1, NARA.

31. Ned Parker, "Sniper Team Tells of Pressure from Above," *Los Angeles Times*, October 5, 2007; Bradley Brooks, "Army Sniper Is Sentenced to 10 Years for Murder of Iraqi Civilian," Associated Press, February 10, 2008.

32. Ewell and Hunt, *Sharpening the Combat Edge*, Chapter 6, "Tactical Refinements and Innovations," pp. 134–135; Buckley, "Pacification's Deadly Price," pp. 42–43.

33. The 1st Infantry, 25th Infantry, and 1st Cavalry divisions are singled out for praise in Ewell and Hunt, *Sharpening the Combat Edge*, Chapter 10, "Corps Level Operations," pp. 194, 224.

34. Correspondence, "Casualties Caused by Friendly Forces in Chon Thanh District, Binh Long Province," February 11, 1969; "Report of Investigation Surrounding the Death of Seven Woodcutters," Inspector General, 1st Cavalry Division, Records of the Office of Inspector General, RG 472, NARA.

35. "Report of Investigation Surrounding the Death of Seven Woodcutters," Inspector General, 1st Cavalry Division, Records of the Office of Inspector General, RG 472, NARA.

36. Correspondence, "Shooting of Lumber Workers," March 4, 1969; "Report of Investigation Surrounding the Death of Seven Woodcutters," Inspector General, 1st Cavalry Division, Records of the Office of Inspector General, RG 472, NARA.

37. Ewell and Hunt, *Sharpening the Combat Edge*, Chapter 10, "Corps Level Operations," p. 207.

38. Investigation summaries by the Inspector General, Casualties Caused by Friendly Forces in Chon Thanh District, 1969, Records of the Office of Inspector General, RG 472, NARA.

39. Ibid.

40. Report of Investigation, "Firing Incident Involving Vietnamese Nationals During Combat Operations," September 5, 1970, Records of the Office of Inspector General, RG 472, NARA.

41. Memorandum for Record, "Meeting with Province Chief, BIN LONG Province Concerning Death of Ten Indigenous Individuals During a Combat Operation on 26 August 1970 Vicinity of XT572688," August 28, 1970; Report of Investigation, "Firing Incident Involving Vietnamese Nationals During Combat Operations," Records of the Office of Inspector General, RG 472, NARA.

42. Case summaries, Hartmann Incident (Sugarman Allegation), Delamain Allegation (Mooradian Incident), Vietnam War Crimes Working Group, War Crime Allegations Case Files, RG 319, Boxes 3 and 5, NARA.

43. Case summary, Duffy-Lanasa Incident, Vietnam War Crimes Working Group, War Crime Allegations Case Files, RG 319, NARA; William Thomas Allison, *Military Justice in Vietnam: The Rule of Law in an American War* (Lawrence: University Press of Kansas, 2007), pp.111–112.

44. http:gravelocator.cem.va.gov.

## CHAPTER FOUR

1. Case summary, Bumgarner incident, Vietnam War Crimes Working Group, RG 319, Box 15, NARA; sworn statements of witnesses; records of courts-martial of Roy E. Bumgarner, May 26, 1969; army response to Peter Berenbak's Freedom of Information Act request.

2. Military service record, Roy Edward Bumgarner Jr., National Personnel Records Center, St. Louis, Missouri.

3. Statement of James Carl Rodarte, February 27, 1969, Vietnam War Crimes Working Group, RG 319, NARA.

4. Case summary, Bumgarner Incident, Vietnam War Crimes Working Group, RG 319, Box 15, NARA; sworn statements of witnesses; records of courts-martial of Roy E. Bumgarner, May 26, 1969, army response to Peter Berenbak's Freedom of Information Act request.

5. Military service record, Roy Edward Bumgarner Jr., National Personnel Records Center.

6. Fox Butterfield, "For Handful of Americans, Vietnam Is Almost Home," *New York Times,* March 31, 1972.

7. Letter to the editor, April 1, 1972, Bumgarner Incident, Vietnam War Crimes Working Group, RG 319, Box 15, NARA.

8. Letter to U.S. Rep. Peter H. B. Frelinghuysen, April 21, 1972, Bumgarner Incident, Vietnam War Crimes Working Group, RG 319, Box 15, NARA.

9. Military service record, Roy Edward Bumgarner Jr., National Personnel Records Center; Obituaries, January 28, 2005, *Hickory Daily News*; http:gravelocator.cem.va.gov/.

10. Memorandum for Record, "Report of Interview," March 4, 1968, Judge Advocate General Command; army response to Peter Berenbak's Freedom of Information Act request.

11. Memorandum for Record, "Substantiation," March 4, 1968, Judge Advocate General Command; army response to Peter Berenbak's Freedom of Information Act request.

12. Ewell and Hunt, *Sharpening the Combat Edge,* Chapter 10, "Corps Level Operations," pp. 194–195.

13. Report of Investigation, March 3, 1970, Delamain Allegation (Mooradian Incident), Vietnam War Crimes Working Group, RG 319, Box 5, NARA.

14. Investigator's statement, Report of Investigation, Delamain Allegation (Mooradian Incident), Vietnam War Crimes Working Group, RG 319, Box 5, NARA.

15. Report of Investigation, March 3, 1970, Delamain Allegation (Mooradian Incident), Vietnam War Crimes Working Group, RG 319, Box 5, NARA.

16. Statement of Hoang Van Nho, February 20, 1970, Report of Investigation, Delamain Allegation (Mooradian Incident), Vietnam War Crimes Working Group, RG 319, Box 5, NARA.

17. Case summary, Delamain Allegation (Mooradian Incident), Vietnam War Crimes Working Group, RG 319, Box 5, NARA.

18. Massacre survivors and local government officials differed on the date of the first massacre. Survivors said it took place April 1, 1966, on the Vietnamese lunar calendar (May 20, 1966, on western calendars). Officials insisted it was April 1, 1967 (May 9, 1967, on western calendars), and that's the date that went on the memorial.

19. October 1968, 5th Marines Command Chronology, U.S. Marine Corps History Center, Quantico, Virginia.

20. December 5, 1969, 7th Marines Command Chronology; 1st Battalion, 7th Marines Journal, U.S. Marine Corps History Center, Quantico, Virginia.

21. Gary D. Solis, *Son Thang: An American War Crime* (Annapolis, Md.: Naval Institute Press, 1997); Allison, *Military Justice in Vietnam,* pp. 103–109.

22. Heonik Kwon, *After the Massacre: Commemoration and Consolation in Ha My and My Lai* (Berkeley: University of California Press, 2006), p. 29.

23. Ibid., p. 124.

## Chapter Five

1. Don Wagner, "Fort Belvoir News: Belvoir Honors Top Employees," www.belvoir.army.mil/news.asp?id=topemployees.

2. Fact sheet, "Allegations of War Crimes Other Than Son My," for "Chief of Staff, US Army," September 8, 1972, Vietnam War Crimes Working Group, RG 319, Box 5, NARA.

3. Neil Sheehan, "Taylor Says by Yamashita Ruling Westmoreland May Be Guilty," *New York Times,* January 9, 1971; Neil Sheehan, "Five Officers Say They Seek Formal War Crimes Inquiries," *New York Times,* January 13, 1971; Henry Raymont, "Vietnam Inquiry Urged by Taylor," *New York Times,* July 7, 1971.

4. Michael D. Sallah, Mitch Weiss, and Joe Mahr, "Buried Secrets, Brutal Truths," *Toledo Blade,* October 19–22, 2003.

5. See appendix.

6. Henry Allegation, Vietnam War Crimes Working Group, RG 319, Box 5, NARA.

7. Fact sheet, "Allegations of War Crimes Other Than Son My," for chief of staff, U.S. Army, dated September 8, 1972; Memorandum, "Status of Individual," for John Dean, Office of Special Counsel, May 21, 1971, Vietnam War Crimes Working Group, RG 319, NARA.

8. Memorandum, "Fact Sheets—Allegations of War Crimes Other Than Son My," Army Staff, dated September 12, 1972, Vietnam War Crimes Working Group, RG 319, NARA.

9. There were certainly other atrocities committed, and some likely were investigated and prosecuted, but the legal staff involved in the review rejected the suggestion that any crime against a Vietnamese was a war crime. The army applied a narrow definition enunciated in a 1975 report by the staff judge advocate: "Serious incidents involving assault, rape, and murder that were not directly connected with military operations in the field were not characterized as war crimes but were reported through military police channels." Prugh, *Law at War,* p. 76.

10. Case summaries, fact sheets, and case files, Vietnam War Crimes Working Group, RG 319, NARA. I tracked the fate of 191 suspects in violent war crimes against Vietnamese. I did not include forty-nine men accused of crimes solely involving property or desecration of corpses. In that group, nine were tried and seven convicted, and none received a prison sentence. The most gruesome case involved a master sergeant who ordered a subordinate to decapitate a corpse. The sergeant boiled the head in water and later traded the skull for a radio. He was fined $500 and reduced in rank to staff sergeant.

11. U.S. Justice Dept. data, 2004–2007, as reported by Transactional Records Access Clearinghouse, Washington, D.C. State courts reported a 59 percent conviction rate according to the most recent report from the Bureau of Justice statistics.

12. Ed Pound, "Unequal justice: Military courts are stacked to convict–but not the brass. The Pentagon insists everything's just fine," *U.S. News and World Report*, December 16, 2002.

13. The war-crime archive very likely contains a significant portion of war crimes that were tried by courts-martial but not a complete set. In *Final Report of the Research Project: Conduct of the War in Vietnam*, May 1971, U.S. Army, an official defense of Westmoreland's record, the unnamed authors mention the conviction of Sgt. Patrick Condron, who received a life sentence in 1966 for shooting two unarmed Vietnamese laundry workers at his camp. The case was not included as a war crime in the archive compiled by Westmoreland's staff, probably for the reasons noted in note 9. The length of actual time served was not available.

14. Walter Rugaber, "Senate PX Study Finds Wide Guilt: Panel Says Servicemen, Big Business and Pentagon Shared in Corruption," *New York Times*, November 3, 1971; Associated Press, "General in Service Club Inquiry Pleads Guilty to Gun Charges," April 10, 1971; "The Military Mafia," *Time*, October 17, 1969.

15. Case summary, Byrne Allegation, Vietnam War Crimes Working Group, RG 319, Box 17, NARA.

16. Allison, *Military Justice in Vietnam*. pp. 93–102; William G. Eckhardt, "My Lai: An American Tragedy," 2000. www.law.umkc.edu.

17. *Toth v. Quarles*, 350 U.S. 11 (1955).

18. Memorandum for the Assistant Attorney General (Office of Legal Counsel), "Trial of Discharged Servicemen for Violation of the Law of War," December 2, 1969, Office of Legal Counsel.

19. Robert M. Smith, "26 Are Investigated in Vietnam Deaths," *New York Times*, November 22, 1969.

20. Peter D. Trooboff, ed., *Law and Responsibility in Warfare: The Vietnam Experience* (Chapel Hill: University of North Carolina Press, 1975), pp. 54–62.

21. Richard Halloran, "Aide to Mitchell Opposes Any Curb on Surveillance," *New York Times*, March 10, 1971; Sanford J. Ungar, "Controversy Mounts Over Arrests Here," *Washington Post*, May 6, 1971; Sanford J. Ungar and William Chapman, "Reverses Lower Court Decision," *Washington Post*, June 19, 1971.

22. Jules Witcover and Ronald J. Ostrow, "Chronology of Justice Department's Pentagon Papers Battle," *Los Angeles Times*, July 4, 1971.

23. "8 Green Berets Head for Home: Backers Voice Bitterness over Army Treatment," *New York Times*, October 3, 1969; Joseph B. Treaster, "Ex-Green Beret Still Puzzled by Case," *New York Times*, December 26, 1969.

24. Paul South, "A Step Toward Avenging War-Crime Victims; Jones Fought, at an Ex-Pilot's Behest, for a Law to Prosecute War Criminals," *Virginian-Pilot*, August 29, 1996; Congressman Walter B. Jones Web site, "Jones Bills Passed into Law," http:jones.house.gov/content.cfm?id=365.

25. Clinton Statement on Signing of War Crimes Act of 1996, August 22, 1996, U.S. Newswire.

26. Michael John Garcia, "The War Crimes Act: Current Issues: Updated October 2, 2006," American Law Division, Congressional Research Service, Library of Congress, Washington, D.C., http:handle.dtic.mil/100.2/ADA458725.

27. Agent statement of interview with William Taylor, September 27, 1973, and Final Report of Investigation, Henry Allegation, Vietnam War Crimes Working Group, RG 319, Box 5, NARA.

28. Final Report of Investigation, January 16, 1974, Henry Allegation, Vietnam War Crimes Working Group, RG 319, Box 5, NARA.

29. Tim McGirk, "Collateral Damage or Civilian Massacre in Haditha?" *Time*, March 19, 2006.

30. "Viet Prober for Army Found Dead," from news dispatches, *The Washington Post*, April 18, 1971; Kenneth Reich, "Head of Army Atrocity Probe Called Suicide," *Los Angeles Times*, April 17, 1971; United Press International, "Army Investigator in War Crime Case Dies of Gun Wound," *New York Times*, April 18, 1971.

31. Statement of William E. Legat, April 19, 1971, Public Correspondence, Vietnam War Crimes Working Group, RG 319, Box 6, NARA.

32. Statement of Dolores A. Hensley, May 12, 1971, Public Correspondence, Vietnam War Crimes Working Group, RG 319, Box 6, NARA.

## CHAPTER SIX

1. Memoranda, "Fact Sheets—Allegations of War Crimes Other Than Son My," September 11, 1972, Vietnam War Crimes Working Group, RG 319, NARA.

2. Felix Belair Jr., "House Team Asks Army to Cure Addicts," *New York Times,* May 28, 1971; Michael Getler, "U.S. Vows Crackdown on Heroin Flow to GIs," *Washington Post,* May 28, 1971; Carroll Kilpatrick, "Nixon Seeks National War on Drug Use," *Washington Post,* June 18, 1971; Lewis M. Simons, "Army Turns to Yale for Drug Abuse Aid: 132 Officers, Men Attend Special Courses on Narcotics," *Washington Post,* December 16, 1971.

3. Kendrick Oliver, *The My Lai Massacre in American History and Memory* (Manchester: Manchester University Press, 2006), p. 76; John R. Brown III to Henry Kissinger, "Possible My Lai Commission," 2 Dec 1969 folder, Alexander Haig Special File Box 1004, National Security Council Files, Nixon Presidential Materials, NARA.

4. U.S. Marine Corps, Office of the Judge Advocate General, Winter Soldier Investigation files; Guenter Lewy, *America in Vietnam* (Oxford: Oxford University Press, 1978), p. 350. The Air Force and Navy received similar directives. Lewy reports that the Air Force did not have many atrocities to report, and the Navy had no mechanism for discerning war crimes from ordinary violations of the UCMJ.

5. War Crimes Allegations Talking and Information Papers, and Congressional Backup Sheets, Central File, Vietnam War Crimes Working Group, RG 319, NARA.

6. Telephone transcript, "Telecon: Secretary Laird, 11/21/69 3:50 p.m.," Kissinger Telcons, National Security Archive, Washington D.C.

7. Melvin R. Laird, "Iraq: Learning the Lessons of Vietnam: Setting the Record Straight," *Foreign Affairs* 84, no. 6 (November/December 2005).

8. The Nixon administration entertained the possibility of obtaining an injunction to stop the media from reporting atrocities. In a December 1969 letter, Maj. Gen. Kenneth J. Hodson, army judge advocate general, mentioned that the Justice Department was considering such an action. Michael Sallah and Mitch Weiss, *Tiger Force: A True Story of Men and War* (New York: Little, Brown and Co., 2006), p. 363.

9. Medina was Calley's commander. At his court-martial, Calley accused Medina of ordering him to kill civilians at My Lai. Medina was tried in August 1971 and acquitted of all charges. William Thomas Allison, *Military Justice in Vietnam: The Rule of Law in an American War* (Lawrence: University Press of Kansas, 2007), pp. 98–102.

10. "Introduction," *Final Report of the Research Project: Conduct of the War in Vietnam,* Department of the Army, Washington, D.C., May 1971, p. 1.

11. Neil Sheehan, "Taylor Says by Yamashita Ruling Westmoreland May Be Guilty," *New York Times,* January 9, 1971.

12. Ibid.

13. "Responsibility for War Crimes," *Final Report of the Research Project: Conduct of the War in Vietnam,* p. 84.

14. Ibid., p. 97. The "children of Hamelin" refers to the story of the Pied Piper.

15. By the time the chief of staff's office stopped keeping count, probably in 1974 or 1975, there were at least 246 numbered case summaries in the war-crime files.

16. Prugh, *Law at War: Vietnam 1964–1973,* p. 74.

17. See Chapter 5 for an analysis of the war-crime allegations. Cases involving more than three hundred allegations were officially substantiated; at least fifty-three others were confirmed but still classified as unproven for a variety of reasons.

18. Prugh, *Law at War: Vietnam 1964–1973,* p. 78.

19. Ibid.

# APPENDIX A:
## CASE SUMMARIES OF U.S. WAR-CRIME INVESTIGATIONS COMPILED BY ARMY STAFF DURING THE VIETNAM WAR

## Cases Classified as Founded by Army Investigators[1]

| CASE # | ALLEGATIONS | DIVISION/ BRIGADE | YEAR | PROVINCE | SUSPECTS | COURTS-MARSHAL[2] | CONVICTIONS | CONFINEMENT[3] |
|---|---|---|---|---|---|---|---|---|
| 1 | Prisoner with a broken leg and wound in his abdomen was shot to death by a first lieutenant. | 173rd Airborne Brigade | 1969 | Binh Dinh | 1 | 1 GCM | — | — |
| 2 | First lieutenant and three other members of his unit killed an unarmed man in front of his family. | 9th Infantry Division | 1969 | Long An | 4 | 2 GCM | 1 | 1 |

[1] Most investigations were conducted by the U.S. Army Criminal Investigation Division, renamed the U.S. Army Criminal Investigation Command in 1971 and referred to as "CID." The chart provides selected allegations from each case, not a complete list.

[2] Number of suspects tried by general court-martial (GCM) or special court-martial (SPCM). A special court-martial is the equivalent of a misdemeanor proceeding in the civil court system. Approximately sixty suspects who were not tried by courts-martial received administrative penalties only, such as fines, reprimands or reductions in rank.

[3] Number of convicted suspects who served time in confinement as part of their sentence.

| # | Description | Unit | Year | Province | | | | |
|---|---|---|---|---|---|---|---|---|
| 3 | Unprovoked fatal shooting of a boy, 14, and wounding of his friend, 13, as they biked past a camp's guard tower. Eight empty beer cans were found among the shell casings on the tower floor. | 20th Engineer Brigade | 1969 | Binh Duong | 1 | 1 GCM | 1 | 1 |
| 4 | Captain ordered combat patrol to shoot into huts across a canal, killing a woman and wounding her nephew. | 9th Infantry Division | 1969 | Dinh Tuong | 2 | — | — | — |
| 8 | Helicopter crew threw a North Vietnamese army body from an airborne helicopter on the captain's order. | 82nd Airborne Division | 1969 | Gia Dinh | 5 | — | — | — |
| 9 | Massacre of thirty-nine to ninety civilians as they huddled in bunkers or ran for their lives in My Khe on the same day as My Lai. | 23rd Infantry Division | 1968 | Quang Ngai | 2 | — | — | — |
| 20 | Vietnamese "Kit Carson" scouts kicked and beat detainees as U.S. soldiers watched. | 25th Infantry Division | 1969 | Hau Nghia | 1 | — | — | — |
| 23 | Helicopter crew spotted three women in a rice paddy, landed, forced a 19-year-old woman into the aircraft, assaulted her, and released her a half hour later. | 1st Aviation Brigade | 1969 | Kien Phong | 4 | — | — | — |

CASES CLASSIFIED AS FOUNDED BY ARMY INVESTIGATORS, *continued*

| CASE # | ALLEGATIONS | DIVISION/ BRIGADE | YEAR | PROVINCE | SUSPECTS | COURTS MARSHALL | CONVICTIONS | CONFINEMENT |
|---|---|---|---|---|---|---|---|---|
| 28 | First lieutenant captured and killed a toddler and a boy, about 8, "for no apparent reason," while leading a combat patrol. Four more bodies were found at the site. (He was charged with attempted murder.) | 23rd Infantry Division | 1970 | Quang Ngai | 1 | 1 GCM | – | – |
| 29 | Member of a Rangers team executed a cooperative, unarmed man in front of his young son after an ID check. | 9th Infantry Division | 1969 | Long An | 1 | – | – | – |
| 30 | U.S. Customs in Oakland, California, intercepted three severed ears and photos of Vietnamese corpses shipped to a soldier's home. The soldier's sworn statement said he took two of the ears from a North Vietnamese army soldier he shot with twenty rounds from his M-16 and then stabbed forty-five times in the chest in revenge for North Vietnamese army/Vietcong mutilation of U.S. soldiers. | 173rd Airborne Brigade | 1970 | Binh Dinh | 1 | – | – | – |
| 32 | Henry allegation: In a months-long string of atrocities, soldiers crushed a man with an armored personnel carrier, ambushed and killed five women, tossed a detainee over a cliff, executed a young boy and two old men, and massacred nineteen civilians. | 4th Infantry Division | 1967– 1968 | Quang Nam | 9 | – | – | – |
| 36 | Medic killed a female Vietcong with a severe head wound based on the belief nothing could be done for her. | 4th Infantry Division | 1970 | Binh Dinh | 1 | – | – | – |

| | Description | Unit | Year | Province | | | | |
|---|---|---|---|---|---|---|---|---|
| 39 | Staff sergeant fatally shot two unarmed teenage brothers in a fishing boat as their mother watched from shore. The captain reported them as two Vietcong killed in action. | 4th Infantry Division | 1967 | Quang Ngai | 2 | 1 GCM | 1 | — |
| 40 | Sergeant detained and shot an innocent civilian at close range, killing him. | 173rd Airborne Brigade | 1970 | Binh Dinh | 2 | 1 GCM | — | — |
| 49 | First lieutenant and private scalped two enemy corpses, removed fingers and ears, faked an ambush, and blew up the bodies to destroy the evidence. | 173rd Airborne Brigade | 1970 | Binh Dinh | 2 | 2 SPCM | 2 | — |
| 54 | After his sniper team killed a man in a North Vietnamese army uniform, a soldier severed the man's ears. | 101st Airborne Division | 1970 | Thua Thien | 2 | 1 SPCM | — | — |
| 57 | Crews in two gunships fired machine guns and grenade launchers at the ground, killing one civilian and wounding sixteen others. | 1st Airborne Brigade | 1970 | An Xuyen | 8 | — | — | — |

Cases Classified as Founded by Army Investigators, *continued*

| CASE # | ALLEGATIONS | DIVISION/ BRIGADE | YEAR | PROVINCE | SUSPECTS | COURTS MARSHALL | CONVICTIONS | CONFINEMENT |
|---|---|---|---|---|---|---|---|---|
| 58 | Herbert allegation: U.S. interrogators tortured detainees with water and field phones; South Vietnamese forces executed eight detainees in a U.S. adviser's presence. The case led to wider investigation of torture by the 172nd Military Intelligence Detachment which identified twenty suspects in more than one hundred allegations of torture and cover-up over an eighteen-month period. | 173rd Airborne Brigade | 1968– 1969 | Binh Dinh | 20 | — | — | — |
| 61 | Sergeant threw a man in a well, tossed in a grenade, and then shot him. Unproven allegations included rape, burning and pillaging villages, crop destruction, and shooting livestock. | 23rd Infantry Division | 1968 | Quang Tin | 1 | — | — | — |
| 69 | Soldier shot a POW while his hands were bound; on a separate occasion, the same soldier assaulted another POW. | 198th Infantry Brigade/ 23rd Infantry Division | 1970 | Quang Ngai | 2 | 1 GCM | — | — |
| 75 | First lieutenant ordered the killing of a civilian, whose arm then was severed by a medic; the same officer led a combat patrol that shot two fishermen, killing one. The wounded man was killed by an unidentified soldier. | 11th Infantry Brigade/ 23rd Infantry Division | 1968 | Quang Ngai | 5 | — | — | — |

| | | | | | | | | |
|---|---|---|---|---|---|---|---|---|
| 77 | Squad beat eight civilians and torched a building after discovering two green North Vietnamese army uniforms in a rice bin. | 11th Infantry Brigade/ 23rd Infantry Division | 1970 | Quang Ngai | 5 | 1 SPCM | — | — | — |
| 78 | Soldier left a jar with a human ear on his commanding officer's desk as a gift. Inspection of enemy bodies killed by suspect's unit revealed one corpse was missing an ear. | 1st Cavalry Division | 1971 | N/A | 1 | — | — | — | — |
| 86 | Brigadier general and two lieutenant colonels were implicated in multiple allegations of civilian killings and cover-up, including the abduction of a man later thrown from an airborne helicopter. An investigation found that one of the lieutenant colonels ordered a soldier to shoot and kill an unarmed male riding a bicycle on a trail. | 11th Infantry Brigade | 1968– 1969 | Quang Ngai | 3 | — | — | — | — |
| 93 | Head of Vietcong, blown off by a rocket, was put on display. | 12th Aviation Group | 1971 | N/A | 5 | — | — | — | — |
| 96 | Member of an advisory team used an ear severed from a Vietcong corpse for horseplay. | Advisory Team 66 | 1971 | Dinh Tuong | 1 | — | — | — | — |
| 97 | Captain threw a concussion grenade at children begging for food, wounding one. | 12th Aviation Group | 1970 | Long Khanh | 1 | — | — | — | — |

CASES CLASSIFIED AS FOUNDED BY ARMY INVESTIGATORS, *continued*

| CASE # | ALLEGATIONS | DIVISION/BRIGADE | YEAR | PROVINCE | SUSPECTS | COURTS MARSHALL | CONVICTIONS | CONFINEMENT |
|---|---|---|---|---|---|---|---|---|
| 98 | Soldiers failed to remove North Vietnamese bodies before detonating explosives; sergeant embedded a 5th Infantry Division patch in a corpse's head, and the first lieutenant took photos. | 5th Infantry Division | 1971 | Quang Tri | 4 | — | — | — |
| 100 | Captain and staff sergeant punched, kicked, and beat detainee with fists and a bamboo stick. | 196th Brigade/23rd Infantry Division | 1970 | N/A | 2 | — | — | — |
| 105 | Soldier killed three unarmed farmers working in the fields. | 11th Infantry Brigade/23rd Infantry Division | 1968 | Quang Ngai | 1 | — | — | — |
| 110 | Second lieutenant removed an ear from a Vietcong corpse and displayed it on a jeep antenna. | 4th Infantry Division | 1966 | Phu Yen | 1 | — | — | — |
| 111 | Three soldiers beat a POW to death. | 9th Infantry Division | N/A | N/A | 3 | 3 GCM | — | — |
| 112 | Captain ordered a lieutenant to have a POW killed. Three GIs carried out the execution. Only the three low-ranking soldiers were convicted. | 1st Cavalry Division | 1967 | Binh Dinh | 5 | 5 GCM | 3 | 3 |

| | | | | | | | | |
|---|---|---|---|---|---|---|---|---|
| 113 | A staff sergeant decapitated the bodies of two enemy soldiers with an axe. Officers from his unit then posed for photos with the corpses. | 25th Infantry Division | 1967 | Binh Duong | 5 | 1 GCM | 1 | — |
| 116 | An interrogator raped an 11-year-old detainee in an interrogation hut. | 196th Infantry Brigade | 1967 | N/A | 1 | 1 GCM | 1 | 1 |
| 117 | Interrogators made detainees lie on their backs with their arms and legs in the air, then struck them with a baseball bat. | 196th Infantry Brigade | 1967 | Quang Tin | 2 | — | — | — |
| 119 | Acting on a dare from a TV news cameraman, two GIs cut ears off a Vietcong corpse. | 1st Infantry Division | 1967 | Binh Duong | 2 | 2 SPCM | 2 | — |
| 120 | Suspected Vietcong assaulted, forced to shave off his beard until he told the truth. | 9th Infantry Division | 1967 | N/A | 1 | — | — | — |
| 121 | As second lieutenant watched, four GIs robbed fourteen civilians during a search-and-clear patrol. | N/A | 1967 | Quang Nam | 5 | — | — | — |
| 122 | While riding in a vehicle, a captain pulled out his pistol and shot a Cambodian national to death. | 5th Special Forces Group | 1967 | Gia Dinh | 1 | 1 GCM | — | — |

CASES CLASSIFIED AS FOUNDED BY ARMY INVESTIGATORS, *continued*

| CASE # | ALLEGATIONS | DIVISION/ BRIGADE | YEAR | PROVINCE | SUSPECTS | COURTS MARSHALL | CONVICTIONS | CONFINEMENT |
|---|---|---|---|---|---|---|---|---|
| 124 | Field telephones were wired to the "sensitive areas" of three men and a woman interrogated by a captain, a first lieutenant, and four sergeants. | 5th Special Forces Group | 1968 | Phuoc Tuy | 6 | — | — | — |
| 125 | Newspaper photo showed a U.S. soldier sitting on a Vietcong suspect as Vietnamese interrogators applied water torture. | 1st Cavalry Division | 1968 | Quang Nam | 1 | 1 SCM | 1 | — |
| 127 | Soldier cut off the ears of several Vietcong killed in a firefight. | 173rd Airborne Brigade | 1968 | Quang Tri | 1 | — | — | — |
| 129 | Master sergeant ordered a subordinate to decapitate a Vietcong corpse. When the subordinate hesitated, the master sergeant threatened him with jail. The master sergeant then boiled the head, removed the flesh, and traded the skull for a radio. | 199th Infantry Brigade | 1968 | Bien Hoa | 2 | 1 GCM, 1 SPCM | 1 | — |
| 133 | Two teenage girls, 14 and 17, were taken into custody with nine other detainees. Soldiers handed a male detainee an M-16 and told him to kill one of the girls. He shot her, fatally wounding her in the throat. The other girl was sodomized and raped for several days. | 198th Infantry Brigade/ 23rd Infantry Division | 1968 | Quang Tin | 8 | 4 GCM | 4 | 3 |
| 135 | While driving through a hamlet, a soldier fired a burst from his M-60 machine gun at a house without reason, killing a 16-year-old girl. | 13th Artillery | N/A | N/A | 1 | 1 GCM | 1 | 1 |

| | | | | | | | | |
|---|---|---|---|---|---|---|---|---|
| 136 | GI assaulted two detainees and shot an unarmed man to death. He severed both ears and a finger at another soldier's urging "to prove himself a man." | 173rd Airborne Brigade | 1968 | Binh Dinh | 3 | 2 GCM | 2 | — |
| 137 | Soldier shot and wounded a civilian; members of his unit then returned to the scene and killed the man. | 23rd Infantry Division | 1968 | Quang Ngai | 5 | 1 GCM | — | — |
| 139 | Home invasion by first lieutenant and four other soldiers led to the sexual assault of two girls, 15 and 17. | 23rd Infantry Division | 1968 | Quang Ngai | 3 | 2 GCM | 2 | 2 |
| 140 | At urging of his platoon, a GI kidnapped a young girl from her home and raped her in a bunker. | 23rd Infantry Division | 1968 | N/A | 2 | 2 GCM | 1 | — |
| 141 | Two soldiers beat two detainees, requiring their hospitalization. | 196th Infantry Brigade | 1968 | Quang Tin | 2 | 1 SPCM | 1 | — |
| 142 | Squad encountered a group of Vietnamese and opened fire when they ran away. A wounded villager raised his hands in surrender. But when informed of the situation by radio, the captain told a second lieutenant to kill him. Soldiers shot the man as well as another detainee kneeling on the ground with his hands tied behind his back. | 82nd Airborne Division | 1968 | Thua Thien | 3 | 1 GCM | — | — |

Cases Classified as Founded by Army Investigators, *continued*

| CASE # | ALLEGATIONS | DIVISION/BRIGADE | YEAR | PROVINCE | SUSPECTS | COURTS MARSHALL | CONVICTIONS | CONFINEMENT |
|---|---|---|---|---|---|---|---|---|
| 143 | POWs were routinely beaten and given electric shocks. Suspects admitted shocking and assaulting detainees. Maltreatment was "common knowledge." | 173rd Airborne Brigade | 1968 | N/A | 5 | 3 SPCM | 1 | — |
| 144 | Detainee died of "natural causes" during an abusive interrogation. | 55th Military Intelligence Detachment | 1968 | Binh Dinh | 1 | — | — | — |
| 145 | Soldier opened fire on a POW camp, killing one and wounding one. | 23rd Infantry Division | 1968 | Quang Tin | 1 | — | — | — |
| 147 | Bumgarner incident: Platoon leader detained two young duck herders and an irrigation worker, shot them to death, decapitated them with a fragmentation grenade, and planted weapons to support his claim of three Vietcong killed in action. | 173rd Airborne Brigade | 1969 | Binh Dinh | 2 | 2 GCM | 1 | — |
| 148 | Sergeant entered the home of a man, 65, accused him of being a Vietcong, and executed him. | 173rd Airborne Brigade | 1969 | Binh Dinh | 1 | 1 GCM | — | — |
| 149 | Soldier cut off dead man's ears as retribution for the death of a close friend. | 101st Airborne Division | 1969 | N/A | 1 | 1 SPCM | 1 | — |
| 150 | Four soldiers kidnapped a girl, raped her over several days, and then executed her. | 1st Cavalry Division | 1966 | Binh Dinh | 4 | 4 GCM | 2 | 2 |

| # | Description | Unit | Year | Location | | | | |
|---|---|---|---|---|---|---|---|---|
| 154 | Two intoxicated soldiers fired into a group of civilians, killing one and wounding one. | 39th Engineer Battalion | 1970 | Quang Ngai | 2 | 1 GCM | – | – |
| 155 | Helicopter bearing a red cross emblem was used to deliver ammunition. | 1st Cavalry Division | 1970 | N/A | 2 | – | – | – |
| 156 | Helicopter crew dropped the body of an enemy soldier from the air, retrieved it, and dropped it into a river. | 1st Cavalry Division | 1970 | N/A | 4 | – | – | – |
| 157 | Second lieutenant subjected detainees to electrical torture during interrogations, forced civilians picked at random to walk point on his patrols, and almost daily opened fire on Vietnamese in farm fields and hamlets. | 173rd Airborne Brigade | 1970 | Binh Dinh | 1 | 1 SPCM | – | – |
| 158 | Soldiers faked the execution of one detainee and used a Vietcong corpse to extract information from others. | 11th Armored Cavalry Regiment | 1970 | Binh Duong | 3 | – | – | – |
| 159 | Two soldiers killed an unarmed civilian woman. | 23rd Infantry Division | 1969 | Quang Nam | 2 | 2 GCM | – | – |
| 160 | Three soldiers gang-raped a Vietnamese female. | 173rd Airborne Brigade | 1969 | N/A | 3 | 3 GCM | – | – |

CASES CLASSIFIED AS FOUNDED BY ARMY INVESTIGATORS, *continued*

| CASE # | ALLEGATIONS | DIVISION/ BRIGADE | YEAR | PROVINCE | SUSPECTS | COURTS MARSHALL | CONVICTIONS | CONFINEMENT |
|---|---|---|---|---|---|---|---|---|
| 162 | Green Beret Incident: A colonel, two majors, three captains, and two other members of a special forces unit were implicated in the execution of a Vietnamese man believed to be a double agent for U.S. and Communist forces. The secretary of the army intervened and dismissed the charges. | 5th Special Forces Group | 1969 | Khanh Hoa | 8 | - | - | - |
| 163 | Unarmed civilian man died after being stabbed by a GI. | N/A | 1968 | N/A | 1 | 1 GCM | - | - |
| 209 | Four helicopter gunships shot up two friendly villages, killing ten civilians, wounding fifteen, and destroying three hootches and eight sampans. | 23rd Infantry Division | 1969 | Quang Tin | 4 | - | - | - |
| 210 | Soldiers killed an unarmed man after being ordered to shoot anything that moved in a free-fire zone. | 101st Airborne Division | 1966 | Phu Yen | 3 | - | - | - |
| 219 | A U.S. helicopter "hunter-killer" team and South Vietnamese army platoon opened fire on a Cambodian village filled with civilians. Eight were killed, fifteen were wounded. Instead of assisting the wounded, soldiers pillaged a motorcycle and presented it to the commanding officer. | 1st Cavalry Division | 1971 | Cambodia | 7 | - | - | - |

| | | | | | | | | |
|---|---|---|---|---|---|---|---|---|
| 221 | Tiger Force: Soldiers in an elite platoon assaulted and killed numerous unarmed Vietnamese. The allegations were classified as "unsubstantiated" in a case summary, but in 2003 the *Toledo Blade* obtained documents showing CID secretly substantiated at least ten incidents involving ten killings, several assaults, and multiple corpse mutilations. The *Blade* presented additional evidence from documents and interviews that scores of noncombatants were slain. | 101st Airborne Division | 1967 | Quang Ngai | 8 | – | – | – |
| 226 | A major and captain ordered bodies of ten to twelve Vietcong sappers to be buried instead of buried after a fierce battle in which thirty Americans died. | 196th Infantry Brigade/ 23rd Infantry Division | 1971 | Quang Tin | 2 | – | – | – |
| 232 | Hoag allegation: Members of a reconnaissance platoon opened fire on civilians in two huts, killing at least nine unarmed children and women. They were reported as enemy killed in action. A teenager was captured and killed, and a girl was raped. | 196th Infantry Brigade/ 23rd Infantry Division | 1969 | Quang Nam/ Quang Tin | 7 | – | – | – |
| 235 | Soldiers attached an enemy corpse to the fender of a tank and hung another body by the ankles from a gun tube. The first lieutenant and others at the base took photographs. | 173rd Airborne Brigade | 1971 | Binh Dinh | 4 | – | – | – |

CASES CLASSIFIED AS FOUNDED BY ARMY INVESTIGATORS, *continued*

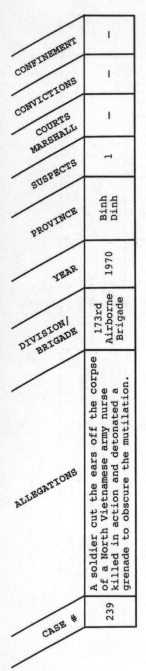

| CASE # | ALLEGATIONS | DIVISION/ BRIGADE | YEAR | PROVINCE | SUSPECTS | COURTS MARSHALL | CONVICTIONS | CONFINEMENT |
|---|---|---|---|---|---|---|---|---|
| 239 | A soldier cut the ears off the corpse of a North Vietnamese army nurse killed in action and detonated a grenade to obscure the mutilation. | 173rd Airborne Brigade | 1970 | Binh Dinh | 1 | – | – | – |

## CASES CLOSED BY ARMY INVESTIGATORS AS UNSUBSTANTIATED, UNFOUNDED, OR DUE TO INSUFFICIENT EVIDENCE[4]

| CASE # | ALLEGATIONS | DIVISION/ BRIGADE | YEAR | PROVINCE |
|---|---|---|---|---|
| 5 | Helicopter Crew Attacked A Boy In A Sampan. Killing Confirmed, Found Within Rules Of Engagement. | 13th Aviation Battalion | 1969 | An Giang |
| 6 | Elderly Vietnamese male was shot, other civilians were mistreated. Case "closed." | 196th Infantry Brigade/23rd Infantry Division | N/A | N/A |
| 7 | Captain said he refused an order by a lieutenant colonel to arrange for the execution of a POW. The detainee later was shot by South Vietnamese security forces. The investigation concluded he was shot while attempting to escape. Case "closed." | 5th Special Forces Group | 1969 | Tay Ninh |
| 10 | Troops opened fire on six unarmed children at the platoon leader's command, killing four and wounding two. CID confirmed, but classified them as combat-related civilian casualties and closed the case as "unsubstantiated." | 196th Infantry Brigade/23rd Infantry Division | 1969 | Quang Tin |

[4] Investigators confirmed incidents in more than a quarter of the cases, but for reasons indicated, the army designated them otherwise. Those are marked in bold. Six case summaries were not available; the outcomes of those cases could not be determined. Selected allegations from each case are provided, not a complete list.

Cases Closed by Army Investigators, *continued*

| CASE # | ALLEGATIONS | DIVISION/ BRIGADE | YEAR | PROVINCE |
|---|---|---|---|---|
| 11 | Team commander ordered the bombing of a Vietcong hospital marked with a red cross. Case "completed." | 5th Special Forces Group | 1968 | Phuoc Long |
| 12 | **U.S. troops shot civilians, slaughtered livestock, burned huts, tossed a grenade into a bunker, and destroyed a temple after a land mine killed a GI. The investigation confirmed a temple was destroyed after troops received hostile fire. CID also uncovered evidence that an elderly detainee died after a beating by a U.S. soldier, but did not determine whether the beating caused his death. The case was classified as "unsubstantiated."** | **18th Engineer Brigade** | **1968** | **Quang Ngai** |
| 13 | A staff sergeant reported rape, mutilation, torture, and murder of detainees. After interviewing 112 men from his unit, CID closed the case, citing "insufficient evidence" to prove or disprove the allegations. Some of the incidents involved the Tiger Force platoon, later tied to numerous atrocities in a secret CID investigation. | 101st Airborne Division | 1966– 1967 | N/A |
| 14 | Complainant witnessed and participated in several atrocities. Case "closed." | 23rd Infantry Division | 1968 | N/A |
| 15 | Soldier asked for investigation of a magazine article that described members of his unit as "Hatchet Men" who mutilated bodies of dead Vietcong. Case "closed." | 23rd Infantry Division | 1967 | N/A |
| 16 | U.S. troops were told to "make no difference between soldiers and civilians" during the "Johnson City" combat operation. Case "closed." | 1st Infantry Division | 1967 | Tay Ninh |
| 17 | Hospitalized air force veteran confided to another patient that POWs were pushed from helicopters. Case "closed." | N/A | N/A | N/A |
| 18 | Canadian nurse said men at a U.S. soldiers' club in Quang Ngai often boasted about killing people. Case "closed." | N/A | N/A | Quang Ngai |

| # | Description | Unit | Year | Location |
|---|---|---|---|---|
| 19 | GI reported witnessing repeated killings and other atrocities against civilians. He recanted under questioning by CID. Case "closed." | 173rd Airborne Brigade | 1969 | N/A |
| 21 | **A South Vietnamese soldier under the watch of U.S. soldiers stabbed a POW in the back. Investigators confirmed the stabbing but were told the detainee had been trying to escape. Case "closed."** | **N/A** | **1969** | **N/A** |
| 22 | Ten to twenty-five POWs who vanished overnight were either shot or released. Classified "unsubstantiated." | 1st Cavalry Division | 1969 | Quang Ngai/Binh Dinh |
| 24 | Patients at a hospital in Da Nang told a military reporter about a gang rape, the murder of an old woman, and a grenade thrown into burning hooch with a crying baby. Case "closed." | N/A | N/A | Da Nang |
| 25 | Soldiers at psychiatric aid stations told a captain, who was serving as social worker, of numerous atrocities, including indiscriminate helicopter firing on villages in Vietnam, Laos, and Cambodia. Case "closed." | N/A | N/A | N/A |
| 26 | Neighbor reported that a veteran bragged about serving in an elite "murder unit" that committed war crimes. The veteran denied ever making such a statement when questioned by CID. Case "closed." | 101st Airborne Division | 1965–1968 | N/A |
| 27 | N/A | N/A | N/A | N/A |

CASES CLOSED BY ARMY INVESTIGATORS, *continued*

| CASE # | ALLEGATIONS | DIVISION/BRIGADE | YEAR | PROVINCE |
|---|---|---|---|---|
| 31 | In a letter to his parents, a captain serving as a military adviser to the South Vietnamese army told of participating in "many My Lai type operations where a lot of innocent civilians have been killed." He told CID he was referring to "search and destroy" operations that resulted in civilian casualties. Case "closed." | 25th Infantry Division | 1968–1970 | N/A |
| 33 | Imprisoned GI deserter claimed to have film depicting civilian killings. He was unable to produce the rolls, and CID closed the case due to insufficient evidence. | N/A | N/A | Quang Nam/Quang Ngai |
| 34 | Citizens Commission of Inquiry on U.S. War Crimes in Vietnam (1970: Washington, DC): Warrant officer testified at a public forum that a helicopter crew killed thirty-three civilians. The former commanding officer told CID that eight to ten armed enemy combatants were killed and that several weapons were retrieved. A soldier dispatched to conduct ground policing told investigators he found the bodies of fourteen men and women and one child. He saw no weapons, but said they may have been collected before he arrived on the scene. CID found "insufficient evidence" to determine whether the allegations were true or false. | 1st Cavalry Division | 1967 | Quang Ngai |
| 35 | Member of a helicopter crew reported that he was ordered to kill a civilian and witnessed the killing of six others. The crew declined to give written statements to CID and their commanders denied the allegations. Classified "unsubstantiated." | 101st Airborne Division | 1968 | Quang Tri |

| | | | | |
|---|---|---|---|---|
| 37 | Letter to Nixon from two reservists said training camp instructors who had served in Vietnam talked about "widespread use of brutality and murder" by U.S. troops. Classified "unsubstantiated." | N/A | N/A | N/A |
| 38 | Members of a ranger team shot five woodcutters, killing three. CID confirmed the shootings but concluded the soldiers acted reasonably. Classified "unfounded." | 75th Infantry Rangers | 1970 | Phu Bon |
| 41 | Sergeant reported that two soldiers killed two Vietcong suspects who were lying on the ground surrendering. One suspect admitted the shooting to CID; the second suspect denied it. Case closed as "unsubstantiated." | 101st Airborne Division | 1969 | Quang Nam |
| 42 | Three soldiers on reconnaissance patrol killed a Vietnamese man. The soldiers admitted to killing the man but said he was holding a grenade. Case "closed." | 1st Infantry Division | 1970 | Binh Duong |
| 43 | N/A | N/A | N/A | N/A |
| 44 | Two male and two female Vietnamese were shot during a "search and clear" operation; one fell into a pond and died. CID confirmed the shootings but considered them combat-related casualties. | 198th Infantry Brigade/23rd Infantry Division | 1970 | Quang Ngai |
| 45 | Airmobile assaults took place inside Cambodia. CID found "insufficient evidence" to determine whether the allegations were true or false. | 25th Infantry Division | 1969 | Cambodia |
| 45 | Sixteen-year-old was tortured with a field telephone. CID investigation found "insufficient evidence" to determine whether the allegations were true or false. | 23rd Infantry Division | 1969 | N/A |

Cases Closed by Army Investigators, *continued*

| CASE # | ALLEGATIONS | DIVISION/ BRIGADE | YEAR | PROVINCE |
|---|---|---|---|---|
| 46 | Lieutenant colonel ordered the camp dump "off limits," resulting in the killing of two children playing in trash; he also ordered a hamlet destroyed with heavy equipment. The allegations were corroborated but described as combat-related incidents. The case was closed as "unfounded." | 35th Engineer Group | 1968 | Quang Ngai |
| 47 | Former military police officer wrote a letter to Nixon describing the assault of civilians and female POWs. Classified "unsubstantiated." | 89th Military Police Group | 1968 | Long Binh |
| 48 | Citizens Commission of Inquiry: Captain witnessed the destruction of thirty to forty villages in "free fire zones" and the murder of a POW by South Vietnamese soldiers. An investigation found "insufficient evidence" to determine whether the allegations were true or false. | Military Assistance Advisory Group | 1968– 1969 | Quang Nam |
| 48 | Citizens Commission of Inquiry: Army surgeon was told to keep a POW alive only long enough for interrogation; he gave CID photos depicting inhumane treatment of a Vietcong suspect and water torture of a detainee. Investigation confirmed mistreatment of male and female detainees by South Vietnamese police. Case closed as "unfounded." | 11th Armored Cavalry | 1968 | Binh Duong |
| 48 | Citizens Commission of Inquiry: Twelve POWs were pushed from U.S. helicopters by South Vietnamese soldiers. CID found "insufficient evidence" after an "extensive investigation." | 5th Special Forces Group | 1963 | Saigon |
| 50 | Helicopter gunships sank one hundred sampans on Sang Cau River, killing scores of women and children. A pilot and two officers denied the allegations. Classified "unsubstantiated." | 1st Aviation Brigade | 1967 | N/A |

| # | Description | Unit | Year | Location |
|---|---|---|---|---|
| 51 | Peter Martinsen allegation: He witnessed the beating and electric torture of detainees, including two who died. Classified as "unsubstantiated." CID later confirmed multiple instances of detainee abuse from 1968 to 1969 by the 173rd Airborne Brigade. See case number 58. | 101st Airborne Division/173rd Airborne Brigade | 1966–1967 | N/A |
| 51 | Robert Stemme and Frederick Brown reported that interrogators used electrical shock and other abusive measures on detainees with the approval of superiors. Classified as unsubstantiated. However, records from case number 58 show CID later confirmed the allegations. | 173rd Airborne Brigade | 1968–1969 | Binh Dinh |
| 52 | U.S. helicopter gunships killed 100 to 300 Montagnards (indigenous Central Highlands people) as Vietcong forced them to march toward Pleiku. U.S. interrogators subjected detainees to electric shock and other forms of abuse. Other members of the unit told CID about detainee torture and killing of 125 to 200 Montagnard civilians but gave conflicting reports on who was responsible. Commanders denied the massacre; confirmed the killing of 200 Vietcong around same time. Classified "unsubstantiated." | 4th Infantry Division | 1968 | Pleiku |
| 53 | Vietcong suspect, stabbed in the head during an interrogation, died. CID confirmed death, attributed it to combat injury. Classified "unsubstantiated." | 23rd Infantry Division | 1970 | Quang Tin |
| 55 | Twenty-seven civilians were killed in a village as a tank fired into homes with cause. Report says complainant declined to cooperate. Case "closed." | 101st Airborne Division | 1968 | N/A |
| 55 | Vietcong suspect was tortured by wiring a jeep battery to his genitals; a suspect's throat was cut; corpses were wired together and dragged through villages. Report says complainant declined to cooperate. Case "closed." | 25th Infantry Division | 1966–1967 | N/A |

Cases Closed by Army Investigators, *continued*

| CASE # | ALLEGATIONS | DIVISION/ BRIGADE | YEAR | PROVINCE |
|---|---|---|---|---|
| 55 | A South Vietnamese soldier burned a POW with cigarettes during an interrogation; Vietcong bodies were dumped outside the tent of George S. Patton III as a "tribute" to his father. Report says complainant declined to cooperate. Case "closed." | 11th Armored Cavalry | 1968 | N/A |
| 56 | Platoon leader gunned down frightened a 12-year-old boy after a botched interrogation. Report says complainant declined to cooperate with CID. Classified "insufficient evidence." | 23rd Infantry Division | 1968 | N/A |
| 56 | U.S. soldiers killed twenty-six unarmed women and children on a beach. Allegation retracted. Classified "unsubstantiated." | 173rd Airborne Brigade | 1968 | Binh Dinh |
| 59 | Woman says that her brother, killed by military police, was murdered; he had sent her letters and photos detailing war crimes, and his life had been threatened by superiors. Classified "unsubstantiated." | 173rd Airborne Brigade | 1969– 1970 | N/A |
| 60 | Soldier's letter to his wife cited the massacre of an entire village after children fitted with booby traps killed a GI who gave them candy. Classified "unsubstantiated." | 25th Infantry Division/199th Infantry Brigade | 1970 | N/A |
| 62 | Army medic told complainant he smothered a hospitalized Vietcong suspect. Classified "unsubstantiated." | N/A | 1970 | N/A |
| 63 | Citizens Commission of Inquiry: Former soldier stated he overheard Gen. Westmoreland say, "The pacification program is out. I want more bodies." Classified "unfounded." Army Staff was directed to pursue discharge of the complainant from the reserves due to his "irresponsible, unsubstantiated public statements and his affiliation with the Citizens Commission of Inquiry." | Military Assistance Command, Vietnam | 1967– 1968 | N/A |

| # | Citizens Commission of Inquiry | Unit | Year | Location |
|---|---|---|---|---|
| 64 | Citizens Commission of Inquiry: Combat photographer saw a second lieutenant kill an unarmed, elderly civilian. Suspect declined to talk to CID on advice of counsel. A witness corroborated the killing; said the suspect panicked. Classified "unsubstantiated" due to "insufficient evidence." | 25th Infantry Division | 1967 | Quang Ngai |
| 65 | Four GIs killed a wounded POW and dumped the body in a river with their captain's knowledge. Witnesses interviewed by CID corroborated the account. The soldier who made the allegation passed a polygraph exam. The captain declined to talk. CID turned the case over to the captain's commander, who declined to take action. Classified "insufficient evidence." | 25th Infantry Division | 1967 | Quang Ngai |
| 66 | Citizens Commission of Inquiry: Soldier's unit routinely destroyed villages; three POWs were released and then shot for allegedly escaping; a girl was raped and then shot to death as she ran away. CID interviewed the complainant and closed the case. Classified "insufficient evidence." | 199th Infantry Brigade | 1968 | N/A |
| 67 | Citizens Commission of Inquiry: Two former soldiers testified that members of their unit threw a baby and an elderly woman into a well, followed by grenades; dragged five unarmed men from a bunker and killed them; and destroyed ten villages. CID contacted the complainants and then closed the case. Classified "insufficient evidence." | 23rd Infantry Division | 1969–1970 | N/A |

CASES CLOSED BY ARMY INVESTIGATORS, *continued*

| CASE # | ALLEGATIONS | DIVISION/ BRIGADE | YEAR | PROVINCE |
|---|---|---|---|---|
| 68 | Citizens Commission of Inquiry: Fifteen to twenty North Vietnamese soldiers were killed while surrendering on one occasion; on another occasion, fifteen Vietcong were executed by gunship while surrendering. Complainant later saw a report on the second incident in his division's daily journal. CID obtained his written statement and closed the case. Classified "insufficient evidence." | 1st Cavalry Division | 1969 | Quang Tin |
| 70 | Citizens Commission of Inquiry: A man and a woman found in a hut were shot; a wounded POW was killed. CID found corroboration for the killing of the wounded Vietcong and the man from hut. Case listed as "in progress" as of 1973. | 198th Infantry Brigade/23rd Infantry Division | 1968 | Quang Tin |
| 71 | Citizens Commission of Inquiry: GI showed slides of his unit torturing Vietcong suspects during interrogations. CID reported complainant "would answer no questions." Case "closed." | 23rd Infantry Division | N/A | N/A |
| 72 | Citizens Commission of Inquiry: In the Mekong Delta, U.S. troops killed three civilians without cause at a commanding officer's order. A woman and a child were killed in an ambush. Heavy firepower was used routinely on hamlets without regard for civilians. CID interviewed complainant, closed case. Classified "unfounded." | 9th Infantry Division | 1969 | N/A |
| 73 | Citizens Commission of Inquiry: Vietnamese female intelligence agent was killed without cause; a wooden peg was shoved into a POW's ear, killing him; two POWs were pushed from a helicopter to frighten four others into divulging information. Case investigated, classified "unsubstantiated." | 525th Military Intelligence Group; III Marine Amphibious Force | 1967– 1968 | N/A |

| 74 | Citizens Commission of Inquiry: Huey gunship attack on hamlet killed at least ten Vietnamese. CID interviewed the complainant and closed the case. | 199th Infantry Brigade | 1967 | Long An |
|---|---|---|---|---|
| 76 | Soldier reported to CID that one POW was subjected to water torture and another was executed at Landing Zone English. He provided photos of mutilated POW corpses. The team leader denied the allegation. Classified "unsubstantiated." A separate CID investigation found interrogators at LZ English routinely used water and electric torture. See case number 58. | 173rd Airborne Brigade | 1969 | Binh Dinh |
| 79 | A platoon executed a nurse wounded in an ambush of unarmed Vietcong suspects. The platoon leader told CID that his unit killed three men and two women carrying medical supplies. He denied that a wounded woman was executed. CID concluded the dead were "members of a North Vietnamese Propaganda Team." Classified "unsubstantiated." | 173rd Airborne Brigade | 1967 | Phu Yen |
| 80 | POWs often were tortured with field telephones under the battalion commander's supervision. The unit also was ordered to kill civilians and livestock and to "level villages." Investigators contacted the complainant and closed the case. Classified "insufficient evidence." | 23rd Infantry Division | 1969–1970 | N/A |
| 80 | Vehicle convoys frequently fired on friendly Vietnamese. CID contacted the complainant and closed the case. Classified "insufficient evidence." | 1st Logistical Command | 1968–1969 | N/A |

Cases Closed by Army Investigators, *continued*

| CASE # | ALLEGATIONS | DIVISION/ BRIGADE | YEAR | PROVINCE |
|---|---|---|---|---|
| 81 | Winter Soldier Investigation forum sponsored by Vietnam Veterans Against the War, Detroit, Jan. 31–Feb. 2, 1971: Two of five POWs were pushed from a helicopter. Soldiers were offered a three-day pass if they could prove they killed a POW, resulting in murder and mutilation. CID contacted the complainant and closed the case. Classified "insufficient evidence." | 173rd Airborne Brigade | 1967–1968 | Binh Dinh |
| 82 | Captain used a grenade launcher to gas a group of children, ages 3 to 12, who had gathered near a burning trash pile. Other members of the company confirmed the incident but said the captain acted to disperse children from a danger zone. Classified "unfounded." | 4th Infantry Division | 1970 | Pleiku |
| 83 | GI's letter to a neighbor detailed the unwarranted killing of detained men, women, and children. The writer recanted when interviewed by CID. Classified "unsubstantiated." | 23rd Infantry Division | 1971 | N/A |
| 84 | Case summary says only "See File." The complainant, a West Point captain who served as an aide to the division commander, also testified at a congressional hearing in 1971. He described village burnings, a white phosphorous mortar attack on a hamlet that left ten women and children burned to death, electric torture of detainees, and the deliberate bombing of a Cambodian hospital. Other records show CID concluded that none of the allegations were "criminal in nature." Case closed. | 25th Infantry Division | 1968 | Binh Duong |
| 85 | Squad leader ordered his men to fire at a group of villagers the day after the booby-trap death of a popular GI; thirty civilians died, but the squad leader reported them as Vietcong. Investigation found that the squad reported twenty-seven enemy killed in action. CID said the evidence indicated civilians may have been caught in the "crossfire." Classified "unfounded." | 11th Infantry Brigade | 1969 | Quang Ngai |

| | | | | |
|---|---|---|---|---|
| 87 | At an impromptu Fort Bliss press conference, a gunner told TV reporters that he murdered Vietnamese on orders and demanded that the army arrest him. Classified "unsubstantiated." | 1st Aviation Brigade | 1967–1968 | Hau Nghia |
| 88 | Letter, written by a veteran in English class and forwarded by his teacher to the defense secretary, described an ambush set up to kill civilians trying to steal food from base. He was surprised that the letter was mailed and declined to discuss it with CID. Case closed as "unsubstantiated." | N/A | N/A | Binh Dinh |
| 89 | Lieutenant executed a POW for no reason; a soldier displayed the genitals cut from an enemy corpse; a diamond was carved into the chest of another corpse; photos were taken of a severed head. Closed as "unsubstantiated/insufficient evidence." | 5th Infantry Division | 1971 | Quang Tri |
| 90 | Former assistant province adviser for psychological operations reported that the Phantom Program, which used Cobra helicopters to control enemy forces, killed and wounded numerous women and children. He witnessed gunships strafe a herd of water buffalo and six or seven "buffalo boys" tending the animals. Hospitals reported an increase in wounded peasants despite a drop in ground combat. The adviser submitted a memorandum to the senior province adviser asking for termination of the Phantom Program. A witness told CID he saw explosions among the buffalo but did not know what happened to children riding them. "Other personnel" told CID they agreed with the memorandum. Case classified "insufficient evidence." | N/A | 1968–1969 | Bac Lieu |
| 91 | N/A | N/A | N/A | N/A |

CASES CLOSED BY ARMY INVESTIGATORS, *continued*

| CASE # | ALLEGATIONS | DIVISION/ BRIGADE | YEAR | PROVINCE |
|---|---|---|---|---|
| 92 | April 26, 1971, *New York Times* article contained an account of Cobra gunships killing 350 villagers in retaliation for the death of one GI and a similar incident that killed thirty to forty fleeing villagers. Classified "unfounded." | N/A | N/A | N/A |
| 94 | TV footage showed a human skull displayed on an armored personnel carrier (APC). An investigation confirmed the incident but recommended no action be taken. Classified "unfounded." | 5th Infantry Division | 1971 | Quang Tri |
| 95 | A former army physician wrote a letter to then ambassador George Bush, stating that he and other medical personnel tortured prisoners. The physician declined to talk to CID. Classified "insufficient evidence." | 1st Cavalry Division | 1966– 1967 | Binh Dinh |
| 99 | Sergeant and a fellow GI killed a POW on a commanding officer's order while on a "search and destroy" mission. Classified "insufficient evidence." See case numbers 13 and 221. | 101st Airborne Division | 1967 | Quang Tin |
| 101 | Team leader killed a wounded, unarmed Vietcong soldier. CID confirmed the killing but attributed it to a sudden movement by the injured man. Classified "unfounded." | 1st Cavalry Division | 1971 | Binh Tuy |
| 102 | Staff sergeant ordered his Rangers team to fire on a small group of people who were thought to be wearing uniforms. No fire was returned. They killed one adult and wounded one boy. The investigation confirmed the deaths but concluded that the killings conformed to the rules of engagement. Classified "unfounded." | 75th Infantry Rangers | 1971 | Binh Dinh |

| # | Description | Unit | Year | Location |
|---|---|---|---|---|
| 103 | GI fired blindly in a free-fire zone after hearing voices, killing one of four unarmed boys. The investigation confirmed the killings and found the shootings violated the rules of engagement. Letters of reprimand were issued, but the case was classified "unsubstantiated." | 173rd Airborne Division | 1971 | Binh Dinh |
| 104 | GIs tied a detainee to the ground in a spread-eagle position, abused him, and threatened him with a knife during interrogation. The captain in charge confirmed tying him to the ground to keep him from escaping and covering his mouth to keep him quiet, but denied using unnecessary force. Case classified "unfounded." | 23rd Infantry Division | 1971 | Quang Nam |
| 106 | *TRUE* magazine ran an account of a GI decapitating a wounded Vietcong detainee with a hatchet and another GI playfully showing the head to reporters. Unit members told investigators that the detainee tried to throw a grenade, and the GI attacked "in a fit of rage" because a popular member of the unit had been killed. "Because of the unfavorable publicity associated with the incident, the battalion immediately discontinued the use of the hatchet," the case summary noted. Classified "unsubstantiated." | 101st Airborne Division | 1965 | Binh Duong |
| 107 | News report said a commander ordered his men to blast shut a cave with ten to three hundred civilians and enemy soldiers inside. Investigation concluded the cave had been cleared before the blast, and no one was knowingly trapped. Classified "unsubstantiated." | 25th Infantry Division | 1966 | N/A |
| 108 | GIs dropped Vietcong corpses from a helicopter. The commanding officer told investigators he had the bodies removed from the area because they posed a health hazard. The report does not say how they were removed. Classified "unfounded." | 1st Infantry Division | 1966 | Tay Ninh |

CASES CLOSED BY ARMY INVESTIGATORS, *continued*

| CASE # | ALLEGATIONS | DIVISION/ BRIGADE | YEAR | PROVINCE |
|---|---|---|---|---|
| 109 | A prize-winning *Washington Post* photo showed a Vietcong soldier, who appeared to be alive, being dragged behind an armored personnel carrier. Members of the unit told investigators that the man was dead, they were dragging his body in case it was booby-trapped, and "the clawing fingers were a result of rigor mortis." Classified "unsubstantiated." | 1st Infantry Division | 1966 | N/A |
| 114 | GI stole money from a POW. Case "completed" with no action taken. | N/A | 1967 | N/A |
| 115 | POW was hit and deprived of food. Classified "unsubstantiated." | 9th Infantry Division | 1967 | Dinh Tuong |
| 118 | Four detainees captured by U.S. troops were injured by South Vietnamese army interrogators. An investigation confirmed the allegations but concluded no U.S. soldiers were present during the assaults. Classified "unsubstantiated." | 9th Infantry Division | 1967 | Go Cong |
| 123 | Captain ordered the execution rather than capture of an unarmed Vietcong suspect. Classified "unsubstantiated." | 4th Infantry Division | 1967 | Quang Ngai |
| 126 | Bodies of two dead Vietcong were mutilated. Classified "insufficient evidence." | 101st Airborne Division | N/A | N/A |
| 128 | N/A | N/A | N/A | N/A |
| 130 | Commanding officer ordered the killing of a wounded Vietcong soldier with a satchel charge. An investigation concluded he was a threat, and the order was justified. Classified "unsubstantiated." | 815th Engineer Battalion | 1968 | Pleiku |

| | Description | Unit | Year | Location |
|---|---|---|---|---|
| 131 | In a letter to relatives, GI told of killing four Vietnamese nationals to avenge a friend killed in action. He told CID the killings were "figments of my own imagination." Classified "unfounded." | 97th Artillery Group | 1966 | N/A |
| 132 | Vietnamese female reported that she had been raped by ten U.S. soldiers. CID report says one soldier admitted he "had intercourse" with her. Classified "unsubstantiated." | 173rd Airborne Brigade | 1968 | Binh Dinh |
| 134 | Detainee was tortured during interrogation. Classified "unfounded." | 4th Infantry Division | 1968 | N/A |
| 138 | U.S. platoon discovered what appeared to be mutilated bodies in nine graves. An investigation determined that the corpses were decomposed but not mutilated. | 101st Airborne Division | 1968 | Thua Thien |
| 146 | Unidentified U.S. adviser, quoted in a newspaper article, condoned killing wounded POWs. The article implied that he had just committed a revenge killing. Military Assistance Command,Vietnam was asked to "continue surveillance of such incidents." Classified "completed." | N/A | 1968 | N/A |
| 151 | GI beat an innocent civilian that he suspected of being a Vietcong soldier. Classified "unsubstantiated." The same soldier was convicted and fined for abusing a detainee in case number 125. | N/A | N/A | N/A |
| 152 | Soldier stripped a dead Vietcong of clothing and severed one ear, then showed the items to a neophyte team member to impress him. Suspect told CID that the ear had been already disconnected when he picked it up. Classified "insufficient evidence." | 1st Cavalry Division | 1970 | Phuoc Long |

CASES CLOSED BY ARMY INVESTIGATORS, CONTINUED

| CASE # | ALLEGATIONS | DIVISION/ BRIGADE | YEAR | PROVINCE |
|---|---|---|---|---|
| 153 | Three GIs tied a slain Vietcong soldier to the fender of an army truck. CID confirmed the incident and a reprimand was issued, yet the case was classified as "unsubstantiated." | 101st Airborne Division | 1970 | Thua Thien |
| 161 | Sergeant accused Gen. Creighton W. Abrams Jr. of being present in a village near Saigon when interrogators subjected detainees to water torture and beatings. Secretary of Army Stanley Resor concluded there was no evidence that Abrams was aware of any maltreatment when he visited the troops. The report does not say whether the maltreatment occurred. Classified "unsubstantiated." | 23rd Infantry Division | 1968 | Binh Duong |
| 164 | Three hundred Vietnamese were massacred during the army's "Operation Russell Beach" and marines' "Operation Bold Mariner." The army turned the investigation over to the marines, who classified the allegations as "unfounded." | 26th Marine Regiment | 1969 | Quang Ngai |
| 165 | Winter Soldier Investigation: Former medic testified that he and Special Forces members tortured a Vietcong suspect with a cigarette and suspended a naked detainee from a tree. Later, he told *Life* magazine that he helped treat forty-three civilians wounded by indiscriminate firing into a village. CID closed the case after an interview with the former medic and an unsuccessful attempt to find other suspects. Classified "unsubstantiated." | 1st Cavalry Division; Special Forces | 1966– 1967 | Binh Dinh/ Pleiku |
| 166 | Winter Soldier Investigation: Soldiers fired mortar rounds at civilians scavenging in a garbage dump, resulting in civilian deaths. CID reported the complainant had no firsthand information. Case closed, classified "insufficient evidence." | 1st Cavalry Division | 1969 | Tay Ninh |

| | Description | Unit | Years | Location |
|---|---|---|---|---|
| 167 | Winter Soldier Investigation: GIs killed five or six unarmed POWs, committed rapes on ten to fifteen occasions, and allowed a scout dog to attack a helpless family. CID could not locate complainant. Classified "insufficient evidence." | 198th Infantry Brigade/23rd Infantry Division | 1967–1968 | N/A |
| 168 | Winter Soldier Investigation: Sergeant said he killed a civilian on a commander's orders. Members of his unit raped three females, routinely used tear gas on civilians, frequently mutilated bodies, and destroyed all homes encountered during field operations. Another member of the unit said the complainant had killed a civilian but not on a commander's order. Other members denied the allegations. Classified "insufficient evidence." | 1st Cavalry Division | 1969–1970 | Thua Thien |
| 169 | Winter Soldier Investigation: Low-flying U.S. aircraft deliberately shot a civilian; speeding vehicles ran over civilians; two GIs broke a 12-year-old boy's arm during a vicious beating; soldiers removed skulls from graves for use as candle holders on several occasions; they destroyed crops and villages. CID said the complainant declined to cooperate. Classified "insufficient evidence." | 11th Armored Cavalry | 1969–1970 | Binh Long |
| 170 | Winter Soldier Investigation: A detainee was thrown from a helicopter, civilians were shot, villages and rice supplies were burned. CID said the complainant declined to cooperate. Classified "insufficient evidence." | 198th Infantry Brigade/23rd Infantry Division | 1967–1968 | N/A |
| 171 | Winter Soldier Investigation: Helicopters "played games" by blowing down huts and civilians, once killing a small boy. POWs were beaten. The complainant gave hydraulic fluid to children to drink. CID could not locate him after the forum. Classified "insufficient evidence." | 1st Cavalry Division | 1967–1968 | Binh Dinh |

CASES CLOSED BY ARMY INVESTIGATORS, CONTINUED

| CASE # | ALLEGATIONS | DIVISION/ BRIGADE | YEAR | PROVINCE |
|---|---|---|---|---|
| 172 | Winter Soldier Investigation: Young girl was brutalized for resisting sex with ten GIs. An elderly man was beaten. CID said the complainant declined to cooperate. Classified "insufficient evidence." | 1st Logistical Command | 1968– 1969 | N/A |
| 173 | Winter Soldier Investigation: Unit massacred civilians after high U.S. casualties and shot another civilian as villagers buried the dead. GIs shot two young children; POWs under the control of U.S. soldiers were dropped from helicopters on two occasions; right ears were cut off corpses for verifying body counts; indiscriminate firing into villages wounded women and children. CID said the complainant declined to cooperate. Classified "insufficient evidence." | 101st Airborne Division | 1965– 1967 | Phu Yen |
| 174 | Winter Soldier Investigation: Commanding officer ordered his unit to kill all wounded enemy; North Vietnamese army soldiers were pushed from helicopters. CID said the complainant declined to cooperate. Classified "insufficient evidence." | 1st Cavalry Division | 1968– 1969 | Tay Ninh |
| 175 | Winter Soldier Investigation: Commanding officer ordered strafing of livestock. The pilot refused. CID closed the case after the complainant provided a sworn statement. Classified "unsubstantiated." | 5th Special Forces Group | 1969 | Kontum |
| 176 | Winter Soldier Investigation: Squadron's standard operating procedure was to fire rockets, miniguns, and grenade cannons at every hooch, stack of crops, and Vietnamese who ran away. Women and children were included in the body count. A major dropped the bodies of his unit's enemy kills at the brigade tactical operations center to prove his body count. CID could not locate complainant. Classified "insufficient evidence." | 1st Cavalry Division | 1968– 1969 | Long An |

| | | | | |
|---|---|---|---|---|
| 177 | Winter Soldier Investigation: Civilian bled to death after being hit by truck; a girl was crippled by a random shot fired. CID reported that complainant later said the incidents were accidents. Classified "insufficient evidence." | 45th Engineer Group | 1967–1968 | Saigon |
| 178 | Winter Soldier Investigation: POWs were routinely abused with electric shock, by prodding their open wounds and by scaring them with scout dogs. CID said the complainant declined to cooperate. Classified "insufficient evidence." | 23rd Infantry Division | 1968–1969 | Quang Ngai |
| 179 | Winter Soldier Investigation: Child was killed for refusing to leave a garbage dump; livestock and crops were needlessly destroyed; a village was burned. CID said the complainant declined to cooperate. Classified "insufficient evidence." | 9th Infantry Division | 1967–1968 | Long An |
| 180 | Winter Soldier Investigation: POW nearly drowned during an interrogation; a water buffalo was shot and villages were burned for no reason. CID said the complainant declined to cooperate. Classified "insufficient evidence." | 9th Infantry Division | 1968–1969 | Long An |
| 181 | Winter Soldier Investigation: Villagers were gassed, and their homes and farms senselessly destroyed; fishing boats were targeted for sport. CID said the complainant declined to cooperate. Classified "insufficient evidence." | 23rd Infantry Division | 1969–1970 | Quang Ngai |
| 182 | Winter Soldier Investigation: Door gunner shot a civilian in a sampan after dark; complainant's unit used excessive firepower, causing civilian and American deaths; a POW was severely beaten. CID said the complainant declined to cooperate. Classified "insufficient evidence." | 1st Cavalry Division | 1968–1969 | Saigon |

CASES CLOSED BY ARMY INVESTIGATORS, CONTINUED

| CASE # | ALLEGATIONS | DIVISION/ BRIGADE | YEAR | PROVINCE |
|---|---|---|---|---|
| 183 | Winter Soldier Investigation: Indiscriminate firing on a village killed seven civilians and wounded sixteen; a mortar unit fired illuminating rounds into another village just to watch people flee. CID said the complainant declined to cooperate. Classified "insufficient evidence." | 25th Infantry Division or 9th Infantry Division | 1966–1967 | Binh Duong |
| 184 | Winter Soldier Investigation: Elderly woman and two children were killed when a grenade was thrown into a bunker. CID interviewed the complainant and closed the case. Classified "insufficient evidence." | 198th Infantry Brigade/23rd Infantry Division | 1967–1968 | Quang Tin |
| 185 | Winter Soldier Investigation: Shells were fired into villages at night without determining if civilians were in the target area. CID interviewed the complainant and closed the case. Classified "insufficient evidence." | 1st Infantry Division | 1967–1969 | N/A |
| 186 | Winter Soldier Investigation: A helicopter crew tossed stones at sampans, sinking a boat and killing or wounding a fisherman. A captain ordered a helicopter gunner to kill several animals. CID said the complainant declined to cooperate. Classified "insufficient evidence." | 155th Assault Helicopter Company | 1968–1969 | Phu Yen |
| 187 | Winter Soldier Investigation: A platoon called in five hours of artillery and air strikes after being ambushed in a village, destroying the town. CID could not locate the complainant. Classified "insufficient evidence." | 101st Airborne Division | 1968 | Phuoc Long |

| | Description | Unit | Year | Location |
|---|---|---|---|---|
| 188 | Winter Soldier Investigation: CIA and Military Assistance Command, Vietnam agents killed a man believed to be a Laotian prince and then threatened to file desertion charges against complainant's team if they revealed the incident. A POW was thrown out of a helicopter. A village was leveled by gunships and declared "pacified." CID could not locate complainant. Classified "insufficient evidence." | 5th Special Forces Group | 1968–1969 | Quang Nam/Laos/Cambodia |
| 189 | Winter Soldier Investigation: While serving at the brigade tactical operations center, the complainant reported that three women and one infant had been killed by a gunship, but an officer refused to accept the report until the incident was deleted. CID said the complainant declined to cooperate. Classified "insufficient evidence." | 4th Infantry Division | 1970 | Pleiku |
| 190 | Winter Soldier Investigation: GIs turned in severed ears to accumulate "Sat Cong" (kill Cong) badges from the commanding officer for R&R leaves. The complainant gave CID copies of the orders authorizing the badges. A major and a captain confirmed the badge program but denied proof of kill was required. Classified "unsubstantiated." | 9th Infantry Division | 1969 | N/A |
| 191 | Winter Soldier Investigation: Fragmentation grenade was placed under a wounded combatant; villages were routinely destroyed. CID said the complainant declined to cooperate. Classified "insufficient evidence." | 101st Airborne Division and Marines | 1969 | Quang Tin |
| 192 | Winter Soldier Investigation: Village was forcibly evacuated and destroyed, livestock were slain, and rice was dumped into wells. CID said the complainant declined to cooperate. Classified "insufficient evidence." | 25th Infantry Division | 1967 | Binh Duong |

CASES CLOSED BY ARMY INVESTIGATORS, CONTINUED

| CASE # | ALLEGATIONS | DIVISION/BRIGADE | YEAR | PROVINCE |
|---|---|---|---|---|
| 193 | Winter Soldier Investigation: Three POWs were pushed from a helicopter; C-ration cans were thrown to children from moving vehicles, resulting in some being run over. CID said the complainant declined to cooperate. Classified "insufficient evidence." | 79th Engineer Group/34th Engineer Group | 1966–1967 | N/A |
| 194 | Winter Soldier Investigation: Detainee was tortured with a field phone; children were gassed at a garbage dump. Complainant provided a sworn statement to CID. CID interviewed a second member of the unit who denied knowledge of the incidents. Classified "insufficient evidence." | 101st Airborne Division | 1969 | Thua Thien |
| 195 | Winter Soldier Investigation: Interrogator forced his M-16 rifle suppressor up the nose of a POW; dead enemy were mounted on vehicles; villages were destroyed. Complainant showed slides that substantiated most of his testimony. CID said the complainant declined to cooperate. Classified "insufficient evidence." | 9th Infantry Division | 1967–1968 | N/A |
| 196 | Winter Soldier Investigation: POWs were beaten by South Vietnamese soldiers and locked in barbed-wire cages in the presence of U.S. advisers. CID closed the case after interviewing the complainant. Classified "unsubstantiated." | 5th Special Forces Group | 1963 | Long An |
| 197 | Winter Soldier Investigation: A base camp was built on top of a Vietnamese cemetery; U.S. troops staged "mad minutes" in which everyone would gather at the perimeter fence and fire their weapons indiscriminately. CID found that the graves were relocated before construction began. Classified "insufficient evidence." | 101st Airborne Division | 1968–1969 | Phuoc Long |

| # | Investigation | Unit | Years | Location |
|---|---|---|---|---|
| 198 | Winter Soldier Investigation: Artillery unit shot forty-six rounds at an area known to contain a leper hospital, killing civilians. Two or three children were injured when struck by C-ration cans thrown hard from a moving convoy. The complainant told CID that members of convoy were reprimanded by military police and that the hit on the hospital was not intentional. Case closed, classified "unsubstantiated." | 1st Infantry Division | N/A | Binh Duong |
| 199 | Winter Soldier Investigation: Troops executed a POW; opened a grave to partially expose a corpse and reported it as a new kill for the body count. CID closed the case after interviewing the complainant. Classified "insufficient evidence." | 25th Infantry Division | 1966–1967 | N/A |
| 200 | Winter Soldier Investigation: Lieutenant executed an unarmed civilian. The complainant was ordered to stop providing medical treatment to wounded civilians. CID said the complainant declined to cooperate. Classified "insufficient evidence." | 25th Infantry Division | 1968 | N/A |
| 201 | Winter Soldier Investigation: Ten unarmed civilians were killed by field operations over six weeks while tending gardens. CID said the complainant declined to cooperate. Classified "insufficient evidence." | 173rd Airborne Brigade | 1969–1970 | Binh Dinh |
| 202 | Winter Soldier Investigation: U.S. dropped 6,500 pounds of bombs in Saigon area when 600 Vietcong were believed to be in the area, reportedly killing 1,300 to 1,400 people. Case closed after CID interviewed complainant. Classified "unsubstantiated." | 524th Military Intelligence Detachment | 1968 | Saigon |

CASES CLOSED BY ARMY INVESTIGATORS, CONTINUED

| CASE # | ALLEGATIONS | DIVISION/ BRIGADE | YEAR | PROVINCE |
|---|---|---|---|---|
| 203 | Winter Soldier Investigation: Commanding officer sent men out to draw ambushes whenever the body count was low, resulting in higher U.S. casualties and civilian deaths. Track vehicles, firing indiscriminately, killed two children and an old man in a house. Complainant accidentally struck a motorcycle, but the military police refused to help the unconscious driver. The bodies of two Vietcong were dragged behind vehicles; later, their ears were cut off and gold was removed from their teeth. CID said the complainant declined to cooperate. Classified "insufficient evidence." | 25th Infantry Division | 1968 | Bin Duong |
| 204 | Winter Soldier Investigation: Vietnamese interrogator killed a POW without cause in the presence of U.S. troops; artillery fired into civilian homes, killing a woman and wounding her baby; a village was needlessly evacuated, pillaged, and destroyed. CID said the complainant declined to cooperate. Classified "insufficient evidence." | 9th Infantry Division | 1968– 1969 | Kien Hoa |
| 205 | Winter Soldier Investigation: Wounded POW's throat was slit; others were subjected to beatings and water torture by U.S. officers and South Vietnamese Tiger Scouts. CID said the complainant declined to cooperate. Classified "insufficient evidence." | 9th Infantry Division | N/A | Kien Hoa |
| 206 | Winter Soldier Investigation: Soldiers shot at civilians in the presence of their commanding officer. (No civilians were hit.) Tear gas was routinely used on civilians scavenging in dumps. Graves were desecrated. CID closed the case after interviewing the complainant and failing to get corroboration from other members of his unit. Classified "unfounded." | 101st Airborne Division | 1968– 1969 | Thua Thien |

| | | | | |
|---|---|---|---|---|
| 207 | Soldier reported that he heard that combatant bodies were mutilated. Case closed after CID interviewed complainant and other members of unit did not corroborate. Classified "unfounded." | 101st Airborne Division | 1971 | Quang Tri |
| 208 | U.S. Customs found a skull in a captain's luggage. An inquiry found no evidence that the captain had severed the head from a body. Classified "unfounded." | 23rd Infantry Division | 1971 | Quang Tri |
| 211 | U.S. Customs in Seattle intercepted a skull that a GI shipped to relatives. He did not respond to a letter seeking information about the skull. Classified "unsubstantiated." | 1st Cavalry Division | 1971 | N/A |
| 212 | Americal Daily News Sheet reported that two Vietcong hospitals had been destroyed. Investigation confirmed the presence of operating tables and medical supplies at the site, but concluded the structures were part of an enemy base camp, not fixed medical buildings. Classified "unsubstantiated." | 11th Infantry Brigade | 1971 | N/A |
| 213 | Soldier at his discharge hearing said he witnessed U.S. troops fire and injure children trying to steal gas from a pipeline, and that he saw detainees beaten. When questioned by CID, he said he would prefer to drop the matter. The case was closed after an unsuccessful effort to get more information. Classified "unfounded." | N/A | 1968–1969 | Khanh Hoa |

Cases Closed by Army Investigators, continued

| CASE # | ALLEGATIONS | DIVISION/ BRIGADE | YEAR | PROVINCE |
|---|---|---|---|---|
| 214 | U.S. Rangers killed two woodcutters and then took their chainsaw and bicycle. The killings took place in a newly designated "strike zone." An investigation found that the hamlet chief had learned the area was off limits only a day earlier, so he did not have time to warn residents. The shooters claimed the victims had AK-47s. The investigator said the evidence indicated the victims were merely woodcutters and noted that some of the Ranger team members carried AK-47s. The case was closed and classified "unfounded." | 1st Cavalry Division | 1972 | Bien Hoa |
| 215 | Lieutenant colonel received a bronze star for valor after taking credit for kills by his subordinates. CID interviewed a witness who said the officer landed his helicopter at an ambush site and shot two enemy who were motionless and appeared to be dead. The officer denied the allegation and then declined to answer questions. The report said the evidence "tends to substantiate the allegation that LTC . . . did shoot two dead enemy soldiers, but it is questionable whether he knew they were dead." The case was closed and classified "insufficient evidence." | 101st Airborne Division | 1971 | N/A |
| 216 | U.S. Customs in Seattle intercepted a skull sent from a GI in Vietnam to a soldier in the United States. Attempts to reach the two men by mail were unsuccessful. Classified "unsubstantiated." | 101st Airborne Division | 1971 | N/A |
| 217 | Customs inspectors in Da Nang confiscated two skulls from two soldiers trying to ship them home. Classified "unsubstantiated." | N/A | 1971 | Quan Tin |
| 218 | U.S. Customs in Tacoma, Washington, intercepted a human arm bone in a soldier's possessions. Classified "unsubstantiated." | 44th Artillery | 1971 | N/A |

| | Description | Unit | Year | Location |
| --- | --- | --- | --- | --- |
| 220 | OZ magazine (London) published a deserter's story of war crimes in Vietnam, including POWs being pushed from helicopters. When CID contacted the complainant, he retracted his allegations. Classified "unsubstantiated." | N/A | N/A | Long Binh |
| 222 | U.S. Customs in Oakland, California, confiscated a severed ear and photos of corpses that a U.S. Ranger shipped to his home. The suspect said an unidentified member of his unit gave him the ear to commemorate his first enemy kill. Classified "insufficient evidence" of a crime. | 1st Cavalry Division | 1971 | N/A |
| 223 | Vietcong suspect was killed by a booby trap while walking point with a U.S. reconnaissance patrol. An investigation confirmed the incident but found the patrol had not acted improperly. Classified "unsubstantiated." | 173rd Airborne Brigade | 1970 | N/A |
| 224 | Helicopter crew on a reconnaissance patrol in U Minh Forest spotted three males running into a hut, fired on the house, and fatally shot two youths, 11 and 14, as they fled the flames. Their father and two other family members were injured. An investigation confirmed the deaths and injuries but noted they occurred in free-fire zone. The commanding officer was admonished for failing to ensure the team followed rules of engagement. Classified "insufficient evidence." | 16th Cavalry Regiment | 1971 | Minh Hai |
| 225 | Interrogators told a wounded POW that he'd be thrown from a helicopter if he didn't cooperate. Classified "unsubstantiated." | 519th Military Intelligence Battalion | 1971 | Long Binh |
| 227 | U.S. Customs in Fort Lewis, Washington, confiscated an ear given to a soldier as a "parting gift" by his unit. Classified "insufficient evidence." | 173rd Airborne Brigade | 1970 | N/A |

CASES CLOSED BY ARMY INVESTIGATORS, CONTINUED

| CASE # | ALLEGATIONS | DIVISION/ BRIGADE | YEAR | PROVINCE |
|---|---|---|---|---|
| 228 | U.S. Customs in Fort Lewis, Washington, confiscated a skull, jawbone, and leg bone. The soldier told CID he found them laying on the ground and sent them home as souvenirs. Offense of mutilation was classified as "unfounded"; offense of grave desecration was classified "insufficient evidence." | 173rd Airborne Brigade | 1971 | Binh Dinh |
| 229 | Customs inspection in Tacoma, Washington, found a human ear in the possession of a sergeant. The suspect told CID that an unidentified member of 75th Rangers gave him the ear as a going-away gift. CID could not determine the identity of the Ranger after interviewing seventy-seven former members of unit. Classified "unsubstantiated." | 173rd Airborne Brigade | 1971 | Binh Dinh |
| 230 | U.S. Customs in Seattle intercepted a skull sent from Vietnam to a woman in Florida. CID interviewed the sender, who said he found the skull in a barracks locker. Classified "unfounded." | 173rd Airborne Brigade | 1971 | Binh Dinh |
| 231 | Vietcong nurse killed after a razor blade she inserted into her vagina injured a platoon leader during an attempted rape. CID investigation found no firsthand evidence the hearsay report was true. Classified "unsubstantiated." | 5th Infantry Division | 1968 | N/A |
| 233 | Human skull was removed from a GI's luggage as he boarded a plane at Da Nang. Classified "unsubstantiated." | 3rd Brigade, 82nd Airborne Division | 1972 | Da Nang |
| 234 | A man and woman collecting firewood in an off-limits zone were killed by U.S. troops. An investigation confirmed their deaths but found they were killed when they hit a trip wire that detonated claymore mines. Classified "unfounded." | 1st Cavalry Division | 1972 | Bien Hoa |

| # | Description | 173rd Airborne Brigade | N/A | Binh Dinh |
|---|---|---|---|---|
| 236 | **Soldier on patrol shot an unarmed farmer. The suspect said he shot the farmer when he did not halt and subsequently found Vietcong papers on him. Classified "unfounded."** | 173rd Airborne Brigade | N/A | Binh Dinh |
| 237 | Battalion commanding officer instructed a helicopter pilot to kill a man working in a rice paddy and ordered the destruction of a village and all occupants. An investigation uncovered a second allegation that the commanding officer ordered the execution of another farmer. Case "in progress" as of June 1973. | 25th Infantry Division | 1969 | N/A |
| 238 | Skull confiscated from a soldier's room during the routine health inspection of troops' billets. The suspect told an investigator that another soldier had desecrated a grave to obtain it. He added that a helicopter on an assault mission opened fire on twelve to fifteen civilians. The commanding officer told the investigator it was a South Vietnamese army mission. "Investigation in progress" as of June 1973. | 1st Cavalry Division | 1969 | Quang Tin |
| 240 | Anti-war activist reported that he had seen a photo of a mutilated body of a girl. Classified "insufficient evidence." | U.S. Army Special Forces | N/A | N/A |
| 241 | While flying overhead, a lieutenant saw the bodies of women and children near the Tiger Force reconnaissance platoon's temporary base camp. The suspects confirmed the presence of the bodies but denied being responsible and told CID that the lieutenant had a reputation for exaggerating. The case was closed and classified "insufficient evidence." The Toledo Blade in 2003 reported on secret CID investigation files revealing multiple war crimes committed by members of Tiger Force. | 101st Airborne Division | 1967 | N/A |

CASES CLOSED BY ARMY INVESTIGATORS, CONTINUED

| CASE # | ALLEGATIONS | DIVISION/ BRIGADE | YEAR | PROVINCE |
|---|---|---|---|---|
| 242 | Captain ordered his men to shoot enemy bodies to make sure they were dead. He denied the allegation and disparaged the complainant. Other members also denied the allegation. CID said the complainant expressed regret that the army had conducted an official investigation. Classified "unfounded." | 25th Infantry Division | 1966 | N/A |
| 243 | Helicopter gunship killed a male civilian and three children. Investigators confirmed the deaths and located a 12-year-old witness who said the shooters wore camouflage uniforms. U.S. Rangers were in the vicinity but reported no engagement. Classified "unsubstantiated." | 1st Cavalry Division | 1972 | Binh Duong |
| 244 | N/A | N/A | N/A | N/A |
| 245 | Two soldiers attempted forcible sodomy and indecent assault on a woman. Classified "unfounded." | 4th Infantry Division | 1968 | Quang Nam |
| 246 | N/A | N/A | N/A | N/A |

# APPENDIX B:
## ARMY RESPONSE TO A WHITE HOUSE REQUEST FOR A LIST OF U.S. WAR-CRIME ALLEGATIONS OTHER THAN THE MY LAI MASSACRE

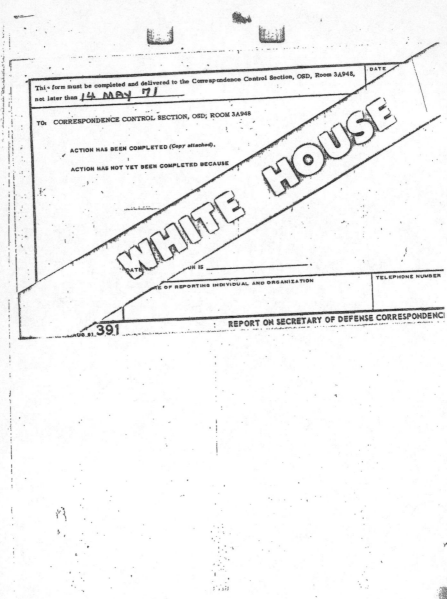

This form must be completed and delivered to the Correspondence Control Section, OSD, Room 3A948, not later than **14 MAY 71**

DATE

TO:   CORRESPONDENCE CONTROL SECTION, OSD; ROOM 3A948

ACTION HAS BEEN COMPLETED *(Copy attached).*

ACTION HAS NOT YET BEEN COMPLETED BECAUSE

WHITE HOUSE

DATE _____ UN IS _____

...E OF REPORTING INDIVIDUAL AND ORGANIZATION          TELEPHONE NUMBER

REPORT ON SECRETARY OF DEFENSE CORRESPONDENC...

AUG 61 **391**

THE WHITE HOUSE

WASHINGTON

May 10, 1971

MEMORANDUM FOR:            THE JUDGE ADVOCATE GENERAL

FROM:                      JOHN W. DEAN, III
                           COUNSEL TO THE PRESIDENT

In your letter of May 5, 1971, you attached an information sheet
entitled "Allegations of War Crimes Other than Son My." I would
like to request additional information elaborating upon the
statistics cited in that information sheet, including:

    1. An individual case breakdown of those convicted by
Court Martial; a description of charges brought against these
individuals and charges for which defendants were convicted;
an individual breakdown as to sentences imposed by the military
court and time actually served in prison.

    2. A listing and description of the cases in which
commissioned officers were acquitted.

    3. A status report on the investigations now in progress
relating to alleged war crimes.

I would like this information as soon as possible.

Thank you.

THRU BRIGADIER GENERAL JAMES D. HUGHES

WH  9207

**DEPARTMENT OF THE ARMY**
OFFICE OF THE JUDGE ADVOCATE GENERAL
WASHINGTON, D.C. 20310

JAGW 1971/1096                                                    21 May 1971

Mr. John W. Dean, III
Office of Legal Counsel
The White House
Washington, D.C.   20500

Dear Mr. Dean:

This is in further response to your memorandum of 10 May 1971 in which
you requested additional information concerning allegations of war
crimes other than Son My.

The Army maintains records relating to such allegations both as to the
number of cases involved and the number of identified individuals
involved.  A case, in this context, may be the file relating to a particular incident or the file relating to allegations made by a particular
person or persons.  A case may involve personnel whose identity has not
been established.  Data concerning individuals, however, pertain solely
to persons who have been specifically identified.

At Inclosure 1 is an analysis of the cases monitored by my office reflecting the number involving unidentified personnel and those involving
identified individuals.  It also reflects the number of cases as to which
final action has and has not been taken.

At Inclosure 2 is a set of figures reflecting the status of individuals.
As you expressed a particular interest in officers, a separate figure
for such personnel has been included.

At Inclosure 3 is a summary of the trials by court-martial in which
officers were acquitted.

At Inclosure 4 is a summary of cases in which individuals were convicted
by court-martial.  You should be aware that many records of trial are not
forwarded to my office for custody.  Accordingly, within the time frame
available, it was necessary to rely upon narrative or telegraphic reports.
In each case, the best available information was used.

At Inclosure 5 is a report of the current status of cases under investigation.  You will note that Inclosure 1 reflects four more cases as to
which final action has not been taken than the number reported as under
investigation.  Three cases are pending action at Headquarters, United
States Army, Vietnam and one has been referred to trial by court-martial.

21 May 1971

JAGW 1971/1096
Mr. John W. Dean, III

With respect to the time served in confinement, the figures submitted should be accurate with a range of plus or minus fifteen days. This should, I believe, be sufficiently precise for comparative purposes.

I trust this information is fully responsive to your inquiry.

Sincerely yours,

5 Incl                                KENNETH J. HODSON
As stated                             Major General, USA
                                      The Judge Advocate General

2

CASES MONITORED BY THE OFFICE OF THE JUDGE ADVOCATE GENERAL
RELATING TO WAR CRIMES ALLEGATIONS OTHER THAN SON MY
(As of 20 May 1971)

|  |  |  |  |
|---|---|---|---|
| Initially Opened |  | 148 |  |
| Transferred to Son My<br>Investigation | 2 |  |  |
| Transferred to United<br>States Marine Corps | 1 | -3 |  |
| Total |  | 145 |  |
|  |  |  |  |
| Cases Involving Unidentified Personnel |  |  | 42 |
| Final Disposition Made |  | 31 |  |
| Final Disposition Not Made |  | 11 |  |
| Total |  | 42 |  |
|  |  |  |  |
| Cases Involving Identified Individuals |  |  | 103 |
| Final Disposition Made |  | 80 |  |
| Final Disposition Not Made |  | 23 |  |
| Total |  | 103 |  |
|  | TOTAL |  | 145 |

FOR OFFICIAL USE ONLY

STATUS OF INDIVIDUAL

| | Total | Officers |
|---|---|---|
| Investigation in Progress | 31 | 13 |
| USARV Action Pending | 8 | 3 |
| Unsubstantiated/Unfounded | 44 | 17 |
| Charges Dismissed After Article 32 Investigation | 15 | 9 |
| Referred for Trial | 8 | 0 |
| Convicted by Court-Martial | 29 | 4 |
| Punished Under Article 15 | 16 | 2 |
| Adverse Administrative Action | 8 | 6 |
| Acquittal or Dismissed After Arraignment | 31 | 7 |
| Killed in Action or Died Before Final Disposition | 3 | 1 |
| Found to be Insane | 2 | 1 |
| Granted Immunity to Testify in Case of Another Accused | 3 | 0 |
| Not Tried for Various Grounds | 15 | 3 |
| | 213 | 66 |

FOR OFFICIAL USE ONLY

CASES INVOLVING OFFICERS ACCUSED WHO WERE ACQUITTED

### Case No. 1

Accused        1LT ██████████████

Charge         UCMJ, Article 118, Premeditated Murder.

Allegation     Murder of an oriental male human being whose name is unknown
               by shooting him with a rifle.

Type of Court  General Court-Martial.

### Case No. 28

Accused        1LT ██████████████

Charge         UCMJ, Article 80, Attempted Murder.

Allegation     Attempted murder of an unidentified Vietnamese child approximately
               four years of age by shooting him with a rifle.

Type of Court  General Court-Martial.

### Case No. 112

Accused        CPT ██████████████

Charge         UCMJ, Article 118, Unpremeditated Murder.

Allegation     Murder, jointly with 1LT ████████ and three enlisted men, of a
               male Vietnamese by shooting him with a rifle and a pistol.

Type of Court  General Court-Martial.

### Case No. 112

Accused        1LT ██████████████

Charges        UCMJ, Article 118, Unpremeditated Murder.
               UCMJ, Article 133, Conduct Unbecoming an Officer.

Allegations    (1) Murder, jointly with CPT ████ and three enlisted men, of a
               male Vietnamese by shooting him with a rifle and a pistol.
               (2) Failure to control troops under his command by permitting
               them to murder the same male Vietnamese who had been detained
               on the field of battle.

Type of Court  General Court-Martial.

Incl 3

Case No. 140

Accused          2LT ████████████████

Charge           UCMJ, Article 134, Assault with Intent to Commit Rape
                                      Lewd Acts

Allegations      (1) Assault with intent to commit rape on a Vietnamese girl.
                 (2) Commission of a lewd act on the body of a Vietnamese girl,
                     under 16 years of age.

Type of Court    General Court-Martial.


Case No. 142

Accused          CPT ████████████████

Charge           UCMJ, Article 118, Premeditation.

Allegations      (1) Murder an unknown Vietnamese prisoner by shooting him with
                     a rifle.
                 (2) Murder an unknown Vietnamese prisoner by shooting him with
                     a rifle.

Type of Court    General Court-Martial.


Case No. 157

Accused          2LT ████████████████

Charges          Not specifically known.  Probably UCMJ, Article 134.

Allegations      (1) Compelling Vietnamese to walk at the point position on patrols.
                 (2) Maltreatment of a Vietnamese by attaching an electric device
                     to his person during an interrogation.

Type of Court    Special Court-Martial.

Incl

## INDIVIDUALS CONVICTED BY COURT-MARTIAL

#### Case No. 2

Accused:  ILT ████████████

Charges:  UCMJ, Art 81  - Conspiracy
          UCMJ, Art 118 - Premeditated Murder
          UCMJ, Art 107 - False Official Statements
          UCMJ, Art 133 - Conduct Unbecoming an Officer

Findings of Guilty:  UCMJ, Art 81  - Conspiracy
                     UCMJ, Art 119 - Voluntary Manslaughter
                     UCMJ, Art 133 - Conduct Unbecoming an Officer

Summary:  The accused was alleged to have conspired in and taken part in the
          killing of a Vietnamese, believed to be an ARVN soldier absent
          without leave.

Sentence: To be confined for 6 months and to forfeit $250.00 per month for
          6 months.

Period Served:  Not specifically known.  Probably 5 months, i.e., sentence
                adjudged less time off for good behavior.

Type of Court:  General Court-Martial

Remarks:  None


#### Case No. 3

Accused:  PFC ████████████

Charges:  UCMJ, Art 118 - Premeditated Murder

Findings of Guilty:  UCMJ, Art 118 - Unpremeditated Murder
                     UCMJ, Art 128 - Assault with a Dangerous Weapon

Summary:  From a base camp guard tower, the accused fired a rifle at two
          Vietnamese boys, age 13 and 14, as they passed by on a motor bike.
          One victim died, and the other was wounded.

Sentence: To be dishonorably discharged from the service, to forfeit all pay
          and allowances, to be reduced to the lowest enlisted grade, and
          to be confined at hard labor for 7 years.

Period Served:  Still in confinement.

Type of Court:  General Court-Martial.

Remarks:  None

Case No. 39

Accused:  SSG ████████████

Charge:  UCMJ, Art 118 - Unpremeditated Murder

Findings of Guilty:  As charged

Summary:  More than four years prior to trial, the accused was alleged to
          have murdered a Vietnamese boy.  The boy was in a boat fishing
          when he was seen by the accused's unit, which was enroute to a
          field position.  The boy was shot when he did not return to
          shore as ordered.

Sentence:  No punishment

Period Served:  None adjudged

Type of Court:  General Court-Martial.

Remarks:  Appellate review not complete.


Case No. 49

Accused:  1LT ████████████

Charge:  UCMJ, Art 92 - Violation of a Lawful Order.

Findings of Guilty:  As charged

Summary:  The subject scalped and cut off the fingers and ears of two
          dead enemy soldiers.

Sentence:  To forfeit $50.00 per month for 2 months.

Period Served:  No confinement adjudged.

Type of Court:  Special Court-Martial.

Remarks:  Involved in the same incident as PFC ████████████

2

FOR OFFICIAL USE ONLY                                    Incl

Case No. 49

Accused:  PFC ████████████

Charge:  UCMJ, Art 92 - Violation of a Lawful Order

Findings of Guilty:  As charged

Summary:  The subject scalped and cut off the fingers and ears of two
          dead enemy soldiers.

Sentence:  To forfeit $50.00 per month for two months.

Period Served:  No confinement adjudged.

Type of Court: Special Court-Martial.

Remarks:  Involved in the same incident as 1LT ████████████


Case No. 112

Accused:  SSG ████████████

Charge:  UCMJ, Art 118 - Unpremeditated Murder

Findings of Guilty:  As charged

Summary:  Jointly with CPT ███ 1LT ████████ and two other enlisted men, subject
          murdered a Vietnamese male detained during operations.

Sentence:  (As fully affirmed after appellate review.)  To forfeit all
           pay and allowances and to be confined at hard labor for 2
           years.

Period Served:  Approximately 19 months.

Type of Court:  General Court-Martial.

Remarks:  Co-accused with CPT ████ 1LT ████████ SP5 ████████████ and
          PFC ████████████

3

FOR OFFICIAL USE ONLY

FOR OFFICIAL USE ONLY

Case No. 112

Accused:  SP5 ███████████

Charge:  UCMJ, Art 118, Unpremeditated Murder

Findings of Guilty:  As charged

Summary:  Jointly with CPT ████ 1LT ████████ and two other enlisted men, subject murdered a Vietnamese male detained during operations.

Sentence:  (As finally affirmed after appellate review.)  To be discharged from the service with a bad conduct discharge, to forfeit all pay and allowances, to be reduced to the lowest enlisted grade, and to be confined at hard labor for 2 years.

Period Served:  Approximately 14 months.

Type of Court:  General Court-Martial.

Remarks:  (1) Under post-review clemency, the Bad Conduct Discharge was suspended.

　　　　　(2) Co-accused with CPT ████ 1LT ██████ SSG ████████ and PFC ██████


Case No. 112

Accused:  PFC ██████████████

Charge:  UCMJ, Art 118 - Unpremeditated Murder

Findings of Guilty:  UCMJ, Art 119 - Voluntary Manslaughter

Summary:  Jointly with CPT████ 1LT ████████ and two other enlisted men, subject killed a Vietnamese male detained during operations.

Sentence:  To be reduced to the lowest enlisted grade, to forfeit all pay and allowances and to be confined at hard labor for 6 months.

Period Served:  6 months and 9 days.

Type of Court:  General Court-Martial.

Remarks:  Co-accused with CPT ████ 1LT ████████, SSG ████████ and SP5 ██████

4

FOR OFFICIAL USE ONLY

FOR OFFICIAL USE ONLY      Incl

Case No. 113

Accused: SSG ██████████

Charge: UCMJ, Art 134 - Conduct to the Prejudice of Good Order and Discipline

Findings of Guilty: As charged

Summary: The accused decapitated two enemy bodies.

Sentence: To be reduced to the grade of Corporal (E-4).

Period Served: No confinement adjudged.

Type of Court: General Court-Martial

Remarks: None


Case No. 116

Accused: SP5 ██████████████

Charges: UCMJ, Art 120 - Rape
UCMJ, Art 128 - Assault

Findings of Guilty: (As finally affirmed after appellate review.)
UCMJ, Art 134 - Indecent Acts with a Child
UCMJ, Art 118 - Assault

Summary: The accused, an intelligence interrogator, molested an 11-year-old Vietnamese detainee.

Sentence: (As finally approved after appellate review.) Partial forfeiture of pay and allowances and to be confined at hard labor for 1 year.

Period Served: 7 months, 16 days.

Type of Court: General Court-Martial.

Remarks: None

5

Case No. 119

Accused:  SP5 ████████████████████

Charge:  UCMJ, Art 134 - Conduct to the Prejudice of Good order and
         Discipline.

Findings of Guilty:  As charged.

Summary:  The accused cut off the ear of a dead enemy.

Sentence:  To be reduced to the grade of Specialist E-4 and to forfeit
           $110.00 per month for 4 months.

Period Served:  No confinement adjudged.

Type of Court:  Special Court-Martial.

Remarks:  Involved in the same incident as SP4 ████████████

Case No. 119

Accused:  SP4 ████████████████████

Charge:  UCMJ, Art 134 - Conduct to the Prejudice of Good Order and
         Discipline.

Findings of Guilty:  As charged.

Summary:  The accused attempted to cut off the ear of a dead enemy.

Sentence:  To be reduced to the grade of Private E-1 and to forfeit
           $68.00 per month for 2 months.

Period Served:  No confinement adjudged.

Type of Court:  Special Court-Martial.

Remarks:  Involved in the same incident as SP5 ████████████

6

Case No. 125

Accused:  PFC ▆▆▆▆▆▆▆

Charge:  Not specifically known.

Findings of Guilty:  Not specifically known.

Summary:  The accused knelt on the chest of a Vietcong suspect, while
          a Vietnamese soldier poured water on a towel covering the
          suspect's face.

Sentence:  Reduction in grade and partial forfeiture of pay.

Period Served:  No confinement adjudged.

Type of Court:  Special Court-Martial.

Remarks:  This summary incorporates all information included in the
          report furnished by the command concerned.


Case No. 129

Accused:  MSG ▆▆▆▆▆▆▆▆

Charge:  UCMJ, Art 92 - Violation of a Lawful Order

Findings of Guilty:  As charged.

Summary:  The accused ordered a subordinate to decapitate the corpse
          of an unknown enemy soldier and to boil the head in a pot
          of water.

Sentence:  To pay to the United States a fine of $500.00 and to be
           reduced to the grade of E-5.

Period Served:  No confinement adjudged.

Type of Court:  General Court-Martial.

Remarks:  None.

Case No. 133

Accused:  CPT ████████████████

Charge:  UCMJ, Art 134 - Conduct to the Prejudice of Good Order and Discipline

Findings of Guilty:  As charged

Summary:  The accused permitted a female detainee to die while in the custody of his unit, thus failing to enforce safeguards.

Sentence: To be reprimanded and assessed a partial forfeiture of pay.

Period Served:  No confinement adjudged.

Type of Court:  General Court-Martial.

Remarks:  Appellate review not completed.  Involved in the same incident are SP4 ██████ and SP4 ████████████


Case No. 133

Accused:  SP4 William Ficke

Charge:  UCMJ, Art 125 - Sodomy

Findings of Guilty:  As charged

Summary:  The accused committed sodomy on a captured enemy nurse who was held overnight for detention.

Sentence: To be reduced to the lowest enlisted grade, assessed a partial forfeiture of pay, and to be confined at hard labor for 12 months.

Period Served:  Approximately 8 months.

Type of Court:  General Court-Martial.

Remarks:  Involved in the same incident as CPT ████████ and SP4 ██████████ By postreview clemency, the unexecuted portion of the sentence was remitted.

8

Case No. 133

Accused: SP4 ███████████

Charges: UCMJ, Art 120 - Rape

Findings of Guilty: As charged

Summary: The accused raped a captured enemy nurse who was being held in overnight detention.

Sentence: (As finally affirmed after appellate review.) Partial forfeiture of pay and allowances, reduction to the lowest enlisted grade, and to be confined at hard labor for 2 years.

Period Served: Approximately 7 months.

Type of Court: General Court-Martial.

Remarks: Involved in the same incident as CPT ████████ and SP4 ████████


Case No. 135

Accused: PFC ███████████

Charges: UCMJ, Art 119 - Involuntary Manslaughter

Findings of Guilty: As charged

Summary: The accused, while riding on an Army truck which was passing through a populated area, fired his rifle at a house. A 16-year-old Vietnamese girl was killed.

Sentence: (As finally affirmed after completion of appellate review.) To forfeit all pay and allowances, to be reduced to the lowest enlisted grade, and to be confined at hard labor for 1 year.

Period Served: Approximately 9 months.

Type of Court: General Court-Martial.

Remarks: None

Incl

Case No. 136

Accused:    PFC ████████████████

Charges:    UCMJ, Art 128 - Assault
            UCMJ, Art 134 - Conduct to the Prejudice of Good Order and
            Discipline

Findings of Guilty:  As charged.

Summary:    The accused assaulted a Vietnamese national and mutilated an
            enemy corpse by cutting off the ears and fingers.

Sentence:   Partial forfeitures, reduction to the lowest enlisted grade, and
            confinement at hard labor for 10 months.  The convening authority
            suspended the execution of the confinement.

Period Served:  Very brief.  From the date the sentence was adjudged until
                the convening authority acted thereon.

Type of Court:  General Court-Martial.

Remarks:    None


Case No. 139

Accused:    1LT ████████████████

Charge:     UCMJ, Art 134 - Indecent Acts with a Minor

Findings of Guilty:  As charged.

Summary:    A group of soldiers led by the accused entered an inhabited area
            near the unit field position and molested young Vietnamese girls.

Sentence:   (As modified during appellate review.)  To be dismissed from the
            service, to forfeit all pay and allowances and to be confined at
            hard labor for 30 months.

Period Served:  9 months and 10 days.

Type of Court:  General Court-Martial.

Remarks:    Involved in the same incident as SP5 ████████████

10

Incl

Case No. 139

Accused: SP5 ████████████████

Charges: UCMJ, Art 134, Assault with Intent to Commit Rape

Findings of Guilty: As charged.

Summary: The accused entered an inhabited area near a field position and assaulted a young Vietnamese girl.

Sentence: (As affirmed after completion of appellate review.) To be discharged from the service with a bad conduct discharge, to forfeit all pay and allowances, and to be confined at hard labor for three years.

Period served: Approximately 26 months.

Type of Court: General court-Martial.

Remarks: Involved in same incident as 1LT ████████████


Case No. 140

Accused: PFC ████████████████

Charges: UCMJ, Art 134 - Assault with Intent to Commit Rape

Findings of Guilty: As charged.

Summary: Accused took a young Vietnamese girl from her home and assaulted her in a bunker.

Sentence: Unknown.

Period Served: Unknown.

Type of Court: Special Court-Martial.

Remarks: This summary included all information currently available.

FOR OFFICIAL USE ONLY                          Incl

Case No. 141

Accused:  SGT ▇▇▇▇▇▇

Charges:  UCMJ, Art 128 - Assault

Findings of Guilty:  As charged.

Summary:  The accused beat two Vietnamese detainees, causing injuries
          which required hospitalization of one of the victims.

Sentence:  To forfeit $100.00.

Period Served.  No confinement adjudged.

Type of Court:  Special Court-Martial.

Remarks:  None.


Case No. 143

Accused:  SP4 ▇▇▇▇▇▇▇▇

Charges:  UCMJ, Art 128 - Assault.

Findings of Guilty:  As charged.

Summary:  The accused pushed and struck an enemy prisoner.

Sentence:  Reduction and partial forfeitures.

Period Served:  No confinement adjudged.

Type of Court:  Special Court-Martial.

Remarks:  None.

FOR OFFICIAL USE ONLY

Case No. 147

Accused:  PSG Roy E. Bumgarner

Charges:  UCMJ, Art 118 - Premeditated Murder.

Findings of Guilty:  Same article - Unpremeditated Murder.

Summary:  The accused shot three Vietnamese civilians and then detonated
          a grenade near the bodies claiming they were Vietcong.

Sentence:  To be reduced to the lowest enlisted grade and to forfeit
           $97.00 per month for six months.

Period Served:  No confinement adjudged.

Type of Court:  General Court-Martial.

Remarks:  None.


Case No. 149

Accused:  SSG ██████████████

Charges:  Not specifically known.

Findings of Guilty:  Not specifically known.

Summary:  The accused cut off the ears of an enemy body.

Sentence:  Reduction in grade and partial forfeiture of pay.

Period Served:  No confinement adjudged.

Type of Court:  Special Court-Martial.

Remarks:  This information contains all of the information currently
          available.


13

FOR OFFICIAL USE ONLY

Case No. 150

Accused:    PFC ████████████

Charges:    UCMJ, Art 118 - Unpremeditated Murder
            UCMJ, Art 120 - Rape

Findings of Guilty:  (On rehearing.)  UCMJ, Art 118 - Unpremeditated Murder

Summary:    A group of enlisted men took a Vietnamese girl on patrol with them,
            raped her, and then murdered her.

Sentence:   (On rehearing and as affirmed after completion of appellate review.)
            To be dishonorably discharged from the service, partial forfeiture
            of pay, to be reduced to the lowest enlisted grade, and to be
            confined to hard labor for 22 months.

Period Served:  Approximately 28 months.

Type of Court:  General Court-Martial.

Remarks:    Involved in the same incident as SGT████████ and PVT████████  The
            sentence on rehearing was adjudged after accused had served 28
            months.  He was immediately released.


Case No. 150

Accused:    SGT ████████████

Charges:    UCMJ, Art 118 - Premeditated Murder

Findings of Guilty:  UCMJ, Art 118 - Unpremeditated Murder

Summary:    A group of enlisted men took a Vietnamese girl on patrol with them,
            raped her, and then murdered her.

Sentence:   (As finally affirmed after completion of appellate review.)  To be
            dishonorably discharged from the service, to forfeit all pay and
            allowances, to be reduced to the lowest enlisted grade, and to be
            confined at hard labor for 8 years.

Period Served:  Approximately 38 months.

Type of Court:  General Court-Martial.

Remarks:    Involved in the same incident as PFC████████ and PVT████████

14

FOR OFFICIAL                                                    Incl

Case No. 150

Accused:  PVT ▓▓▓▓▓▓▓▓▓▓▓

Charges:  UCMJ, Art 118 - Premeditated Murder
          UCMJ, Art 120 - Rape

Findings of Guilty:  As charged.

Summary:  A group of enlisted men took a Vietnamese girl on patrol with them,
          raped her, and then murdered her.

Sentence:  (As finally affirmed after completion of appellate review.)  To
           be dishonorably discharged from the service, to forfeit all pay
           and allowances, to be reduced to the lowest enlisted grade, and
           to be confined at hard labor for 8 years.

Period Served:  Approximately 39 months.

Type of Court:  General Court-Martial.

Remarks:  Involved in the same incident as SGT ▓▓▓▓▓▓▓ and PFC ▓▓▓▓▓▓▓

STATUS OF PENDING INVESTIGATIONS

**Case No. 8**

Nature of Allegation:  A newspaper photograph purports to show a prisoner being dropped from a U.S. helicopter.

Personnel Involved:  Unidentified.

Status of Investigation:  Information gathered to date tends to indicate that the victim was dead prior to being dropped.  Investigation is now centering, to date without significant results, on establishing who ordered the body to be dropped.


**Case No. 12**

Nature of Allegation:  A former serviceman alleged that his unit engaged in indiscriminate killing of Vietnamese.

Personnel Involved:  SP5 ▬▬▬▬▬▬▬

Status of Investigation:  Additional investigative leads in Vietnam are being exploited.


**Case No. 13**

Nature of Allegation:  A former serviceman alleged that the personnel named below killed, tortured, raped, and mutilated numerous Vietnamese prisoners and civilians.

Personnel Involved:  CSM ▬▬▬▬▬▬▬
                     SP5 ▬▬▬▬▬▬▬

Status of Investigation:  Additional investigative leads are being developed in Vietnam.


**Case No. 22**

Nature of Allegation:  A former officer alleged that the individual named below killed, or caused to be killed, 10-25 NVA prisoners of war.

Personnel Involved:  1SG ▬▬▬▬▬▬

Status of Investigation:  Still open, but tending toward refutation.


1

Case No. 32

Nature of Allegation:  A former serviceman alleged that his unit participated
in the murder of over 7.0 Vietnamese civilians, including the gang-rape murder
of five Vietnamese women.

Personnel Involved:  CPT Donald Reh
                     (Plt Ldr) John M. Carter
                     (EM) John P. Perry

Status of Investigation:  Investigation to date has not supported the
allegations.


Case No. 41

Nature of Allegation:  A serviceman made a sworn statement to an Army
criminal investigator that he saw the suspects kill two suspected Vietcong
who were surrendering.

Personnel Involved:  1LT ███████████
                     SGT ███████████

Status of Investigation:  ███████ orally admitted that he and ██████████
shot the suspects.  ██████████ denied both the basic allegation and
███████'s statements.  Additional leads in the United States are being
developed.


Case No. 47

Nature of Allegation:  A former serviceman, in a letter to the President,
stated that he could give specifics of numerous war crimes in Vietnam.

Personnel Involved:  Unidentified

Status of Investigation:  The complainant, who is undergoing treatment for
a mental disorder, failed when interviewed to identify persons, locations,
or dates.  Probably this case will shortly be closed.


Case No. 48

Nature of Allegation:  Two former officers and a former serviceman alleged
that villages had been wantonly destroyed, that prisoners had been tortured,
and that prisoners had been pushed out of helicopters.

Personnel Involved:  Unidentified.

Status of Investigation:  Investigation to date has not established veracity
of statements made by these individuals.

FOR OFFICIAL USE ONLY

Case No. 50

Nature of Allegations:  A former serviceman alleged that gunship helicopters destroyed 100 sampans, many of which were loaded with women and children.

Personnel Involved: ██████████ (former CW4).

Status of Investigation: ██████ his former Co and other unit pilots, when interviewed by Army criminal investigators, denied the allegations. Investigation is now attempting to locate additional personnel with knowledge of the incident and to collect topographical and weather data.

Case No. 51

Nature of Allegation:  Three former servicemen made allegations that electrical devices were used to torture Vietnamese during intelligence interrogations.

Personnel Involved:  Unidentified.

Status of Investigation:  Investigation has revealed that on occasion the method described was used during interrogations.  The specific incident or personnel involved have not yet been determined.

Case No. 52

Nature of Allegation:  Three former servicemen have alleged that electrical torture was used on civilian detainees.

Personnel Involved:  Unidentified.

Status of Investigation:  Investigations to date have not established a basis for the allegations.

Case No. 56

Nature of Allegation:  Two former servicemen alleged two separate incidents, one of murder of a 12-year-old Vietnamese boy, the other the murder of 26 unarmed Vietnamese civilians.

Personnel Involved:  Unidentified.

Status of Investigation:  One complainant declined to make a statement to an Army criminal investigator.  The second cannot, to date, be located.

3

FOR OFFICIAL USE ONLY

FOR OFFICIAL USE ONLY

Case No. 58

Nature of Allegations: LTC Anthony B. Herbert, formerly assigned to the
173d Airborne Brigade, in a sworn statement alleged that numerous war crimes
were committed by personnel of that unit from August 1968 to April 1969.
These allegations include murder, looting, and torture.

Personnel Involved: MG ██████████
　　　　　　　　　　COL ██████████
　　　　　　　　　　MAJ ██████████

Status of Investigation: More individuals than the original three suspects
are now involved. Eight offenses alleged by LTC Herbert have been substantiated.


Case No. 59

Nature of Allegation: The sister of a deceased serviceman alleged that
her brother was killed by U.S. personnel because he had knowledge of
war crimes.

Personnel Involved: Unidentified.

Status of Investigation: Investigation appears to indicate a refutation
of this allegation.


Case No. 60

Nature of Allegation: In letters to his wife, the suspect stated that he
had stolen money from the enemy dead, killed a wounded Vietcong, and his
squad had murdered Vietnamese children.

Personnel Involved: SP4 ██████████

Status of Investigation: In an interview with an Army criminal investigator,
Snyder's former platoon sergeant has characterized these allegations as
unfounded. Efforts are now underway to interview ██████ now stationed in
Germany.

4

**Case No. 61**

Nature of Allegation:  A former serviceman, in a letter to the Secretary of
Defense, alleged that his unit destroyed villages and murdered and raped
civilians on a regular basis.  He named seven witnesses to these crimes.

Personnel Involved:   MAJ ▆▆▆▆▆▆▆▆▆▆
                      PSG ▆▆▆▆▆▆▆▆

Status of Investigation:  Efforts are being made to locate and interview
the witnesses.

**Case No. 62**

Nature of Allegation:  It is alleged that a former Army medic smothered an
individual suspected of being a Vietcong in a Vietnamese hospital.

Personnel Involved:   Mr. ▆▆▆▆▆▆▆▆▆▆

Status of Investigation:  Army criminal investigators have interviewed
Yancy, who denies participating in any such incident.

**Case No. 64**

Nature of Allegation:  Former combat photographer has alleged that while
accompanying a platoon in Vietnam, he saw a lieutenant shoot and kill an
elderly unarmed man who had surrendered.

Personnel Involved:   CPT ▆▆▆▆▆▆▆▆▆

Status of Investigation:  Army investigators are attempting to identify
other members of this platoon in order to interview them.

**Case No. 65**

Nature of Allegation:  Former combat photographer who accompanied a company
on a search and destroy mission has alleged that an Army captain ordered four
servicemen to kill a wounded Vietcong.  The men then killed the individual.

Personnel Involved:   CPT ▆▆▆▆▆▆▆▆▆

Status of Investigation:  Army investigators are attempting to identify and
locate other persons who may have witnessed this incident.

FOR OFFICIAL

Case No. 67

Nature of Allegation:  Two former servicemen have alleged that members of their unit had killed unarmed civilians.

Personnel Involved:  Unidentified.

Status of Investigation:  Army criminal investigators have interviewed both men, and both have refused to discuss the matter.


Case No. 70

Nature of Allegation:  Former serviceman has alleged that he had knowledge of two incidents involving the killing of enemy prisoners.  He could not identify individuals involved.

Personnel Involved:  Unidentified.

Status of Investigation:  Investigation continues to identify other possible witnesses to these incidents.


Case No. 76

Nature of Allegation:  Former serviceman allegedly saw an unidentified member of his company kill a captured wounded NVA soldier.  He saw another member of his unit torture an NVA prisoner and kill a captured wounded NVA soldier.

Personnel Involved:  SP4 ████████████████ (KIA - May 1969)

Status of Investigation:  Army investigators interviewed former serviceman, who denied any knowledge of this incident.


Case No. 78

Nature of Allegation:  Subject named below left a jar containing a human ear on his commanding officer's desk.  An enemy body killed in a tactical engagement the previous day had a missing ear.

Personnel Involved:  SP4 ████████████

Status of Investigation:  This case is currently being investigated by personnel of the 1st Cav Div (Airmobile).

6

FOR OFFICIAL USE ONLY                            Incl

## Case No. 79

Nature of Allegation:  A former serviceman alleges that he heard the transmission of orders over a radio to kill a wounded Vietcong nurse.

Personnel Involved:  SP4 ████

Status of Investigation:  No investigative leads yet discovered.

## Case No. 80

Nature of Allegation:  Two former servicemen discribed numerous instances of killing of civilians, torture of prisoners, and destruction of property and livestock by members of their former units.

Personnel Involved:  Unidentified.

Status of Investigation:  One of the former servicemen has refused to discuss the matter with Army criminal investigators.  Efforts to interview the other former serviceman have been unsuccessful.

## Case No. 81

Nature of Allegation:  Former serviceman has alleged that, while serving as an interrogator, he and others cut ears off prisoners to gain information. He also has alleged that an American lieutenant pushed an NVA lieutenant out of a helicopter.

Personnel Involved:  ████████████ others unidentified.

Status of Investigation:  This investigation is now in the initial inquiry stage prior to being forwarded to field agencies.

## Case No. 84

Nature of Allegation:  A former officer has alleged that the individual named below knowingly directed artillery fire on an identified enemy hospital.

Personnel Involved:  MG ████████████

Status of Investigation:  The investigation is in the preliminary inquiry phase.

FOR OFFICIAL USE ONLY

**Case No. 85**

Nature of Allegation:  It is alleged that an unidentified platoon leader ordered the killing of 30 unarmed Vietnamese villagers.

Personnel Involved:  Unidentified.

Status of Investigation:  LTC ▆▆▆▆ was interviewed and, on advice of counsel, declined to make a statement.  Investigative efforts are underway to locate additional witnesses.

**Case No. 86**

Nature of Allegation:  The personnel named below have been charged with premeditated murder involving the alleged shooting of unarmed Vietnamese civilians.

Personnel Involved:  BG ▆▆▆▆▆▆▆▆
                     LTC ▆▆▆▆▆▆▆

Status of Investigation:  The criminal investigation has been completed and court-martial charges have been preferred.  The next step may be an investigation under Art 32, UCMJ.

**Case No. 87**

Nature of Allegation:  Former serviceman alleges that he was ordered to shoot a number of unarmed Vietnamese from a helicopter.

Personnel Involved:  Mr. ▆▆▆▆▆▆▆
                     CW3 ▆▆▆▆
                     WO1 ▆▆▆
                     MAJ ▆▆▆▆

Status of Investigation:  Investigation presently being conducted by 4th MP Gp (CI), Fort Bliss, Texas.

8

FOR OFFICIAL USE ONLY

# INDEX